Connections

Connections
New Ways of Working in the Networked Organization

Lee Sproull
Sara Kiesler

The MIT Press
Cambridge, Massachusetts
London England

Fourth printing, 1994

© 1991   Massachusetts Institute of Technology

This book was set in Sabon and Courier by the MIT Press and was printed and bound in the United States of America.

Library of Congress Cataloging-in-Publication Data

Sproull, Lee.
  Connections : new ways of working in the networked organization
  Lee Sproull, Sara Kiesler.
      p.   cm.
  Includes bibliographical references and index.
  ISBN 0-262-19306-X (hb), 0-262-69158-2 (pb)
  1. Electronic mail systems. 2. Communication in organizations.
  3. Decision-making. I. Kiesler, Sara B., 1940– . II. Title.
HE6239.E54S68   1991
384.3'4—dc20   90-476
                                                                      CIP

This book is dedicated to Allen Newell

Contents

Introduction   ix

1 **A Two-Level Perspective on Technology**   1

Communication Technology at Two Levels   3
New Communication Technology   8
The Networked Organization   12
Conclusion   15

2 **Beyond Efficiency**   19

First-Level Efficiency Effects   21
Second-Level Social Effects   25
Conclusion   35

3 **Do You Know Who You're Talking To?**   37

The Social Information in Computer-Based Communication   40
Let Your Fingers Do the Talking   42
Guiding Behavior   50
Conclusion   54

4 **Electronic Group Dynamics**   57

How Electronic Groups Work   59
Designing and Managing Electronic Groups   70
Conclusion   76

5 **Increasing Personal Connections**   79

Increasing Information and Commitment Through New
Connections   81
Performance Implications   95
Conclusion   101

6 Control and Influence 103

Information Control and Systematic Management 104
Computers and Information Control 106
Social Control 112
Complications of Information Control 114
Controlling Remote Workers 117
Conclusion 122

7 Designing Information Procedures 125

Information Procedures 125
Encouraging Information Sharing 132
Conclusion 141

8 New Ways of Organizing 143

Increasing Organizational Interdependence 145
Solving the "Out of Sight, Out of Mind" Problem 150
Dynamic Structures 154
Conclusion 157

9 Making Connections 159

Getting Started 166
Costs and Predicaments 168
The Future 171

Appendix: A Lesson in Electronic Mail 177

Notes 185
References 189
Index 205

Introduction

In 1986, seven teams of software developers raced against a deadline to design and implement computer-based information systems for their clients. All the teams used a computer network to access databases and programming tools; some also used the network for team communication. Teams that used the network to communicate had fewer meetings but induced greater contributions from their members even though team members were physically dispersed and had divided responsibilities. When the teams completed their projects, those that used network-based communication had created better products but with a work process that was substantially different, with more bottom-up contributions, new coordination procedures, and new subgroup structures.

For the past eight years, we have been conducting social science research on pioneering changes in communication in organizations. In the organizations we have studied, like the software teams, new computer-based communication technology—electronic mail, distribution lists, bulletin boards, conferences—is changing how people work. It can overcome temporal and geographical barriers to the exchange of information. Even more significant, these technologies can connect anyone with anyone or everyone on the same computer communication network. They do not simply cross space and time; they also can cross hierarchical and departmental barriers, change standard operating procedures, and reshape organizational norms. They can create entirely new options in organizational behavior and structure. How will these technologies influence and change organizations? Does a computer network make work groups more effective? How do people treat one another when their only connection is a computer message? What kinds of procedures best suit long-distance management using a computer network? What problems do these technologies alleviate—and what problems do they create?

We think computer-based communication may prove more significant than was the mainframe computer revolution of thirty years ago and the personal computer revolution of ten years ago. Because the technology is used for communication, it has an impact on the most critical process in an organization: whether and how people communicate. Communication determines the connections people have with one another and with their different activities. We have published our research on these topics in academic journals, but we have long felt that the behaviors we have been studying will be so important for organizations that we should write a more accessible book about them. This is that book.

We demonstrate how computer-based communication can alleviate barriers and distortions in organizational communication and can create opportunities for new connections among people. And we also show how it can create new problems that need to be addressed. Ours is a social and organizational view of computer-based communication. We write in the same spirit as social analyses of other technologies—the railroad, telegraph, telephone, steel axes, guns, stirrups, snowmobiles, and CAT scanners.[1] We do not consider technical details of how bits travel over networks or optimum command sequences for creating or reading messages.[2] Others have already reported on how new technology streamlines office and factory work.[3] Our contribution is to document how the technology opens up and stimulates new ways of working and thinking. Our purpose is to discuss how these changes can be exploited by people and to illuminate both the benefits and complications of doing so.

We have conducted our field research in well-established electronic mail communities—those in which large numbers of people already have easy access to good networking technology and information resources. This is our operational definition of a networked organization. In such settings, people typically send and receive between twenty-five and one hundred electronic messages every day. They can't imagine living without these connections. We studied these groups and organizations because we wanted to understand behavioral changes under optimum conditions of use. Good strategies for introducing new technology and building support for it are important policy issues, but they are not the focus of this book. We emphasize what can be anticipated once large numbers of people use the technology routinely. Currently, well-established electronic communities are easy to find in high-technology organizations, universities, and the financial industry. Thus the preponderance of our data comes from those domains. Yet successful networks are also to be found in elementary schools (Levin and Cohen 1985; Newman 1990), scientific disciplines (Hesse, Sproull, Kiesler, and Walsh 1990), and even restaurants (Rule and Attewell 1989).

Our goal is to present an argument that is widely relevant to everyone interested in organizations and new technology. We also have subgoals for four more specialized audiences. Managers and executives should be able to use the ideas in this book to help shape their vision of a new communication environment and policy decisions that carry out this vision. Technology designers and developers should be able to use the ideas in this book to expand their picture of the real-life uses of their inventions, and of the different kinds of people who could use them. People who use information technology in their work should find the ideas helpful in gaining a new perspective on their work environment. Social scientists should find this book a source of research ideas. We have included many citations to and discussions of the relevant research of our academic colleagues. They often appear in the notes rather than in the body of the text to preserve the flow of the main argument.

Although each chapter can be read as an independent essay, the book follows a historical ordering of organizational communication technology over time. Chapter 1 draws on the social history of nineteenth century technologies, such as the railroad, typewriter, and telephone, to introduce a two-level framework for thinking about technology changes in organizations. We then use that framework to explain the surprising early history of networked computer communication. Chapters 2 through 8 use the same two-level perspective to focus on contemporary organizations and contemporary computer-based communication technology. The topics of chapters 2 through 8 proceed from smaller-scale to larger-scale processes and from more prevalent to less prevalent change in today's organizations. Chapters 2 and 3 discuss the first social effects people are likely to notice with these new technologies. Chapter 2 shows how computer-based communication can improve coordination among people. We offer evidence that the most interesting coordination effects will emerge not from letting small numbers of people communicate more efficiently but from letting large groups coordinate their activities in ways that have not been possible previously. Chapter 3 analyzes what happens as technology lets communication cross social barriers as well as physical ones. We describe "electronic etiquette" and why it differs from that of other communication situations. Chapters 4, 5, and 6 focus on specific kinds of changes that are likely to occur in three areas: meetings, connections among peripheral workers, and patterns of control. Chapter 4 demonstrates how group dynamics change when people hold meetings electronically rather than face to face. Chapter 5 shows how computer-based communication can reduce the isolation of physically and socially peripheral workers through increasing organizational participation and personal ties. Chapter 6 examines the other side of participation: how increased information exchange can pose problems of authority, control, and influence. Chapters 7 and 8 discuss longer-range changes that we can expect to see in organizational procedures and structures, respectively, as networked communication becomes more ubiquitous.

Some organizations are already doing or thinking about everything we describe in Chapters 2 through 8. For those organizations, these chapters describe the current state of affairs and offer new interpretations of current behavior. For other organizations, the topics in these chapters represent the future. That is, many organizations are likely to be doing at least some of these things within the next five years. These chapters represent a way to imagine what the future could look like. The final chapter identifies technology developments that are infeasible today but are likely to be practical within the next ten years. It also suggests how to think about moving in a principled way from today's organization and technology into a future with more connections among people and organizations.

We owe a large intellectual debt to Carnegie Mellon University, which provided the initial inspiration for our research. CMU is probably the most computer-intensive university in the world. It not only owns thousands of computers, but also people from all over campus have used the network to create a genuine electronic community. We are grateful as well to specific people for their support and good advice. Allen Newell, who exemplifies our ideal of scientific scholarship, intellectual curiosity, and enthusiastic colleagueship, has supported our work from its beginning. Professor Newell, Professor Herbert Simon, and Braden Walter, CMU's dean of students, worked with us on the CMU Committee on Social Science Research in Computing. The committee's job was to help coordinate people and resources to study the impact of computing on campus. Michael Cohen, John P. Crecine, James G. March, and James Morris advised the committee and encouraged us. Many other colleagues worked with us on the research projects described in this book, especially Mike Blackwell,

Diane Burton, Kathleen Carley, David Constant, Vitaly Dubrovsky, Tom Finholt, Brad Hesse, Chuck Huff, Tim McGuire, Anne Marie Moses, Jane Siegel, John Walsh, Suzanne Penn Weisband, and David Zubrow. Arlene Simon has been our administrative and secretarial mainstay since this research began. Several people read and commented on earlier drafts: Robyn Dawes, Rob Kling, Pat Larkey, Richard Mason, Bob Sproull, and Ivan Sutherland. Lorrie LeJeune, Sandra Minkkinen, and Bob Prior of The MIT Press provided valuable production and editorial guidance. We have received financial support from CMU, the Markle Foundation, the National Institute of Mental Health, the National Science Foundation, the System Development Foundation, and the Xerox Palo Alto Research Center. Finally, we thank the managers and employees who gave us interviews, offered to participate in experiments, and allowed us to analyze internal communications and outcomes in their organizations. (We name some of them at various points in the book; others requested anonymity.) Of the people trying to develop and understand new communication systems, these individuals have the daily experience of new technology. We hope this book shows how it is they who really decide the effects of technology.

Connections

1

A Two-Level Perspective on Technology

The C.E.O. of a billion-dollar-a-year company called his office while he was on a business trip, but he could not reach his assistant, who was away from his desk. Instead, he reached the company's state-of-the-art voice mail system that had been installed to increase the efficiency of handling telephone calls. A disembodied voice instructed the C.E.O. in all the different ways he could leave messages and assured him that someone would return his call as soon as possible. The decision to install the voice mail system had been made at the vice-presidential level; the decision to uninstall it was made then and there by the C.E.O.. He didn't want callers forced to talk to a machine. "That's not the way to treat people," he said.

Predicting the potential consequences of any new technology is an extremely complex problem. Simply forecasting the direct costs of new technology can be hard, and that is the easiest step. Understanding how the technology will interact with ongoing routine practices and policies is even more difficult. Imagining how that technology will lead to long-term changes in how people work, treat one another, and structure their organizations is harder still. A two-level perspective on technology change can help in anticipating potential consequences.

A two-level perspective emphasizes that technologies can have both efficiency effects and social system effects. A social system is a society, organization, group, or other social entity consisting of interdependent people, events, and behaviors. Most inventors and early adopters of technology think primarily about efficiency effects, or first-level effects, of that technology. We argue that second-level system effects are often likely to be more important for organizations.[1] Changes we make to improve efficiency often have other offsetting consequences. Imagine a new rocket-powered ski lift that zooms people to the top of a ski slope. Reducing the time skiers spend going up the mountain improves the efficiency of upward transit. Yet assuming there is no change in how fast people ski down the mountain, the speedy lift leads to longer lines at the bottom and more time waiting to get on the faster lift. The invention also might increase the popularity of the lift and therefore produce more crowds on the slopes and even longer lines at the bottom. Building more lanes on the Bay Bridge in San Francisco causes a bigger backup on the highways leading off the bridge. Drug enforcement overcrowds prisons, which forces criminals back on the streets. Bank teller machines cause people to make smaller but more frequent deposits and withdrawals, which increases banks' costs. In each case the technology causes a self-correcting, or deviation-reducing, reaction in the system. More efficiency in one place can cause less in another.[2]

Technology feedback also can cause second-level effects that are unanticipated deviation-amplifying changes in the system (Maruyama 1963). A simple illustration is a rock with a tiny crack in it. The crack is a small change—the deviation. Water seeps into the crack and freezes, enlarging the crack. The crack is now large enough to admit a bit of soil and seed. A tree grows in the crack, enlarging it further. If this effect multiplies over many rocks, it eventually transforms the rockstrewn landscape into a forest. Important technologies have deviation-amplifying effects. Small changes cause other changes, build up deviation, and cause the system to diverge permanently from its initial state.

An early human technology with deviation-amplifying properties was the stick, made from a branch or antler and sharpened to ease tilling the ground or winning in battle. The stick augmented the bare hand and made the human more efficient. It also led to an agricultural revolution, a new idea of war, and a new social order (Mason 1970). The stick was a better hoe than the unaided hand. Mason notes that if prehistoric people had used cost-benefit analysis, they might have scored the stick pretty well on such criteria as square feet of ground tilled per hour or number of laborers required per square foot of ground tilled. They could have evaluated an investment in stick technology based on a quantitative efficiency measurement, but they could not have predicted the second-level effects.

Deviation-amplifying feedback from new technology can cause people to think and behave in qualitatively different ways. The consequences are more profound and the measurement is much harder than when measuring immediate changes in efficiency. The hoe permitted farmers to dig deeper than they had before and to cultivate previously untillable land. They could raise more food on the same land or work more land. These developments led to a new kind of agriculture in which people could raise sufficient food to stay in one place. They also provided an incentive to improve the hoe itself, to add metal tips, and to invent or improve other implements such as the scythe. The new form of agriculture replaced nomadism as a way of life; skills of farming, husbandry, and defense of territory replaced skills of hunting and gathering. It also led to new values. Individuals owned property. A day-to-day outlook on life gave way to planning and future orientation, to an emphasis on time and control of nature. These changes— new uses of technology, new ways of working and living, new skills, and new ways of thinking—are second-level, deviation-amplifying effects.

This chapter sets a theoretical and historical framework for understanding potential changes from new communication technology. It suggests that second-level system effects—the social and organizational changes—stem mainly from how communication technology changes what and whom people know, what and whom people care about, and system interdependencies. The first section shows first-level and second-level effects through historical experience with earlier communication technology, primarily the typewriter and the telephone. The historical record helps us anticipate the potential consequences of new communication technology. The second section traces the historical development of computer-based communication technology and describes some surprising second-level consequences of the first extensive computer network, the ARPANET. The third section lays out characteristics of a networked organization and suggests the kinds of organizations that will choose to become networked. Our emphasis is not on detailed technical features of new technology, many of which are changing rapidly. Instead we emphasize general principles and technical characteristics that influence the social nature of technology.

Communication Technology at Two Levels

First-Level Effects and Second-Level Effects

Ranked among the most important technological inventions are those that have increased the durability, intelligibility, and portability of information. These "communication technologies" include hieroglyphics, papyrus, and the printing press, as well as modern transportation and communication technologies such as the railroad, typewriter, and telephone (Katz 1989). Today's new communication technologies differ from earlier ones in the greater degree to which, through computer processing power, they span space, time, and preexisting social arrangements.

First-level effects of communication technology are the anticipated technical ones—the planned efficiency gains or productivity gains that justify an investment in new technology. Conventional cost-displacement or value-added analysis often underlies the calculation of these gains. For instance, a firm thinking about installing a voice mail system might estimate how much money could be saved by replacing telephone operators, receptionists, and secretaries with the new technology (cost-displacement analysis). Or if the firm did not intend to fire people whose jobs could be replaced or reduced by the new technology, it would calculate the additional jobs those employees could do when they no longer had to answer the phone (value-added analysis).

Enormous difficulties plague such analyses. Cost estimates of new technologies typically underestimate implementation costs of training and conversion to new ways of working even when they do not underestimate installation costs. According to one analyst, "Less than 20% of the total first year cost of equipping an administrator or professional with a workstation involves equipment expense" (Strassman 1985:82). The remainder involves seeing that people can and do actually use the technology. As the voice mail story at the beginning of this chapter illustrates, analyses of functions to be replaced also typically underestimate the utility of the old technology that is to be replaced. They underestimate or ignore ways that old technology has become usefully embedded in the life of the organization. Finally, these analyses have no way to recognize that the most important effects of a new technology may be not to let people do old things more efficiently but instead to do new things that were not possible or feasible with the old technology.[3] Despite these difficulties, people justify most new technologies a priori by their first-level efficiency gains. Indicative of problems with these justifications are studies discovering that once new technologies have been installed in the name of efficiency gains, often no one keeps figures on their actual costs or the cost savings that are supposed to derive from them (Kling 1987).

Second-level effects from communication technologies come about primarily because new communication technology leads people to pay attention to different things, have contact with different people, and depend on one another differently. Change in attention means change in how people spend their time and in what they think is important. Change in social contact patterns means change in who people know and how they feel about them. Change in interdependence means change in what people do with and for each other and how these coupled functions are organized in norms, roles, procedures, jobs, and departments. Social roles, which codify patterns of attention and social interaction, change. Consider the auto mechanic, hot rodder, and Sunday driver, roles created by the automobile. Hacker, user consultant, and MIS specialist are roles created by the computer. Changes in attention, social contact, and interdependencies do not alter human nature or fundamental processes of society. People still fall in love, care about their boss's evaluations, and work for money. Organizations still are differentiated along lines of status and responsibility; they still respond to market forces. Yet changes in attention, social contact, and system interdependencies do affect peoples' choices and how they behave with others. In analyzing how computers are changing universities, we said, "New and changed roles affect not only those who occupy them but also those who interact with them. Patterns of information exchange are changed. So are working and social relationships. Thus, social [and organizational] structure is changed. So are perceptions of who is important, what is legitimate, what is prestigious" (Kiesler and Sproull 1987:34).

Consider how a new technology from an earlier era, the railroad, not only increased the speed of interurban travel (first-level effect) but also profoundly affected attention and social contact (second-level effects). While traveling by train, passengers saw a new landscape, one passing in a continuous blur. This led impressionist painters to experiment with new ways of depicting passing events, which, in turn, changed our subsequent view of light, color, and motion. The railroad also changed social contact patterns. It brought together strangers for the space of a journey. The metropolitan railroads increased the distance between work and home and were the initial impetus, even before the automobile, for the growth of the suburbs. The suburbs were populated by women and children during the day; husbands and fathers appeared only on nights and weekends. In 1902 the wife of a railroad commuter described "life in the [metropolitan railroad] corridor, life revolving around the departure and arrival of her husband, her daily and seasonal activities outdoors, and her growing hatred of occasional visits to the city, the place of congestion, dirt, and noise" (Stilgoe 1983:283).

Historical Experience

New communication technology has much in common with past communication innovations like the telephone and typewriter. We can learn some lessons from the histories of these other innovations. The typewriter was intended, and succeeded, as an instrument to produce letters efficiently that looked like those of a printing press (first-level effect). Its inventors envisioned its most likely customers as clergymen and writers (Monaco 1988). An unanticipated consequence was fundamental change in the clerical operation of commercial organizations (second-level effect). Before typewriters, male assistants who were learning the trade performed clerical duties. With the new technology, clerical opportunities increased, and typewriting became a safe and respectable occupation for young women. The typewriter greatly expanded paperwork, specialization of office work, and sharp demarcations of status between typists and their male bosses.

In Japan and other East Asian countries, the typewriter did not come into widespread use in business. Because the Japanese language uses two forty-one character phonetic alphabets and more than two thousand ideographs, Japanese typewriters were expensive, difficult to use, and slow. Thus, the organization of Japanese offices developed in a way that was sharply different from Western offices. There was a greater reliance on face-to-face meetings and less on documents. The Japanese office never used many stenographers, typists, and file clerks. While many young women worked as receptionists and hostesses in Japanese organizations, few stayed for more than a few years. Young male assistants typically carried out the duties an executive secretary would do in the United States, such as arranging appointments and keeping track of information. These positions were routine launching points for later executive careers (Lynn 1986).

Like the typewriter, the telephone has had profound second-level consequences. It was envisioned originally as a more efficient replacement for the telegraph and therefore was seen primarily as a tool for business. In 1878, Pittsburgh's first telephone directory had twelve pages on which were printed the names of subscribers—all businesses (Lorant 1988). Telegraph companies offering telephones for lease at $50 a year advertised, "The Telephone has ceased to be a novelty and has become a recognized instrument for business purposes," and emphasized to the business manager, "NO SKILL WHATEVER is required in the use of the instrument." By the late 1920s, the Bell System was marketing the telephone as more than a tool for business and household management. It had begun emphasizing the social character of the telephone with claims such as "friends who are linked by telephone have good times" and "friendship's path often follows the trail of the telephone wire" (Fischer 1985).

Today people use the telephone as much for social and personal reasons as for business reasons, and the technology has had tremendous social and organizational impact (Aronson 1971). The telephone reduced isolation and danger for rural families. City dwellers used it as a babysitter. It reinforced the social phenomenon of the teenage peer group. It led to new social and occupational roles: telephone operator, telemarketer, call girl. It helped the geographic expansion of organizations. People once wondered if the telephone would increase the authority of the boss inside the firm by allowing him to call subordinates at any hour of the day. More than that, it gave employees a chance to call their supervisors, each other, and family members at home.

The telephone had extensive and unanticipated effects in part because it routinely extended attention, social contacts, and interdependencies beyond patterns determined by physical proximity. Reducing the constraints of physical proximity increased people's choice of interactions, whether with family members who had migrated from the farm to the city, or distant employees, or the boss. Amplification occurred because communication networks have a mutually causal, spiraling relationship with information networks, close relationships, conformity, and cultural change. What you know depends on whom you know, and who you know depends on whom you meet. What you buy depends on what other people are buying. What you value depends on what other people value. Why is the teenage peer group so influential? People in the same location—a high school—develop closeness; the telephone (and the automobile) extends the possibilities of interaction in private; the peer group develops more closeness, more conformity, and more influence apart from the influence of older people. Our research demonstrates that, as the telephone did, new computer-based communication technology in some organizations is changing attention, social contact patterns, and interdependencies.

From the history of prior technology we can glean four points useful in thinking about the potential consequences of new communication technology. First, the full possibilities of a new technology are hard to foresee. Therefore inventors and early adopters are likely to emphasize the planned uses and underestimate the second-level effects. Second, unanticipated consequences usually have less to do with efficiency effects and more to do with changing interpersonal interactions, ideas about what is important, work procedures, and social organization. These changes may profoundly alter how each of us works and even the work we do. Third, these second-level effects often emerge somewhat slowly as people renegotiate changed patterns of behavior and thinking. Fourth, second-level effects are not caused by technologies operating autonomously on a passive organization or a society. Instead they are constructed as technology interacts with, shapes, and is shaped by the social and policy environment. Although as humans we decide our own cultural responses to technology, an initial technological change can set the direction of a deviation-amplifying spiral. We can affect technology design and policy and therefore influence the second-level effects as well.

New Communication Technology

The technology whose second-level effects are the subject of this book has a history embedded in the history of computing in organizations. In 1889 Herman Hollerith patented a punch-card, data-tabulating system that increased the speed of data enumeration and expanded the scope of data analysis over previous hand tabulation systems. Its use in the 1890 U.S. census reduced the analysis time by one-third from the previous census and allayed fears that the 1890 analysis would not be finished before the 1900 census began (Beniger 1986). It did better error checking than did hand tabulation. Its use also increased the ability to forecast demographic growth and therefore the ability to anticipate and implement policies and laws such as requests for statehood and congressional redistricting. The 1890 census case prefigured how later computing technology would enormously improve the scope and efficiency of organizational data processing and analysis. It also prefigured some later economic surprises of computing, where technology introduced ostensibly to reduce costs actually increased them instead. "Hollerith's system apparently possessed hidden costs—the great temptation to use the equipment to the hilt. All those millions of cards, those thousands of watts of electricity, those scores of statisticians, had run up a big bill" (Augarten 1984:78, quoted in Beniger 1986).[4]

mail, electronic bulletin boards, and electronic conferencing.[6] We often use the terms *electronic mail* and *electronic communication* as shorthand. Electronic mail makes it possible for people to talk with others over a computer network. It uses computer text processing tools and computer networks to provide a high-speed message processing and exchange service. Unlike data processing applications that typically manipulate fixed-format numerical data, electronic mail lets people use free-format natural language in their messages to one another. Messages can be sent to groups of people as easily as to individuals through use of electronic distribution lists. (See the appendix for more technical information on electronic mail.)

Once electronic mail was available on the ARPANET, large numbers of computer scientists around the country started to exchange ideas rapidly and casually on topics ranging from system design to programming bugs to movie reviews. Graduate students worked with professors and other students who could offer interesting problems and skills without regard to where these colleagues were located physically; some had a kind of free-floating apprenticeship. Scientists could choose their colleagues based on shared interest rather than proximity (Lederberg 1978). A large electronic community formed, filled with friends who didn't know each other and collaborators who had never met in person. We are now beginning to see similar electronic communities develop in organizations that make extensive use of computer-based communication.

Deviation Amplification

Just two key deviations in computer technology made possible the social change from routine data processing and a programmer's leaving messages on a single machine to the creation of entire electronic communities. Electronic mail blossomed because of the confluence of two economic trends that caused both technological breakthroughs and behavior change: the declining costs of computing and of long-distance communications. As is often the case, declining costs led to expanding applications, and both computing and communications were applied in new ways as costs declined. Early data processing applications automated frequent, routine business transactions such as printing a paycheck, writing an invoice, paying a bill, or making an airplane reservation. These transaction-based systems operated on data stored in rigid, fixed formats. As computers became cheaper, the overhead of processing less rigid formats such as text lines and paragraphs became tolerable, and computers were applied to less rigid operations such as word processing. In a similar fashion, early uses of data communications were restricted to high-value applications that required communication, such as connecting to a centralized airline reservation system. As the costs of long-distance lines and the modems to tie them to computers declined, people used digital communication more widely for accessing business databases, for connecting home terminals to computers, for electronic mail, and for other purposes. Declining costs of computation and communication meant computer-based communication could be used by large enough groups to achieve a critical mass for effective communication.

The Networked Organization

The networked organization has both technical and human components and definitions. The technology view of a networked organization is one in which computers are connected to one another through an information transport medium that carries packets of information. The networked organization is defined by its nodes, pathways, and packets. Although these components are necessary, thinking of a networked organization in these terms reinforces an efficiency view of using the technology to increase the speed of information transmission among known, preidentified sources and recipients. The human view of a networked organization is one in which people are connected to one another in diverse forums to exchange ideas and other resources. In this view the networked organization is defined by its people, forums, and resources. Technical components of the networked organization provide necessary technical infrastructure to connect people but by themselves do not create the human networked organization.

Figure 1.1 shows how both data-based and idea-based communication can be supported on one computer network. The network may cover a wide area, a local area, or both. The resources on the network are databases, special data processing capabilities, and people. Database resources can include information on products, orders, customers, markets, administrative and financial records, and libraries. People and computers can access or update these databases over the network. Special data processing resources include expert systems, large-scale modeling programs for design or financial analysis, and simulation programs that run on only one machine

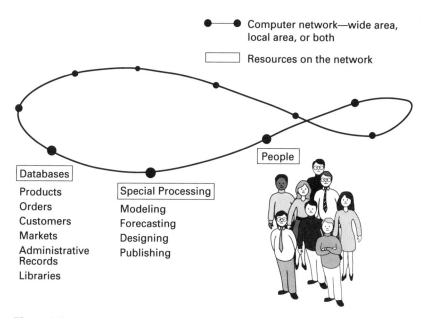

Figure 1.1
Information sharing on computer networks

but accept input and return results over the network. They may include programs that accept requests for services—for special printing, for document delivery, and the like. People are resources on a network if they are accessible using computer-based communication. They can be the source or recipient of ideas, opinions, expertise, and innovation.

Computer networks little resemble older computer technologies. In eerie contrast to the isolation of the mammoth mainframe locked behind glass doors, in 1989 we observed Chinese students who were studying abroad using computer bulletin boards and electronic mail to share their fears, confusion, anger, and information about the suppression of dissent in their homeland. In some companies that use computer networking, communication is strikingly open as employees cross barriers of space, time, and social category to share expertise, opinions, and ideas. In a democracy, people believe that everyone should be included on equal terms in communication; no one should be excluded from the free exchange of information. Independent decision makers expressing themselves lead to more minds contributing to problem solving and innovation. New communication technology is surprisingly consistent with Western images of democracy.

Not everyone will think these possibilities are positive. A new wave of organizations seems on the forefront of the change. These organizations often have employee incentive plans and other special structures to minimize differences between management and workers and to encourage everyone to think about the good of the company. Simultaneously, they rely on the good sense of the individual. There is an emphasis on openness and innovation in the organizational culture, tolerance of deviance, and a participatory style. Yet organizations differ enormously in their attitudes about communication and connections among people, as the following two descriptions show. The first is from an executive vice-president's description of his job at General Motors:

About the same time, I was suddenly inundated with tons of paperwork, the likes of which I had never seen as an executive before or since. There were literally 600 to 700 pages a day to be read and processed. Some of it was important material, such as performance reports from the divisions. Most of it, however, was unimportant at this level of management—like a lease agreement to be signed for a new Buick zone office in St. Louis. . . . Part of this mountain of daily reading material was generated by a practice of "preinformation" for almost every meeting held on The Fourteenth Floor. Each executive attending a meeting was to see in advance the text of any presentation to be given. There were never to be any surprises. (Wright 1979:23)

James Treybig, president of Tandem Computers Incorporated, describes his firm differently:

Almost 99 percent of the people at Tandem have terminals connecting them via electronic mail to every other person in the company. This is essentially a concept of no structure. A person in Switzerland on electronic mail, for example, can request help with a problem. He can say help to 5,000 people (which a person cannot do on the telephone). The next morning he may have 15 answers to the problem, of which 13 are wrong. But he has answers.

Any person can send me a message. In fact, I did something not long ago after which someone wrote a very aggressive mail message to me. That is fair, but he copied it to 5,000 people! (Treybig 1985:14-15)

Our vision of the networked organization builds on four principles. The first is a view of people as people, not as users. In our vision of a networked organization, everyone communicates via the network; therefore the old distinction between users and nonusers of the technology is meaningless and misleading. The second—open access to people and information—follows from the assumption that every employee has something to offer on a network and every employee has something to gain from it. The third principle is providing diverse forums through which people can work together. This principle follows from the assumption that whereas people need to work collectively, collective work is of different kinds. Therefore group communication forums and services are desirable but are not generic. The fourth principle is policies and incentives that encourage information exchange.

Why should an organization become a networked organization? In our view the answer has less to do with efficiency and more to do with characteristics of an organization's personnel, its business or purpose, and its environment. In a networked organization, employee skills and interests need not be tied to a particular physical location. Expertise can be called upon electronically wherever it is needed. If an organization's labor market is plentiful and homogeneous, this may not be a particularly attractive prospect. But if it is scarce and highly differentiated, leveraging employee expertise is a significant task and the network can become a powerful human resource tool.[7] In a networked organization, people can participate in many diverse forums, and group structures can be reconfigured dynamically. If an organization's business is stable or if it is operating within a placid environment with long lead times before predictable changes in markets, suppliers, or customers, then diverse dynamic group structures make little sense. An organization that is operating in a turbulent, unpredictable environment, however, will find that the network can become a powerful strategic tool for flexible management.

Conclusion

The consequences of new technology can be usefully thought of as first-level, or efficiency, effects and second-level, or social system, effects. The history of previous technologies demonstrates that early in the life of a new technology, people are likely to emphasize the efficiency effects and underestimate or overlook potential social system effects. Advances in networking technologies now make it possible to think of people, as well as databases and processors, as resources on a network.

Many organizations today are installing electronic networks for first-level efficiency reasons. Executives now beginning to deploy electronic mail and other network applications can realize efficiency gains such as reduced elapsed time for transactions. If we look beyond efficiency at behavioral and organizational changes, we'll see where the second-level leverage is likely to be. These technologies can change how people spend their time and what and who they know and care about. The full range of payoffs, and the dilemmas, will come from how the technologies affect how people can think and work together—the second-level effects.

Two examples will begin to illustrate how electronic mail can change patterns of attention, social contact, and interdependencies. Neither is revolutionary, but each suggests the potential for deviation-amplifying change. The first example comes from the research laboratories of a Fortune 500 company. The "products" of the laboratories are ideas, and no idea that leaves the laboratories is the product of a single mind. Many ideas are hammered out in lab-wide meetings where they are subjected to exhausting, if not exhaustive, analysis. One laboratory director categorizes his scientists in two groups, the leapers and the plodders. Both groups are equally and exceptionally intelligent, but they have very different ways of working. The leapers dominate the lab meetings because they think quickly on their feet, are witty, and love the punch and counterpunch of intellectual debate. The plodders don't get much air time in the meetings, but when they go back to their offices and think through the implications of an idea, their analyses are just as penetrating. The plodders share their analyses with everyone in the lab using a lab-wide electronic mail distribution list, and in this way are just as influential as the leapers. Without electronic mail, the plodders would not capture their fair share of the laboratory's attention.

The second example comes from the sales organization of a different Fortune 500 company, the Digital Equipment Corporation. Sales of computer systems are complex, and the Digital sales force faces increasing competition from other computing vendors. Digital's sales force uses electronic mail to work with technical support staff and product managers to develop specific customer proposals. Electronic mail allows sales representatives to decrease the turnaround time between a customer's request and Digital's response. This is not exotic behavior; one can imagine using courier services to approximate it without electronic mail. Yet the sales force also uses electronic mail to reduce turnaround time in a way that would be unimaginable without this technology: a sales representative can broadcast an electronic message to all other sales reps worldwide and ask for help with a specific proposal. Often the request is of the form, "I'm trying to close a sale with the XYZ company for our ABC product. Can anyone give me the name of a customer using our ABC product who would be willing to serve as a reference for XYZ?" Or, "Can anyone tell me how your customer handled the QRS problem?" Within hours the sales representative receives replies containing the needed information and can pass it on to XYZ. The sales representative need not know who has the information in order to find it. Any employee located anywhere in the world who reads the message and has the relevant information can easily reply to the message. This behavior stands on its ear the old cliché, "It's not what you know, but who you know that makes you a success." With electronic mail, "It's not who you know, but how you know that makes you a success."

Reprinted with special permission of North America Syndicate

2

Beyond Efficiency

Suppose a major customer encounters a potential showstopper in a new installation of your product. Your on-site representative recognizes the importance of the problem but doesn't know how to solve it. When she calls her boss in the home office, he's at lunch, so she leaves an urgent message for him to return her call. Two hours later he does so, and she explains the problem. He replies that he'll get right back to her and calls: the head of product development—who is in a meeting; the head of manufacturing—who is in transit between one plant and another; the head of research—who is away from his desk; and his wife, to say he'll be late for dinner. By the end of the day, the head of research has returned his call, listened to his explanation of the problem, and promised to ask his staff if they have any ideas for how to deal with it. By the end of the second day, the head of product development and the head of manufacturing agree that they need a joint meeting of their top staff to solve the problem. They discover on the beginning of the third day that the first available day in which all the relevant people can attend such a meeting is ten days away. They decide to meet anyway on the afternoon of the third day with whomever can show up. The head of customer service presents the problem as he understands it from the on-site representative, but some sharp questioning makes it clear to all those in the meeting that they need to hear from the on-site representative directly. They place a call to her at the customer's location, but she does not answer her phone. They leave a message.

This scenario is commonplace in organizations. It derives from three facts of organizational life: people are busy; people are in different places; and information is not always where it is needed.

Organizations try to ensure that employees have enough work to do so that they don't spend too much time sitting around reading the paper or drinking coffee. They try to ensure that people who mostly work on adjacent parts of a product, process, or problem are physically close to one another. And they try to ensure that information flows routinely to those who need it routinely. These arrangements mean that routine matters are usually handled in a reasonable way, but they can lead to big problems when an unusual situation comes up. Unusual situations—problems or opportunities—fall outside the way work and information are usually divided among people and locations in an organization. The difficulties described in the opening scenario are not necessarily signs of an incompetent organization. They are just as plausibly signs of busy people meeting the expected demands of their day as best they can. But handling unusual or unexpected situations effectively is also important to organizational success, so organizations face a dilemma: they can organize to do the routine work efficiently or to do the unusual work effectively. It is hard to do both.

Consider another scenario, one that actually occurred at Tandem Computers Incorporated:

A major telephone company planned to install over 8,000 personal computers in a local area network linked to a Tandem host [computer] via Tandem's [computer network] products. While testing the Tandem environment, the company encountered an urgent design issue that could potentially stop the implementation. The Tandem team knew that the fastest way to solve the design problem would be to poll company experts over Tandem's e-mail network. So, they broadcast the request for design information to customer support, product management, and senior executives. These receivers in turn forwarded the message to many more that might have the answer. From around the world, experts responded with their recommendations to the product manager, who formed the consensus into a single solution for the customer—all in less than 24 hours. (Garbarino 1990)

Processing information and transmitting it from person to person cost time and money. Organizations typically allocate and divide work and information across people and locations in ways that minimize these costs for routine work. Unfortunately this allocation means that these costs can become exorbitant for nonroutine situations. The second scenario demonstrates how computer-based communication can decrease these costs for organizations. These cost savings occur because the technology is fast, asynchronous, and makes one-to-many communication as easy as one-to-one communication.

In this chapter we demonstrate how these three technology attributes can contribute to first-level efficiency effects through accelerating and regularizing the flow of information. We then turn to second-level effects with an examination of how group behavior can change with computer-based communication. Computer-based communication lets groups improve their coordination by having members simultaneously linked with and buffered from one another. Whereas this process can certainly benefit small task groups, it also can support large geographically dispersed groups and group activities that would have been impossible and unimaginable without electronic group communication.

First-Level Efficiency Effects

Accelerating Information Flow: Snail Mail and Telephone Tag
Computer-based communication is extremely fast in comparison with interoffice mail, courier services, or postal mail. A message can be sent down the hall or halfway around the world in seconds or minutes. This rapid transmission speed leads people who use electronic communication to dub the hard-copy alternatives "snail mail." When speed of delivery is important, electronic mail offers clear efficiency gains over hard-copy communication.

Because electronic mail is asynchronous, it also can offer efficiency gains over telephone communication. Some estimates suggest that up to 70 percent of initial telephone call attempts fail to reach the intended party (Philip and Young 1987). But with electronic mail, both parties to a communication do not have to be available simultaneously for it to occur. An electronic message can be sent at the convenience of the sender and read at the convenience of the recipient. This asynchrony reduces the time and frustration of telephone tag. Many telephone conversations do not require a lot of interaction; the substance of the call can often be conveyed in a one-way message. Although most organizations have procedures for taking telephone messages, many featuring the ubiquitous pink slip, they do not eliminate telephone tag. Callers may be reluctant to leave a message with a secretary or receptionist because its contents are too complicated or time-consuming, or they may be unwilling to reveal private information to an intermediary. Leaving an electronic message is an attractive alternative.

The accounting office in a large organization that we have studied demonstrates how electronic mail can efficiently substitute for the telephone. Although standard procedures govern the routine processing of accounts payable information, unusual situations occur frequently. Purchase orders may be missing authorization signatures; shipping orders may have incorrect items; invoices may have inaccurate amounts. The accounts payable supervisor must reconcile all anomalies before authorizing payments to vendors or suppliers. In the office we studied, the supervisor used the telephone to solve many of these problems prior to the introduction of electronic mail, but "it would usually take me several tries to get the person I needed on the phone. Then he wouldn't have the information at his desk and would have to call me back. Sometimes he'd make a mistake when copying down what I needed. It was a mess and it took a long time." Now the supervisor sends electronic mail when she needs information to reconcile discrepancies or resolve anomalies in the accounts payable process. (See box 2.1 for examples of such messages. Names in all messages are pseudonyms.) Most of her messages are answered within 24 hours, and, as a result, she has been able to reduce the late payments from her office.

Some hope that electronic data interchange (EDI) will eliminate the kinds of errors and discrepancies noted in the accounting office. It will not. When orders and shipments are placed and verified electronically and invoices are generated and verified by the same process, both the cycle time and the error rate may indeed decline. But there will always be exceptions, anomalies, and discrepancies that must be resolved by human intervention.

Box 2.1. Accounts payable messages

```
From: A. Reed
Subject: Problems
To: R. Upshaw
Bob,
I need a receiving for po#1014 for Scan Co.
I need a receiving for Color Co for po#1020.
I need a copy of the consulting contract for M.R. Connors for
po968 that has VP's signature on it.
Thanks,
Ann


From: A. Reed
Subject: Signiture Authorization
To: R. Love
Rick,
Mark needs to get signiturre authorization from Nils Schumann
for his budget center #'s 729, 728 and 749.  this can be all on
one memo with his signature and Mark's.
The only other budget center that Mary had authority for was
725 so we need a memo with your signature and Ken Wilson's and
then Mark's.
All other budget center managers said that they wanted to
approve there own freight bills or that they never had anything
to do with freight.
The sooner we get this into effect the better I think.
Ann
```

Companies appreciate the savings that result from reducing telephone tag and snail mail delays and attend to evidence that purports to quantify these savings. For instance, five people in different locations might have the task of preparing a contract bid. Preparing a draft and sending it to the other four locations for comment takes an elapsed time of one day using an overnight courier service and costs $50 to transmit (at $12.50 per copy). Returning comments from each site takes another day and an additional $50. If five drafts are cycled in this fashion, the total elapsed time is nine days, and the total transmission cost is $450. The elapsed time can usually be cut at least in half by using electronic transmission—either fax or electronic mail. The marginal cost of each transmission is also much lower than that of the courier service.[1] The accuracy of numbers such as these is less important for policymakers than people's belief in them. For instance, Manufacturer's Hanover Trust estimated that employees saved an average of 36 minutes a day by using computer-based communication. This translates into an annual net opportunity value of about $7 million (Nyce and Groppa 1983). Digital Equipment Corporation estimated the marginal cost savings to its managers using electronic mail to be $28 million (Crawford 1982).

In considering the benefits that derive from electronic mail's speed and asynchrony, people usually think first about situations in which the alternatives are hard-copy mail or a telephone call, and there is one sender and one receiver who know one another. In these cases electronic mail looks like an information accelerator—firing routine information from one person to another more rapidly and conveniently than could be done by other means. Through this information accelerator, people can work more efficiently than they could do otherwise.

Regularizing Information Flow

Through accelerating information flow, electronic communication may increase efficiency. It also may do so through regularizing information flow. Here, electronic mail's broadcast capability becomes important, along with its speed and asynchrony. Because it is as easy to send a message to a group of any size as it is to one person, previously ad hoc communication can become routinized. All organizations have procedures for disseminating information to groups such as departments (often a memo placed in everyone's mailbox) or to people who work in the same building (often a memo taped on the main entrance and exit doors of the building). The costs of these procedures preclude their being used indiscriminately.

When they are not used, people may learn of potentially useful information only if they happen to overhear it or in some other informal way. Broadcast electronic mail makes it easy to regularize some of these ad hoc communications.

We were interviewing a mid-level manager in his office one day when one of us looked out the window and noticed that a car was on fire in one of the parking lots. The manager first called the fire department, which dispatched a fire truck. Then he turned to his computer and sent an electronic mail message, using a distribution list, to everyone who worked in the building. The message described the fire and said that drivers whose cars were parked in that lot should move them. Obviously hard-copy memos in mailboxes or on doors would have been no use in this situation. The building had no public address system. It did have a fire alarm system, but ringing the alarm, and thereby evacuating the building, was not the appropriate message. Of course, not everyone was reading electronic mail at the moment the fire message arrived, but enough were so that the message was effectively transmitted to everyone in the building. Although the burning car was damaged, employees moved other cars out of the way before they were in any danger. The point here is not that a car or two escaped damage but that broadcast electronic mail made it relatively easy to regularize communication to a group of people, ensuring that no one was inadvertently left out. The efficiency implications of regularizing communication may be more obvious in the next example.

Like many other large organizations, Digital Equipment Corporation runs an extensive training and education program. Classes that are filled during preregistration often get taught with empty seats because of last-minute cancellations. Some of these seats can be filled from waiting lists and instructors' calling around. The training group at Digital now uses electronic mail to broadcast the announcement of last-minute availability of courses. This regularizes the dissemination of this information to everyone who might be able to benefit from it. As a result, more employees receive training for any given course, a direct efficiency gain from the broadcast capabilities of electronic mail.[2]

The previous analyses are based on improving current work demands and routines through reducing transaction time and regularizing communication—important improvements that may provide the initial cost justification for electronic mail. But in the long run, more interesting benefits may emerge because the technology lets people and groups interact in ways that were not possible before.

Second-Level Social Effects

Group Mail and Coordination Costs

The fundamental unit of work in the modern organization is the group, not the individual. Work is organized in departments, subunits, committees, task forces, and panels. All groups incur coordination costs, defined as the time and money necessary to organize and sustain group activity. For instance, meetings must be scheduled, information must be shared, and individual contributions must be meshed.

When groups meet face-to-face, they incur a coordination cost called process loss, the difference between the potential contribution of all group members if each contributed maximally and their actual contribution. For instance, brainstorming groups tend to produce fewer ideas, even fewer good ideas, than the total ideas produced by the individual members of these groups when they work alone (Diehl and Stroebe 1987). One reason for this loss is that in brainstorming groups, people spend time listening to others and telling others their ideas. In an n person group, there are potentially $(n^2 - n)/2$ possible two-way conversations that can occur. There are potentially 2^n teams (of size two and greater) that can form. If everyone talked simultaneously, everyone could have a turn but no one would hear anything. And so conventionally in a face-to-face meeting, only one person talks at a time. When meeting time is limited (and it always is), some good ideas are never heard. Process loss also increases when group time is taken up by one-to-one exchanges—for instance, in repeating information to a late arrival. Because group memory is usually faulty, process loss also occurs when people repeat what was said earlier in the meeting or disagree over what was settled earlier.

As several of our examples have illustrated, electronic mail can be used to communicate to groups of people as well as to one person. An electronic distribution list can be used to send a message to many people as easily as to one person. A list of people's names and computer addresses is given a name—such as "Sales Group" or "Science Fiction Lovers." A sender mails one message to the group name; then the computer automatically mails a copy of the message to every person whose name and address are on the distribution list. The sender does not have to specify—or even to know—the names and addresses of group members in order for them to receive the message. Thus electronic mail makes it possible to have fast, asynchronous group communication, as well as one-to-one communication.

Electronic group mail can decrease group coordination costs just as electronic one-to-one mail decreases one-to-one coordination costs. The scheduling constraints of getting everyone into the same room at the same time vanish. Because electronic mail is asynchronous, everyone can "talk" at his or her convenience; everyone can "listen" at his or her convenience. Because electronic mail is fast, asynchronous messages can approximate real-time interaction. Because electronic mail can archive the complete text of every message, the same group memory is available to every member.

The software development teams described at the beginning of the book demonstrate how groups can use electronic communication for coordination. Each team had seven to ten college seniors completing an intensive management information systems curriculum. Each team's objective was to produce a working software system for a real business client under a four-month deadline. Each team was hierarchically organized with a manager, comanager, and workers and functionally differentiated with different subgroups (sometimes with overlapping membership) responsible for programming, documentation, and training. Although team members were in the same organization, they did not share office space, nor were they working exclusively on this task; each had other responsibilities as well. Each team held regularly scheduled meetings over the course of the project, and communicated by telephone, memo, and informal conversation. Each team also had the opportunity to communicate by electronic mail. Members could send individual messages to one another or to the entire group. Within the groups' electronic mail, we found four kinds of messages related to coordination. (See box 2.2 for examples of such messages.)

Scheduling   All managers who used electronic mail sent group mail announcing or reiterating the time and place of an upcoming meeting. Some managers used electronic mail to solicit information about when people were available. Teams that did not use electronic mail took up face-to-face meeting time trying to schedule the next meeting. When the time or place of a meeting had to be changed, managers using electronic mail could get the word to everyone by sending one message. Managers who did not use electronic mail had to make telephone calls, leave messages stuck on doors, and generally expend much more effort to get people to meetings.

Task assignments   Managers used mail to announce and reiterate task assignments for both individuals and subgroups. Some of these messages organized people for the next meeting, telling them what they should have accomplished by the time of the meeting and what they should bring to it. These messages could increase the productivity of face-to-face meetings by increasing the probability that team members had done their homework before the meeting.

Reporting accomplishments   Team members used electronic mail to report task accomplishments. This mail allowed people to keep up-to-date with others' progress and problems in between meetings, and it meant that not as much time had to be spent in the face-to-face meetings reciting everything that had occurred since the previous meeting.

General awareness   Team members, and especially managers, kept the group generally informed by producing summary messages and by forwarding to the entire group messages of general interest that had been received by one team member.

Did these electronic coordination activities have any payoff? We discovered a very high correlation between use of electronic mail and group productivity—the quality of the software product as judged by the teams' clients. Furthermore, this increased productivity was achieved without an increase in the total amount of communication. The teams that used electronic mail met less often and spent less time on the telephone and writing memos. We cannot definitively rule out two competing explanations for our findings. One is that computer ability in the group was

---

Box 2.2. Group mail for coordination

Announcing a Meeting

```
Date:  Thu 28 Aug 86 10:45:52-EDT
From:  Horatio Nelson <HN03@TB.CC.CMU.EDU>[manager]
Subject:  Meeting Update
To:  Group:
I have arranged a meeting with Robert [client] from 12:30 to 1:00
today.  Anyone who can is free to attend.  A summary of the
meeting and details about next week will follow later today.

Horatio
```

Task Assignment

```
Date:   Thu 25 Sep 86 18:35:51 EDT
From: Oliver Perry <OP12@TD.CC.CMU.EDU> [manager]
Subject: update
To:  PROJECT:  :
```

In lieu of the meeting this week, here's what needs to be going
on at this point:
1) everyone—make sure that you have interviewed your UW people
by Wednesday.Technically,by then we have to meet and pull
together out of the interviews what everyone would like from
the system, and what we can feasibly do.if you ABSOLUTELY can't
do it be then, then by Thursday or Friday, NO LATER. When you
interview them,(or call to set up the interview, introduce
yourself and the system, explain what Claudia has already
suggested,and what Timothy wants, and ask them what information
not already wanted by Timothy or Claudia would be helpful to
them in their decision making process, specifically what kids
of statistics—if they can be that specific.) Claudia's wishes
are explained in clause 7 of the contract and Timothy wants
info for DataMate. Make sure you write down carefully what
they want, since you'll be the only one there, and most likely
we won't have the chance to meet with them again. If you need
help, or can't make your interview see if someone else would be
willing to go in your place.

2) everyone—i assume you got the message from Olson—hardware is
being delivered tomorrw (Friday) to SDS. ANYONE who can be
there to supervise the setting up PLEASE GO!!! (I have to be
at SteelCo. tomorrow, so I can't do it.) It's at 1 in PH 208.
You should go back and reference Olson's message for the
details.

3) Kai, Lynn, Max [group members]—you should continue to work on
the data dictionary for Datamate. No rush at this point but
there's a lot that has to be done, I know.

4) Anne [member], Nancy [assistant manager]—finish setting up
appointments with the chairmen and exec. directors. Let me and
Dylan [member] know if you need people to go to interviews.
Anne, the Gantt
 chart is a last priority, but if you have time.....

5) I have a copy of the R:Base programming manual that Kai
found for us. Anyone who wants to start looking at it let me
know. I've read a couple chapters, and it doesn't look too
bad.

6) Next meeting is our regular meeting on Wednesday, tho i'll
be in touch. Call me—if you have questions or problems.
                      Oliver Perry
```
```

Task Accomplishment

```
Date: Thu 4 Sep 86 15:19:35-EDT
From:J. Johns <JJ76@TD.CC.CMU.EDU> [manager]
Subject:  End of week reports
To: Our-group:
Though I basically know what everyone has done all week it is
probably a good idea to get in the habit of sending weekly
reports. So.... if you would, please try and send them to me
by tomorrow morning.  Thanks.
John (jj76@td)


Date:  Sun. 21 Sep 86 23:38:18 edt
From:  W. Nimitz@andrew.cmu.edu (William Nimitz)[member]
To:  jj76@andrew.cmu.edu (John P. Jones)[manager]
Subject:  End of Week Report 9-14-86
CC:  nimitz@andrew.cmu.edu (William Nimitz)
John-
A synopsis of the weeks effort:
Worked on producing slides for the probdef presentation.
Worked with Dreux on the presentation outline and text.
Well thats realy about it.  Idon't realy know what else to add.
William


Date:  Tue. 16 Sep 86 10:46:03 edt
From: caroline@andrew.cmu.edu (Caroline Shea)[member]
To:  jj76@andrew.cmu.edu (John P. Jones)[manager]
Subject:  Re:  some tasks for me
John,
     A weekly meeting time might be difficult for me since my
schedule is based on when other people want to meet.  (like
bosses and stuff).  How about if we set Monday afternoons at
1:30 aside?  I haven't had a meeting scheduled for that time
slot in a few weeks.
```

responsible for both the volume of electronic mail and the quality of group performance, with no direct link between mail and performance. There were no differences across teams in the computer ability variables we measured, but more sensitive measures might have revealed such differences. A second alternative explanation is that managerial savvy might have been responsible for both volume of electronic mail and quality of group performance. The teams were made up of relatively novice software developers. Their supervisors emphasized that groups should communicate extensively and use electronic mail. Savvy managers might have decided to use electronic mail extensively because their supervisors wanted them to and also to have been better at organizing their teams, with no necessary relationship between the two. If this were the case, the savvy managers would also have to have explicitly decided to reduce their teams' volume of noncomputer communication and to use electronic mail for coordination messages, with no expectation of affecting group performance. There probably is a relationship between managerial savvy and group electronic mail, but we suspect it is a direct one; that is, savvy managers understand how to exploit the technology to benefit the group directly.

In the nonelectronic world, groups use face-to-face meetings to link members with one another and time outside meetings to buffer members from one another. During meetings members become mutually aware of others' attitudes, problems, and accomplishments. They are reminded that their individual work must be meshed with that of other people. During time not spent in meetings, each member can work on his or her individual contribution to the group product. While individual members are working alone and buffered from the rest of the group, they can lose track of group objectives and turn to other responsibilities that have nothing to do with the group project. Or while working on their piece of the group project, they can become so absorbed in their own contribution to the project that they lavish too much attention on each component in striving for perfection (at the expense of meeting deadlines) or pursue tangents that are intrinsically interesting but irrelevant to the project needs.

Electronic group communication lets busy people who aren't in the same place share information rapidly and effectively. In effect it allows group members to be simultaneously linked to and buffered from one another. They are buffered from one another because they can attend to information from the group at their own convenience, and they are linked to the group because group mail reminds them and informs them of other parts of the project, including issues that will affect their own work. When they send group mail, they inform other group members of their own work and simultaneously remind themselves that they are working on a group project.

Although electronic group mail reduces the amount of meeting time needed for coordination activities, it doesn't eliminate the need for face-to-face meetings. Face-to-face meetings are particularly important in getting a group started, in negotiating issues, and in problem solving.[3] But with electronic group mail, there can be less total time devoted to meetings and a higher proportion of meeting time devoted to functions for which face-to-face communication is best suited.

Distributed Groups

The software development teams were small, located in the same place, and concentrating on a shared task. Groups met face-to-face at least once a week. A different kind of group found in all large organizations is the dispersed project group. Its members are drawn from different locations and often from different divisions or sectors. Its function is often to coordinate or set policy for shared or similar activities occurring quasi-independently across the organization. It may hold meetings somewhere between once a month and once a year. The coordination costs of such groups are enormous. Hewlett-Packard engineers describe the typical frustrations of such groups: "Our Council meets once a month . . . half of us have to fly in . . . for a few hours . . . we need to start over each time . . . We can't get anything done!" (Fanning and Raphael 1986). Electronic group mail can allow such groups to sustain and even build productive momentum between meetings by simultaneously linking and buffering their members.

Beneficial Finance communicates with its board of directors between board meetings using electronic mail. Just before one Labor Day weekend, the company received a serious and attractive offer, valid until the following Tuesday, to buy its Western Auto subsidiary. Through electronic mail, the company's top management and its board were able to explore the implications of the offer and craft some counterprovisions over the weekend. The board met the next Tuesday and approved the divestiture. Without electronic mail, according to Finn Caspersen, the company's president, Beneficial Finance would have tried to inform all the relevant parties of the offer by fax or an overnight delivery service, but there would have been no opportunity for board members and management to react to the original proposal or make counterproposals prior to the Tuesday meeting. The divestiture would probably have been approved but with people less informed and terms less favorable.[4]

Electronic group mail can improve the operation of existing groups, even distributed ones, as the software development teams and Beneficial Finance examples illustrate. More significant, it can support groups and group activities that would be impossible and unimaginable without electronic group communication. When sending a message to an electronic distribution list, it doesn't matter if there are five, fifty, five hundred, or five thousand people in the group. The sender still sends only one message. Furthermore, the geographic location of any group member is irrelevant to his or her participation in the electronic communication. Thus the technology of electronic mail can simultaneously link and buffer extremely large geographically distributed groups.

One of the developers of Common LISP, a popular computer language for artificial intelligence, described one such group and its operations. Over sixty people from universities, government, and industry collaborated for three years to produce Common LISP:

The development of Common LISP would probably not have been possible without the electronic messaging system provided by the ARPANET. Design decisions were made on several hundred distinct points, for the most part by consensus, and by simple majority vote when necessary. Except for two one-day face-to-face meetings, all of the language design and discussion was done through the ARPANET message system, which permitted effortless dissemination of messages to dozens of people, and several interchanges per day. The message system also provided automatic archiving of the entire discussion, which has proved invaluable in the preparation of this reference manual. Over the course of thirty months, approximately 3000 messages were sent (an average of three per day), ranging in length from one line to twenty pages. Assuming 5000 characters per printed page of text, the entire discussion totaled about 1100 pages. It would have been substantially more difficult to have conducted this discussion by any other means and would have required much more time. (Steele 1984)

The Common LISP group was constituted for a specific purpose. Although not every member may have personally known every other member, both membership and task were explicitly identified. Thus, it could be considered a kind of dispersed work group in that all members spent at least some of their time working on a common task. The Tandem scenario at the beginning of this chapter illustrates a different kind of totally distributed group. In that case, the group was not specifically formed to solve the customer's problem. But because everyone in the company shared the same computer network and electronic mail system, the product manager could broadcast a request for help to all employees as a standing group. Those who could help solve the problem responded to the broadcast message. The sender did not have to know in advance who those people were. They emerged from the network to make their contribution and then continued with their own work.

An organization's employees represent a vast reservoir of information and experience that can potentially be brought to bear on any particular problem or opportunity. The difficulty is accessing it. When electronic group mail reaches large numbers of employees, they can be treated as an information buffer, a way to organize current information in a readily accessible form.[5] A case from the product development organization of a Fortune 500 company provides another example of how this can occur. Box 2.3 shows a message that a product developer sent to distribution lists that reached thousands of employees. The message described an idea for developing a new product and asked others to contribute their ideas. Within two days, the developer had received twenty-five replies from twenty-two people in five different cities. Within two weeks he had received over one hundred fifty replies, almost all from people he did not know. He did not have to know in advance who those people were, and they did not have to divert a lot of attention from their own work to reply to him.

But It's Not All Rosy
Reducing communication costs is not always and automatically beneficial because faster and easier communication is not always better communication. Because it is so easy to send a message, people may be tempted to speak before they think, and injudicious communication may result. (We discuss this topic in chapter 3.) Moreover, more information is not always better than less information. In the case of the product developer, several thousand people received his message and "only" 150 replied. Presumably the message was irrelevant to most of the people who received it but who didn't reply. Thus the cost of the inquiry was bothering several thousand people with an irrelevant message. We can crudely estimate the "cost" of such a broadcast message. Assume it was sent to three thousand people.

Box 2.3. Electronic message to an entire organization

```
DATE:  12-April-83  10:49:00 PST Tuesday
FROM:  Salamon
SUBJECT:  Spreadsheets
TO: Everyone
REPLY-TO: Salamon
Do you have any opinions about spreadsheet programs (Visicalc,
SuperCalc, MultiPlan, Lotus 1-2-3, MBA etc.etc.)?  I'd like to
hear what you consider to be their strengths and weaknesses.
We're planning some spreadsheet-like additions to [our prod-
uct]; what should we include?

Let me know if you want to get the compiled replies or to join the
discussion on SpreadsheetInterest.
```

Assume one-third of them never saw it or scanned the header but didn't read the message. If it takes 5 seconds to actually read the message, then the two thousand who did read the message spent a total of 167 minutes reading it. If the median annual salary for electronic mail reading employees is $50,000, then the direct cost of reading the message was approximately $75, or $.04 per reader. This ignores any benefits foregone that might have accrued by spending the five seconds in any other way. Was the cost worth it? The product developer would certainly say yes. The people who read the irrelevant message would probably say no.

David Constant, who studied question asking and answering in one company's electronic mail system, has collected data that help us extend the cost-benefit analysis. People who respond to messages such as the one from the product developer estimate it takes a mean of 6 minutes to write a reply. Aggregating the mean reply time over 150 replies yields 900 reply minutes. Using the same salary figures as above yields a direct cost of message reply time of $375. (Again, this ignores any benefits foregone from other time uses.) People such as the product developer who had asked questions estimated the mean value of each reply to them to be $10. (These data came from answers to a question phrased as follows: "If you could award from $0 to $25 for how useful this answer was to you, how much would you award it?") Aggregating across 150 replies yields an estimate of direct benefit to be $1,500 and a net benefit (subtracting the cost of replies) of $1,125. These figures are only rough estimates. Their merit lies more in suggesting the order of magnitude of costs and benefits rather than specifying them precisely.

More information is not always more valuable than less information. Surely not every one of the 150 replies contained unique information. There was certainly redundancy. And the product developer had to filter out the redundant messages. Was it worth it? According to Constant's data, the product developer would probably say yes. These data show that question askers did not downgrade their replies just because of getting too many. What was important to them was the actual expertness of the repliers and the repliers' desires to help their fellow employee. So the developer might even say that redundancy was a sign of consensus and support. The more messages making the same point, the more attention the developer would pay to that point.

Ideally the request would have gone to only the people for whom it was relevant, and only replies containing information not previously sent by someone else would have been returned. Some developers might be tempted to build special-purpose intelligence-gathering systems to target questions and filter replies, thereby reducing some of the costs described. Unfortunately special-purpose systems impose their own costs in both requiring askers to specify their questions precisely and requiring potential answerers to specify their areas of expertise equally precisely. A ubiquitous, general-purpose tool like broadcast electronic mail seems a better compromise between ease of use and costs of possibly inappropriate use.

Conclusion

Because information is not always where it should be, organizations incur information processing and transmission costs. Because people are busy and physically separated, the speed and asynchrony of electronic mail allow it to act like an information accelerator for one-to-one communication. Many organizations have discovered its utility in this domain and wax enthusiastic about its merits in reducing the delays of telephone tag and snail mail. While we think it's fine to reduce telephone tag, we believe that more important organizational consequences may stem from the fact that electronic group communication is as easy as one-to-one communication. By simultaneously linking and buffering people, electronic mail can reduce group coordination costs for conventional groups, and it can support very large groups of physically separated people that would be otherwise impossible.

"Doing new things" is not simply a matter of adding new activities to an unchanging base, like hanging ever more exotic ornaments on a Christmas tree. Doing new things leads to thinking in new ways and thereby to fundamental changes in how people work and interact. In the early days of the automobile, some of its most important potential benefits were expected to come from horse-related savings. (Of course, people were also worried about potential injury to horses involved in accidents with cars.) It strikes us that electronic mail is to telephone tag as the automobile is to horse-related savings—true but ultimately not very important. The more profound impact of the automobile has come from changing patterns of work and residential density and interaction. The more profound impact of computer-based communication may similarly come from changing patterns of organizational interaction.

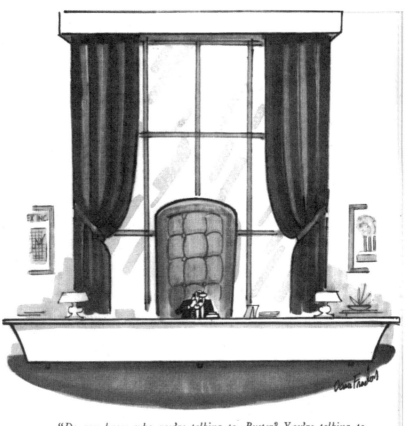

"Do you know who you're talking to, Buster? You're talking to the guy with the biggest desk, biggest chair, longest drapes, and highest ceiling in the business!"

Drawing by Dana Fradon; ©1981
The New Yorker Magazine, Inc.

3

Do You Know Who You're Talking To?

A departmental meeting is about to begin. The clock shows 9:55 A.M.
Chairs surround a rectangular table. People in business dress drift into the
room. They stand near a side table, helping themselves to coffee. Gradually
they seat themselves; most choose a chair near someone they like well. The
department head enters the room at 10 o'clock and sits at the head of the
table. His secretary follows and distributes a memorandum to the people
around the table. The memo says, "Treasure Hunt Clues and Map."
Guffaws rock the room. People jump up and take plastic bags and little
notepads from their briefcases. They run from the room, and soon it is
empty. The time is 10:15 A.M.

The scenario is jarring because the setting is inconsistent with typical
behavior. The time on the clock face, the coffee pot, the conference table
and chairs, the secretary's actions, and peoples' clothes and demeanor are
social cues defining the situation as a business meeting. Yet the participants
do not act according to the norms of a business meeting. The participants
are not crazy; their behavior is perfectly compatible with the norms of a
party. Suppose it is late evening. Chairs haphazardly circle a low table.
Everyone is dressed in jeans. Hosts serve wine and beer. In a corner of the
room, the department head lounges on the floor. Unlike the cues in the
meeting room, these cues suggest a party where loud laughter and a
treasure hunt are appropriate.

Proponents of the efficiency benefits of computer-based communication
often assume that it delivers the same message as any other medium but
simply does so more rapidly. That view is misleading because a message—
even the "same" message—changes its meaning depending on the forum
within which people convey it. For instance, people generally exaggerate
reports of how frequently they do socially desirable acts like voting in
political elections, wearing a seat belt, or attending cultural events. When

people discuss these behaviors in a face-to-face interview, they exaggerate their frequency more than people do who discuss them in an anonymous paper-and-pencil questionnaire.[1] Similarly, people underreport socially undesirable behaviors and do so more in personal interviews than in paper and pencil questionnaires. Further, messages change depending upon to whom people convey them. The cliché is that the boss is always the last to hear the bad news. Research shows that people are reluctant to tell others bad news (in comparison with good news) and are especially reluctant to tell the boss (Rosen and Tesser 1970; O'Reilly and Roberts 1974).

Every familiar communication situation has norms or conventions for appropriate behavior. Many also have explicit rules and regulations. Consider a radio call-in show, a board of directors meeting, an employment interview, and filling out an IRS tax return. Each entails norms and explicit rules for what can be said and how it can be said. There is partial overlap in norms across situations; for instance, it is conventional across a variety of situations for speakers or authors to identify themselves. There is also variation within situations across settings; for instance, conventional behavior in a business meeting of General Motors executives probably differs in some measure from conventional behavior in a business meeting of Motown Records executives.

Three general strategies guide behavior in different communication situations—instruction, experience, and reading cues in the situation itself. Instruction comprises all the ways in which authorities convey advice or rules about appropriate behavior. Instruction ranges from the general rules of social politeness that parents teach children (for instance, "Don't talk with your mouth full") to advice manuals (for instance, "How to run a meeting" or "How to make power phone calls") to rule books (for instance, "The following kinds of questions are illegal to ask when interviewing potential employees. Do not ask them."). Instruction can pertain broadly to many communication situations when it is remembered and is applicable. Because computer-based communication technology is somewhat new, instruction and experience are not as powerful in guiding behavior as they are in other media.

The most immediate guide to behavior is reading cues in the situation itself. When we enter a building with a reception area, the receptionist's appearance and surroundings evoke an image of the correct business visitor. The height of the reception counter says something about the amount of formality or friendliness expected. Even the lighting in the area may be a guide to behavior. The waiting rooms of restaurants, airline baggage claim offices, and dental clinics frequently have dim lights to encourage calm and relaxed behavior in their visitors. Other people's behavior is also an important cue to how to behave (Latane and Darley 1968).

When technological change creates new social situations, traditional expectations and norms lose their power. People invent new ways of behaving. In the early years of the automobile, tourists stopped overnight at campsites in fields or towns along the road. The campsites, precursors of the modern motel, offered greatly reduced privacy as compared with hotels. Travelers went about preparations for meals, sleep, and personal hygiene (and of course automobile repairs) in full view of one another. This situation was a stimulus to other intimacies. Soon a new custom developed—strangers exchanged deep personal secrets but understood that they should keep their surnames to themselves (Belasco 1979).

Computer-based communication today, like the automobile of yesterday, creates a new social situation. Unlike automobile campsites, which were rich in social cues and shared experience, today's electronic technology is impoverished in social cues and shared experience. People "talk" with other people, but they do so alone. Reminders of other people and conventions for communicating are weak. Thus in this new forum, messages are likely to display less social awareness. The advantage is that social posturing and sycophancy decline. The disadvantage is that so, too, do politeness and concern for others.

In this chapter we show how computer-based communication technology creates a new forum for human communication, one whose rules are not like those of any other forum. In the previous chapter, we showed how people could use electronic mail to talk more efficiently and to create new kinds of groups and group interactions. We did not analyze the text of particular messages to see what was said or how it was said. Now we move inside electronic mail exchanges to understand how people talk to one another using this technology. We describe how two characteristics of computer-based communication—plain text and perceived ephemerality of messages—make it relatively easy for a person to forget or ignore his or her audience and how reduced social awareness leads to messages characterized by ignoring social boundaries, self-revelation, and blunt remarks. Then we look at ways to guide behavior in this medium.

The Social Information in Computer-Based Communication

Two features of computer-based communication combine to create a relatively unstructured communication situation. First, computer-based communication relies almost entirely on plain text for conveying messages. Second, the text is ephemeral, appearing on and disappearing from a screen without any necessary tangible artifacts. In combination, these two features make it easy for a sender to forget or ignore his or her audience. Without reminders of an audience, people become less constrained by conventional norms and rules for behavior. (With special software it is possible to restructure the communication situation in a variety of ways. We discuss this topic in chapters 4 and 9.)

When Plain Text Is the Medium
Harold Geneen, the former head of ITT, discovered that his response to the European subsidiaries of ITT was different if they made their request by teletype to him in New York versus talking face-to-face with him in Europe: "In New York, I might read a request and say no. But in Europe, I could see that an answer to the same question might be yes . . . it became our policy to deal with problems on the spot, face-to-face" (cited by Trevino et al. 1987). The richness of face-to-face communication is illustrated in a study that found 93 percent of peoples' intent was conveyed by tone of voice and facial expression (Meherabian 1971). When communication lacks the dynamic personal information of face-to-face communication or even of telephone communication, people focus their attention more on the words in the message than on each other. Communicators feel a greater sense of anonymity and detect less individuality in others. They feel less empathy, less guilt, less concern over how they compare with others, and are less influenced by social conventions (Short, Williams, and Christie 1976; Kiesler, Siegel, and McGuire 1984).

The primary medium of electronic mail is text. Consider how this removes dynamic personal information and feedback. Senders have no way to link the content or tone of messages to the receivers' responses so they can evaluate how their messages are being received. Similarly, without nonverbal tools, it is difficult for a sender to convey nuance, communicate a sense of individuality, or exercise dominance or charisma.

Chapter 2 described the case of a product developer who sent a message to distribution lists reaching thousands of people. We noted that he did not have to know in advance who would have helpful information for him. He did not even have to know the kinds of people who might be helpful—their locations, their organizational positions, their department, and so on. Thus his request and responses to it could be exchanged efficiently. Something else is important about this message. The sender not only did not have to know his audience, but he could not have known his audience, at least not in the same way he would have known them had they been in the same room, or on the telephone with him, or even had he written to them by postal mail. Reread the message in box 2.3. Ask yourself, "Where are the recipients located?" "What is their position in the organization?" "How interested do they seem?" "How likely are they to take the message seriously?" Information about the people who receive the message is lacking. Now consider what the recipients of this message would know about its author. Notice that the message is text alone, as letters or memoranda are, but also that it lacks information about the author's physical setting, organizational position, hierarchical status, departmental affiliation, race, age, appearance, and even gender. The form and style of the message is neither formal nor informal, project specific nor general. It looks like neither a corporate memo nor a note someone might stick on an office door.

Text exchanges contain no dynamic personal information such as tone of voice. Electronic text exchanges also contain little static information that relates to place, position, and person. From the sender's side, the large and easily accessible audience is a social hodgepodge. From the receiver's end, all electronic mail looks pretty much the same. A person receiving a message learns very little about the sender's social position—not even the information that a letterhead or a signature placed at the bottom right side of a letter conveys. An electronic mail message also contains scant information about a situation's norms. Reminders of the sender's setting are unavailable. Of course, people may possess relevant information from other sources, but the message itself provides few cues to evoke that knowledge. Many receivers' only clues to a sender's identity and situation are his or her computer name and address. The practice in many computer systems of giving people IDs that computers understand but people don't removes even this identity cue. Consider the following three computer addresses: AS6Y@ANDREW; DAS@FAS.RI; HAS@A.GP.CS. These are the computer names and addresses of the three employees of our university whose last name is Simon. One is a secretary, one a staff engineer, and one a Nobel prize winner. Who's who?

Ephemeral Communication

Although computer-based communication systems may permanently archive all electronic messages, people perceive the experience of sending and receiving messages as an ephemeral one. The immediate experience is conveyed by fingers moving on a keyboard and phosphor flickering on a screen; messages appear and disappear with the touch of a button. There are no tangible artifacts like someone sitting across a desk or ever growing piles of paper or bulging filing cabinets to remind people of their partici-pation in communications exchanges. The lack of tangible artifacts and perceived ephemerality cause people to lose mental sight of their com-munication partners. As one participant in a pharmaceutical company electronic conference put it, "When I discuss something on DIALOG, in the back of my mind I know somebody else is going to hear it, but it isn't as obvious as if we were all in one room. It's like I know the tape recorder is running, but I kind of block it out" (Zuboff 1988:370).

When people perceive communication to be ephemeral, the stakes of communication seem smaller. People feel less committed to what they say, less concerned about it, and less worried about the social reception they will get. Testimony in the Iran-Contra hearings shows that while the computer system used by the White House staff automatically saved all message traffic, and staffers knew it, people forgot that messages deleted from their screens had not in actuality disappeared. People such as Oliver North took care to disguise and hide their face-to-face discussions and hard-copy memoranda about inappropriate or illegal activity. They were lax about their privacy when they communicated using the electronic mail system.

Let Your Fingers Do the Talking

Ordinarily when people communicate, they aren't just exchanging infor-mation; they are projecting an image of themselves. This knowledge can make them shy in front of others, especially those whose respect they most desire. Ephemerality and plain text in electronic mail reduce the fear of appearing foolish in front of others. By removing reminders of a possibly critical audience, electronic mail induces people to be more open (Sproull and Kiesler 1986).

Ignoring Social Boundaries

Birds of a feather flock together. This aphorism summarizes both what is right and what is wrong about communication in organizations. Limiting interaction and information exchange to like-minded colleagues shields people from unnecessary information. It also can lead to organizational disaster by separating people from information they need to know. Cues in organizational settings reinforce social differences that systematically separate people from one another. Office size and decorating schemes are reminders of status differences.[2] Clothing reminds people of the difference between white-collar and blue-collar jobs. Age, gender, race, beauty, wealth, and composure are "read" from voice and appearance. Reminders of these sources of inclusion or exclusion disappear or fade with computer-based communication.

All communication technologies weaken social differences apparent in face-to-face communication. The telephone eliminates visual cues and therefore reduces one's ability to deduce the other person's social position and to grasp the importance of social differences in the interaction. Over the telephone, though, one retrieves some social information in nonvisual form. The secretary who answers or places calls, variations in standard ways of greeting, and pauses and tone of voice all convey social information.

Shoshana Zuboff (1988) describes how a computer conference system in one firm brought together people from different functional areas and diverse social backgrounds. The remote and textural qualities of the computer, she says, eliminated peoples' advantage or disadvantage over one another. Those who regarded themselves as physically unattractive reported feeling more lively and confident when they expressed themselves in a computer conference. Others with soft voices or small stature felt they no longer had to struggle to be taken seriously in a meeting. One employee said, "DIALOG lets me talk to other people as peers. No one knows if I am an hourly worker or a vice president. All messages have an equal chance because they all look alike. The only thing that sets them apart is their content. If you are a hunchback, a paraplegic, a woman, a black, fat, old, have two hundred warts on your face, or never take a bath, you still have the same chance. It strips away the halo effects from age, sex, or appearance" (Zuboff 1988:371).

As halo effects were removed, peoples' competence and ability became recognized, independent of their position or appearance. Zuboff claims that DIALOG's participants built reputations based on the quality of their messages and their helpfulness in being informative. One participant noted that "lots of people have power that is not knowledge-based: it is forceful and based on their personality or position. In DIALOG, the power lies in the ability to communicate and pass on knowledge. I have extended my power base through my knowledge rather than through intimidation or style. It is strictly now the quality of your ideas, the way you put things in words, or your sensitivity to what others say that now determines your influence" (Zuboff 1988:371).

Self-Disclosure

In the mid-1960s an MIT computer scientist wrote a program named ELIZA that parodied a Rogerian psychotherapist. When a person typed in a statement appropriate for an initial visit to a psychotherapist, ELIZA would reply with a supportive response based on simple pattern matching keyed to a response script. For instance, if the "patient" typed a statement containing the word *mother*, the reply might be, "Tell me more about your mother." The author of ELIZA, Joseph Weizenbaum, was appalled to discover that people found it involving and gratifying to tell their troubles to a computer program.[3] He thought that they should know better than to talk to a computer "as if it were a person who could be appropriately and usefully addressed in intimate terms" (Weizenbaum 1976:7). What perhaps he did not realize is that, far from being appropriate and useful, honest self-disclosure to real people can often be inappropriate, offensive, or ego bruising. Perhaps the people "talking" to ELIZA were so intimate precisely because they knew there was no human being who would hear and judge their remarks.

Today organizations are beginning to use computer-based communication as a way to collect information from customers and employees. Unlike ELIZA, there is always a person at the other end of the question-asking program to read and evaluate the collected information. Market research firms, personnel departments, and hospitals are beginning to experiment with electronic questionnaires. The questions appear on a computer screen, and people type their replies directly into the computer. (We distinguish between this method, which includes informed consent to participate, and random-digit-dialing automated telemarketing, which does not.) The advantage of computer interviews over face-to-face interviews is that the computer always treats everyone the same way and never gets tired. The advantage of these interviews over paper questionnaires is that the computer can ask follow-up questions in a branching design based on respondents' answers. With branching, the questionnaire becomes more like an interview—it can cover more topics tailored to the respondent, is more fun, and seems shorter even when it isn't (Synodinos and Brennan 1988). Because answers go directly into computer memory, the method also eliminates transcription costs.

Computer interviews, like electronic mail, create a feeling of privacy. This sense of safety makes interviewees somewhat more willing to disclose information than they are willing to disclose in face-to-face interviews or on paper-and-pencil questionnaires. One of our research projects monitored the outcome of an official university poll of students. Among the students randomly assigned to fill out a paper-and-pencil version of the survey, only 3 percent admitted using illegal drugs at least once a week for recreational purposes. Among the students assigned to receive the survey by electronic mail, a significantly greater 14 percent made the same admission. In another study, we asked people to describe themselves. The sample was divided into two groups—one that answered an electronic survey and one that answered a paper survey. The respondents were randomly assigned to each group so that other systematic differences between the groups were balanced out. Each group was assured that the survey would be completely confidential and private. (Technically, anyone answering a computer survey can be traced, but people feel more exposed when answering on paper or in a face-to-face interview.) Table 3.1 displays some ways respondents in the study answered questions about their behavior. A significantly higher percentage of those who answered on paper cared about "looking good."

The self-disclosure induced in computer interviews has more honesty than that in other methods. Researchers in Scotland looked at whether a computer interview could be used to measure alcohol consumption. As judged by actual sales of alcohol, traditional survey methods measure only half of consumption. Table 3.2 displays the consumption of alcohol respondents reported to a computer as compared to answers given to an interviewer. The alcohol consumption reported in the computer survey was higher than that reported in the face-to-face interview. Also the consumption figures from the computer interviews much more closely matched alcohol sales figures than did the consumption figures from the face-to-face interviews.

Advances in artificial intelligence, along with the discovery that self-disclosure can be extremely comfortable for people interacting with a computer, have encouraged the development of computer-administered interviews. There are electronic surveys for doing market research, em-

Table 3.1
Percentages who responded "true" to questions about good behavior

	Paper survey	Computer survey
I am always careful about my dress	50	20
I always try to practice what I preach	79	72
I would never think of letting someone else be punished for my wrongdoings	87	57
I never resent being asked to return a favor	74	59

Source: Kiesler and Sproull (1986).

Table 3.2
Weekly consumption of alcohol reported by a sample of men in Scotland

	Personal interview	Computer interview
Glasses of beer	15.0	19.0
Glasses of wine	1.2	1.7
Shots of whiskey	3.4	5.4

Source: Waterton and Duffy (1984).

ployment and personnel evaluations, tutoring, career guidance, psychiatric and medical diagnosis, and even psychological counseling.[4] One such program, named Sexpert, is designed to provide counseling for couples with sexual dysfunctions. The program carries out a series of interviews with the couple, "talking" to each of them independently and to both as a couple. It keeps a record of their responses and uses the information it gleans to determine its next responses and therapeutic plans, including "homework assignments" and coaching. Box 3.1 displays a segment from one session.

Sexpert is one of the few computer interview programs to be evaluated in controlled experiments. In a recent study (Binik, Westbury, and Servan-Schreiber 1989), people used Sexpert for a short time. Before and after this interaction, the researchers administered attitude measures about computerized sex therapy. Two control groups got identical measures but different experimental manipulations. In one, the control group interacted with a computer program unrelated to sex. In the other, they filled out a sex-related paper-and-pencil questionnaire with questions identical to those asked by Sexpert. The results showed that before the experimental manipulations, all participants believed that using a computer for sex therapy was little better than reading a book and far worse than seeing a human expert such as a psychologist or physician. After the experiment, strong attitude shifts in favor of computerized sex therapy occurred in those who had used Sexpert. No attitude changes occurred in the control groups.

Comments about Sexpert suggest that this program simulates an unthreatening, knowledgeable human, inspiring respondents' confidence. The developers of the program report their "amazement" at videotaped sessions in which couples were "clearly engaged" by Sexpert and "seriously discussed their sex life, relationship, and Sexpert's comments with each other." In describing one couple they say, "The couple reported after the session that they had discussed together for the first time several critical

---

Box 3.1. Computer-administered sex therapy

This is a "discussion" that a couple had with a computer. Responses of the couple to the computer are given in italics. We do not include a record of what they said to one another:

```
Rhoda, did your parents talk to you about sex when you were
growing up?
```
no

```
Children often consciously or unconsciously interpret their
parents' silence concerning sex as an indication that sex is
bad or at the least is something not to be talked about.
Obviously, parents who are uncomfortable talking about sex or
who are themselves misinformed may also transmit negative
messages. One way or the other, it isn't very useful to blame
them for this. I suspect they tried their best and were
probably only acting like their own parents. Now it is up to
you to improve on it for yourself.
```

```
Did you learn about sex from other sources such as books,
friends, siblings, school, etc?
```
yes

```
Do you feel the information you got was accurate?
```
yes

```
I'm really pleased to hear that.  Most of my clients do not
feel that way.  Although accurate information about sex is
highly desirable and often helps sexual performance, it is
sometimes not sufficient to insure a pleasurable sex life.

Have you experienced any sex related events such as rape or
incest that were traumatic for you?
1 you have
2 you have not
3 you don't want to talk about it
1
```

[Here the client's answer triggers a "sexual trauma dialogue plan" that temporarily interrupts the dialogue plan related to the discussion of orgasmic concerns.]

```
Ron, are you aware of what happened?
nQ

I'm not sure why you haven't discussed this, however there are
often valid reasons to avoid such a discussion.  The most
immediate reason may be that discussing or even thinking about
what happened can bring back many of the emotions and fears
related to it.  I'm a little concerned that I've raised an
issue that you might not be ready to deal with.  If one or both
of you feel this way, it may be better to further delay discus-
sion.  It may also be highly advisable to see human help
concerning this.

Rhoda, do you want to continue talking about this now?
no

Fine, let me just say that even if we were to discuss the
details of what happened, it would be very difficult for me to
know how your sex life would have developed had this trauma not
occurred.  I hope that it is reassuring for you to know that
there are many women who experienced a sexual trauma but were
able to develop their orgasmic capacity.
```

Source: Servan-Schreiber and Binik (1989: 254–255).

issues concerning their sexuality and that as a result they felt increased intimacy, openness, as well as comfort with their sexual feelings" (Servan-Schreiber and Binik 1989:257).

It may seem curious that people would answer threatening or sensitive questions more honestly on a computer than in other forms. Nearly everyone knows a computer can store everything one says. Yet people interacting on a computer are isolated from social cues and feel safe from surveillance and criticism. This feeling of privacy makes them feel less inhibited with others. It also makes it easy for them to disagree with, confront, or take exception to others' opinions.

Flaming

"If you can't say something nice, don't say anything at all" is a common social convention—and one often forgotten in computer-based communication. Electronic messages are often startlingly blunt, and electronic discussions can escalate rapidly into name calling and epithets, behavior that computer buffs call flaming. (According to *The Hacker's Dictionary* [Steele 1983:65], to flame is "to speak incessantly and/or rabidly on some relatively uninteresting subject or with a patently ridiculous attitude . . . Synonym: Rave.") As a consequence of the low level of social information in computer-based communication and its perceived ephemerality, people lose their fear of social approbation. Moreover, they imagine they must use stronger language to get their message across.

Because a person composing an electronic message lacks tangible reminders of his or her audience, the writer can easily forget the norms appropriate for communicating with that audience. Also, the writer lacks paralinguistic resources to help convey his or her ideas. Resorting to ever stronger language is a common result. Box 3.2 displays a message sent by an employee via an electronic distribution list to all the people who worked in his building. It is inconceivable that the writer would have spoken that message to its three hundred recipients had they all been assembled in an auditorium. It is also highly unlikely that the writer would have posted hard copies of the message on all the bulletin boards and exit doors of the building. (By printing this message in a book, we are distorting its original impact by giving it a tangibility that the original did not have.) Each of those acts would have vividly reminded the author of his audience, leading him to temper his language. Flames such as the one in box 3.2 do not go unremarked when they are distributed electronically. The author of that message quickly received several electronic chastisements and sent another message a few hours later apologizing for his language.

The phenomenon of flaming suggests that through electronic mail, actions and decisions, not just talk, might become more extreme and impulsive. Because reminders of settings and kinds of people are weak or nonexistent, decision makers might feel less bound by convention and less concerned with consequences. Research in nonelectronic settings over the past three decades has examined the phenomenon of deindividuation.

Box 3.2. A flame

This example of flaming was delivered automatically to three hundred employees, including a senior vice president, in the sender's division.

```
Date:   5 May 1983 9:06 am PDT (Thursday)
From:   Tom Jones [technical professional]
Subject:  Damage to my scooter
To:  Div.R and D [building distribution list]

cc:    Motorcyclists [interest group distribution list]


Yesterday, some nameless obscenity move my scooter.  Since the
handle bars were locked, this involved dragging my Vespa
sideways.  This was done with enough vigor to break off one of
the rubber molding strips protecting the foot platform.
        Whoever you are, LEAVE MY MACHINE ALONE — LEAVE MY MACHINE
ALONE LEAVE MY MACHINE ALONE.  I AM ANGRY AT THE M****FER WHO
F***KED WITH MY MACHINE.
        This is my basic transportation.  I don't own a car.  If
you destroy my machine, you deprive me of my mobility.  If I
discover anyone tampering with my scooter again, I will cheer-
fully rearrange your face w/the "generic blunt object" I carry
with me.
```

Deindividuation occurs when people have anonymity or when situations lack reminders of societal mores and values. Large crowds wearing uniforms and focused on an exciting event are one situation creating deindividuation. These situations can inspire agitation, feelings of being "part of something else," and freedom from social or moral strictures—feelings that in turn lead to suggestibility. Under heightened suggestibility, people can behave aggressively—or do whatever a leader or strong cue suggests—far more than they would do in their normal milieu.[5] We speculate that an electronic communication setting could inspire suggestible behavior too if an electronic substitute for the strong leader or cue were present.

Guiding Behavior

Strong social norms eventually become attached to all common communication technologies and situations; people rely on instruction, experience, and cues in the situation to remind them of those norms. Some "on-line communities" already have strong norms and expectations for behavior. Many of these are to be found in the public dial-in bulletin board systems that people join for extracurricular reasons (Besston and Tucker 1984). Members lavish attention on their personas and on elaborate codes of behavior in these settings (Myers 1987), yet there is still extremely wide variation in acceptable behavior across electronic situations. In the workplace people have to negotiate this uncertainty while simultaneously trying to get their work done.

Uncertainties arise from the absence of shared rules and norms. Explicit rules and policies for electronic communication differ from organization to organization. For example, some organizations explicitly forbid extracurricular messages; others do not. Some organizations permit people to send electronic mail to anyone with a mail address; others require that mail be sent through channels. Some organizations explicitly designate an employee as censor to read every broadcast message for inappropriate material. Other organizations allow people to police their own behavior. Not only do rules differ but also there are no strong norms common across organizations. Some people use salutations, and some do not. Some copy their mail to superiors, and some do not. Some answer their messages immediately, and some do not. Some talk about intimate personal subjects, and some do not.

In the face of these uncertainties, people adopt various mechanisms to remind themselves and others that they are social actors in a social situation. They add explicit typographic cues to signal attitude and mood, adopt different personas for different groups, and craft etiquette messages. In the future, just as happened with automobile travel, familiarity with the technology will grow, social expectations will evolve, and norms will stabilize. Some unconventional behavior we see today in electronic communication will settle down as the technology becomes more widespread and people gain more experience with it. Still, so long as electronic communication has little social information and seems ephemeral, it will remain relatively open and unconstrained.

Adding Cues

Conventions for expressing mood or feelings are emerging within some well-established electronic mail communities. FLAMEON is a common warning that an unrestrained message follows. A smiling face, typed rotated as :-) , suggests a joke or happiness. Bad news or unhappiness is conveyed by :-(. Although such cues weakly signal mood, they are flat and stereotyped. The boss's smiling face looks no different from the secretary's. Mild amusement looks no different from hilarity.

It is possible to convey idiosyncrasy, personality, and vibrancy with only plain text. Professional writers have always done so. Some people who belong to multiple electronic groups write messages in a different voice to each group.[6] Box 3.3 shows how two people alter their persona for different groups. But such literary skill is uncommon among organizational participants.

McGrath and Hollingshead's (1990) analyses of how time-related cues influence work groups suggest that electronic communication lacks many such cues. For example, a group in an asynchronous discussion is usually not timed or warned about time, nor is the sequence of contributions or the total time given to the discussion controlled. Often group members aren't aware of who should do, or is doing, what task at what time. This lack of awareness can contribute to deregulation of social behavior. People don't

---

Box 3.3. Changing personas in electronic messages

Person A

Message to UserFeatureForum:

```
I cannot imagine a pathname standard that does not reserve * as
a wildcard.  It's much more than PHC we're dealing with here —
I think most other major operating systems use the same conven-
tions:  TOPS-20, RSX-11W...  Users of these systems are exactly
the few hundred thousand people who are most likely to be our
first customers — people who'll be talking to these other
operating systems via TTY emulation.
```

Message to Cinema:

```
an'I likes Joe Bob.  Shucks, I though tall the humorless prigs
had already migrated to Review.  If'n ya dun lak it, y'all kin
CLICK DELETE once a week on any msg with "Joe Bob" in the
header.  AH HAS SPOKEN!  I suggest directing your brickbats,
kudos, etc. to me rather than subjecting the whole list to any
further meta-discussion.
```

Person B

Message to UserFeatureForum:

```
The easiest interface to learn and use would seem to be the
multiple click for contention  resolution, since it is what
most people already do.  However, I would think the inevitable
small movements of the mouse in the course of clicking would
make implementation difficult, with non-redundant ambiguities
introduced between an unintentional movement while intending to
continue on the contenders list, and an intentional movement to
start somewhere nearby.
```

Message to Rowdies:

```
By the way, there's this convention on TV that flashers run
around in raincoats with no pants.  Now, if memory serves, the
men I've seen more of than I would normally expect were gener-
ally just hanging around near the bottom of the subway steps or
something, with their fly open and their whatever hanging out.
So what I want to know, is whether There really are flashers
that run around without any pants on, or whether that's just
something someone made up for TV so people would get the idea
without getting the picture, so to speak.  Anyone know?  Anyone
have personal experience in the matter? ~1492~
```

Source: Finholt and Sproull (1990: 58).

───

establish or enforce deadlines; they lack norms for smooth teamwork; they fail to resolve inefficient or inequitable time demands. Adding temporal cues and controls in computer-based communication might greatly increase social information and guides to behavior.

Among the time-related social information that influences behavior is information about what time it is now, when a piece of work or meeting is supposed to start and be done, whose time is more (or most) important, and how time should be allocated to different projects or topics. Outside the electronic forum, most organizations respond to these questions with physical reminders such as clocks and bells, notices about agendas, deadlines, and requested work commitments, procedures synchronized according to time, and norms for behavior regulation over time. People respond by monitoring their own time and behavior, by making time commitments, and by tuning in to the flow of tasks and to discussions.

Adding cues such as clocks, dynamic gauges and calendars, scheduling programs, and so forth to electronic mail would reintroduce some of the temporal controls that organizations and groups use. Adding restrictions and rules, such as limited participation and agreements on how much input any individual is allowed to make, would do so also. Yet many would resist such changes. The lack of temporal cues encourages electronic interactions to wander and explore indirect paths and creative solutions. Ample time causes groups to use all the time available but also allows them to improve the quality of their interactions and to give more emotional support to one another. It also encourages wider participation.

The addition of sound and pictures to computer-based communication will dramatically increase social information in computer-based communication. Already visual information close to the quality of hard-copy documents is becoming available. Voice will be next. The abortive history of the picture phone suggests that there are limits to people's eagerness to invest in ever-richer social information, yet the general trend is toward more bandwidth, not less. There are both advantages and disadvantages in including more social information in computer-based communication. (In chapter 9 we discuss these trade-offs.)

Instruction and Etiquette
People usually convey norms by example. Only when groups are new, take on many new members, or have conflict do people discuss norms explicitly. Box 3.4 displays an example of a frequent occurrence in electronic mail communities. It is a message offering a series of suggestions for how to write "civil and useful" messages. Notice that a flame preceded it ("my recent outburst against two frequent contributors") and that it references chastising responses ("numerous private responses") to the flame. In an interesting twist, it is the transgressor who proposes the guidelines.

The specific suggestions from the message in box 3.4 or the hundreds of other similar etiquette messages found in computer-based communication systems can be elevated to a general code of etiquette for electronic mail, a version of which has been offered by Shapiro and Anderson (1985). The code contains sensible advice for senders of messages: assume that any message you send is permanent; have in mind a model of your intended audience; do not insult or criticize third parties without giving them a chance to respond. It also offers advice for recipients of messages: avoid responding while emotional; assume the honesty and competence of the sender; avoid irrelevancies. Someone who had never used electronic mail (or who had not read this chapter) might think it peculiar and condescending to offer such obvious advice to grown men and women. By contrast, we believe it is appropriate, but ironically, the features of computer-based communication that make such advice appropriate also make it unlikely to be remembered when people most need it.

Conclusion

Some organizations consider electronic mail a way to increase the transmission accuracy of information that otherwise would be conveyed more haphazardly. The assumption is that the same message can be delivered with fewer errors than through other means. By contrast, we suggest that the means by which a message is conveyed affects the meaning of the message. In the case of electronic mail, plain text and perceived ephemer-

Box 3.4. Electronic etiquette message

```
Date:  Wed, 9 Aug 89
From:  S. Marks
Subject:  [Statistics distribution list] etiquette
To:  Multiple recipients of [Statistics distribution list]
   I have received numerous private responses to my recent
outburst against two frequent contributors to this list....I
would, however, like to  publicly apologize for my rather
strong language in criticizing their postings.  To avoid such
useless exchanges in future, may I suggest some guidelines for
keeping postings to the list civil and useful?

1.  No one is obliged to reply to a question.  If you find a
question too trivial for your trouble, just ignore it.  But
don't tell the world that it is too trivial:  that only puffs
you up and humiliates the questioner.
. . .
4.  Refrain from attacks on a contributor's intelligence,
competence, patience, or diligence.  It is, however, permis-
sible to attack a *solution* as being incorrect, clumsy,
unworkable, or unclear.  Such an attack should be worded and
interpreted in such a way that these attributes are not to be
ascribed to the person who proposed that solution.  And of
course, it is always permissible to criticize the [organization]
and its personnel, as long as the statements are truthful and
tasteful.
5.  Make sure that your answer will be useful to the person
requesting help, or to other subscribers.  Don't post something
merely to show off your erudition or wit.  (Of course, this
doesn't mean that useful postings can't also be witty.)  In
short:  "If you can't post something useful, don't post any-
thing at all."
```

This message was sent to an electronic distribution list for exchanging information about statistical procedures. It is subscribed to by over a thousand people in more than three hundred different sites. The actual readership may be much larger because each subscriber may duplicate the messages for others in his or her organization.

ality induce relatively open and blunt remarks, little influenced (for better or worse) by social niceties. An important point here is that the change is relative. We do not suggest that electronic communication turns employees into beasts. We do suggest that in comparison with other forms of communication in a given organization, the electronic communication will be relatively franker and will demonstrate relatively less audience awareness.

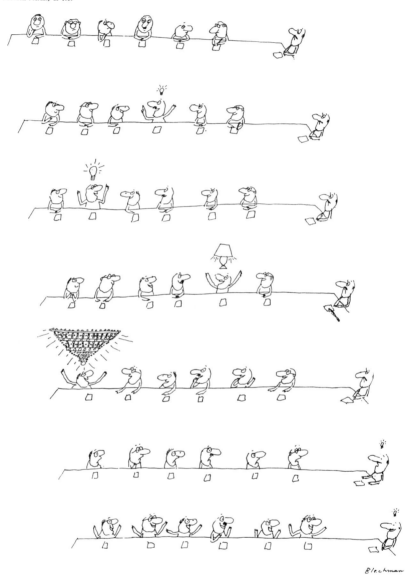

Drawing by Blechman, Courtesy of Punch Publications, Ltd.

4

Electronic Group Dynamics

People in organizations spend much time in meetings and group discussions; managers spend most of their time in this way (Mintzberg 1973; Sproull 1983). Most meetings follow a predictable course. Participation is unequal; one person or a minority clique dominates the floor. Member status predicts who will dominate. Managers speak more than subordinates; men speak more than women; the person at the front of the room speaks more than those at the back. People are polite and considerate, and they avoid controversy. If a decision is necessary, the group converges on a decision over time by narrowing and discarding options through discussion. People prefer options that have obvious popularity. Often we can predict the decision by knowing who dominates the discussion.

The predictability of meetings is often useful. Efficiency is served if one person dominates. When that person has high status, the meeting's outcomes have legitimacy. Mental effort declines if everyone knows how the meeting will come out. Four decades of research on group behavior have documented and described some ways that groups are predictable.[1] *Cohesiveness* is the tendency for group members to stick together. *Egocentrism* is the tendency to reject outsiders and outside ideas. *Group extremitization* describes groups' tendency to adopt more extreme positions than do their individual members. *Groupthink* encompasses egocentrism, conformity pressures, group extremitization, and illusions of invulnerability and morality in groups (Janis 1972). These predictable processes often describe competent groups—but they also can produce disasters. Group decisions ending in lost lives and national confusion led to the 1961 Bay of Pigs invasion of Cuba, the 1980 mission to rescue American hostages in Iran, and the 1986 explosion of NASA's Challenger space shuttle. Bad decisions are not the prerogative of government groups, of course. In 1978, nine hundred members of a religious sect who had fled to Guyana decided to obey their deranged leader by killing themselves.

For good or bad, the dynamics of face-to-face meetings usually are predictable and similar across groups. The dynamics of electronic group meetings, however, differ from those of face-to-face meetings and are less predictable. Managers and software developers interested in putting groups on-line to streamline their operations (a first-level effect) should understand that patterns of participation and the quality of decisions may vary enormously from those of face-to-face groups (a second-level effect). This chapter is about how people behave in electronic meetings. First we compare behavior in electronic meetings with the behavior of the same people in face-to-face meetings. The standard of comparison is face-to-face meetings not because they are always preferable to other forums but because they are ubiquitous. Next we offer suggestions for designing and managing electronic groups.

The evidence in this chapter comes primarily from controlled experiments and not, as in the other chapters, from observation of natural electronic groups in organizations. One might ask why it takes experiments to uncover how electronic communication changes group dynamics. Because people like working in groups, they often do not measure and report their group behavior objectively. Cohesiveness and consensus are pleasant, so group members conclude that their group has done well, whether or not this impression has validity. Experiments can separate perceptions from actual group behavior. An experimental study of brainstorming in a computer-based group decision support system at the University of Arizona illustrates the sometimes incorrect connection between how well group members like a group and how they evaluate its performance. Researchers put a confederate in each group to compare the effect of a critical member with a supportive member. Electronic discussion groups with a planted group member who criticized others produced more new ideas and achieved more than groups whose planted member was highly supportive. Yet group members' perceptions of their success did not match the performance facts. Groups with the critical group member did not like their group and incorrectly thought the group did poorly, whereas groups with the supportive member liked their group and incorrectly thought they did very well (Connolly, Jessup, and Valacich 1990).

Experiments are a way of systematically testing assumptions in a way that cannot be done through natural experience alone. They make it possible to watch the same people (or randomly assigned people) in both electronic and face-to-face groups and thus rule out the possibility that observed differences in behavior stem from personality or job differences that cause people to prefer one type of meeting to another. The disadvantage of experiments is that they never duplicate all the conditions of actual groups. Most troublesome is that experiments usually construct groups from people who do not typically and routinely work together.

Although experimental groups sometimes do not behave as actual groups do, experiments often reveal hidden processes that managers and group members should attend to. For instance, experiments on brainstorming in groups indicates that face-to-face interaction can dampen creativity and productivity. Group members spend too much time listening to each other instead of thinking. They try too hard to please one another. (See, for instance, Diehl and Stroebe 1987.) Actual groups can be given training in brainstorming techniques, but training may not overcome the social pressures on people to listen and to censor their own ideas. New decision-support conference rooms that allow group members to communicate electronically through a local area network make another technique feasible: People meet in the decision room, but prior to discussion, they simultaneously and anonymously contribute ideas to an electronic brainstorming idea pool. This pool of ideas is made the basis of face-to-face discussion. This technique can leverage both the productivity of individual work and the motivating properties of group interaction.

How Electronic Groups Work

Who Participates?

In a face-to-face meeting, only one person can talk a time. In electronic discussions, taking turns is unnecessary because electronic communication is asynchronous. Thus for any given duration of time, more people can "talk" in an electronic meeting than in a comparable face-to-face one.

In a face-to-face meeting, talking time is usually not distributed equally across all participants; often it is very unequal. One person or a minority clique often dominates the discussion, talking most of the time while participation by others falls off rapidly. Sometimes half the members talk only 10 or 20 percent of the time. In electronic discussions, participation is more equal. For instance, in one experiment, three-person groups that held discussions electronically showed twice as much equality of participation as when they talked face to face. Members tended to talk their appropriate one-third of the time in the electronic discussion. Figure 4.1 illustrates differences in participation patterns across many experiments.

In face-to-face groups, the amount a person talks has a high correlation with his or her prestige and social status. Status imbalance has been documented in classrooms, hospitals, personnel interviews, performance appraisals, and decision-making meetings.[2] Status within a group derives in part from status in the outside world, as well as from work in the group. In other words, people carry their status from group to group, though some of their standing in any particular group depends on their particular group role and expertise. Thus, for instance, in face-to-face groups, managers talk more than subordinates; men talk more than women. These behaviors hold

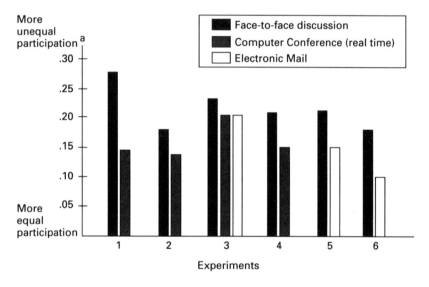

a. In the scale, 1.0 represents perfect inequality, when one person does all the talking. Zero represents perfect equality, when everyone talks the same amount.

Figure 4.1
Equalization of participation in computer-mediated discussions: Results of six experiments (source: Results of experiments 1–3 are from Siegel, Dubrovsky, Kiesler, and McGuire [1986]; of experiment 4 are from McGuire, Kiesler, and Siegel [1987]; of experiment 5 are from Dubrovsky, Kiesler, and Sethna [in press]; and of experiment 6 are from Weisband [in press])

even when the generally higher-status (and more vocal) members are not more expert on the topic under consideration.

Status hierarchies in groups have been of strong interest to social scientists and to people whose business is to improve decision making in organizations. Status has particular relevance to decisions and problems that require a series of steps to reach a solution or choice, with each step dependent on the previous one. Because a consistent strategy is needed to solve the problem, group members may interfere with, rather than complement, one another's efforts. This difficulty was discovered by James Davis and Frank Restle in 1963; they found that groups working through long problems requiring sequential solutions had difficulty in identifying their most expert members. High-status members tended to make comments, whether or not their comments were worthwhile. As a result, discovery of correct solutions depended on factors other than competence, in particular, feelings about who should contribute to the group and who shouldn't—the status of those making suggestions.

Because it is harder to read status cues in electronic messages than it is in other forms of communication, high-status people do not dominate the discussion in electronic groups as much as they do in face-to-face groups. For instance, when groups of executives met face-to-face, the men in the groups were five times as likely as the women to make the first decision proposal. When those same groups met via computer, the women made the first proposal as often as the men did (McGuire, Kiesler, and Siegel 1987). When pairs of graduate students and undergraduates met face-to-face to decide their joint project, the pairs were likely to choose the topic preferred by the graduate student. When equivalent pairs of students discussed and decided electronically, they were equally likely to choose the topic initially preferred by the undergraduate (Huff and King 1988).

We compared face-to-face discussion with discussion by electronic mail in groups with one M.B.A. graduate student and three college freshmen (Dubrovsky, Kiesler, and Sethna in press). Everyone in the groups considered the M.B.A. student to be higher in prestige and experience—a status imbalance that influenced the face-to-face discussions, where the M.B.A. student talked more than the freshmen. The M.B.A. student also was more likely to take the initiative in advocating a decision. (This domination occurred most strongly for career choice decisions about which the M.B.A. student was more knowledgeable. It happened also, but less so, in decisions concerning the freshman year curriculum, about which the M.B.A. student was no more expert than others.) Electronically, status differences were smaller. The high-status group member participated less when the group communicated electronically. Simultaneously, the low-status members spoke more, reducing (but not obliterating) the impact of status differences (figure 4.2).

Another important difference between the two forms of group meeting was that anyone—or everyone—in the electronic discussion could advocate a decision early before "listening" to others, whereas only one member (usually the high-status one) could talk first when discussions were face-to-face. This difference in ability to talk led to a qualitative change in the dynamics of the electronic meetings in thirty-eight of forty-eight electronic discussions studied, two or more members jumped in at the beginning of the discussion with a "first" advocated position (figure 4.3). The consequence of this change was to diminish the credibility and impact of the high-status members. When high-status members were first advocates in face-to-face discussion, they tended to influence the group's decision

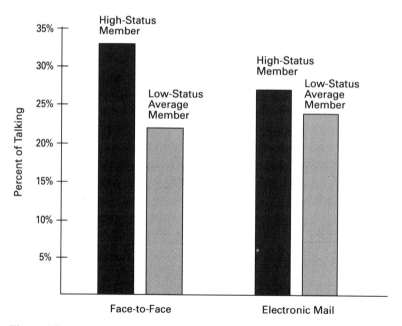

Figure 4.2
Participation in decision-making groups: High-status versus low-status (average) members (source: Dubrovsky, Kiesler, and Sethna in press)

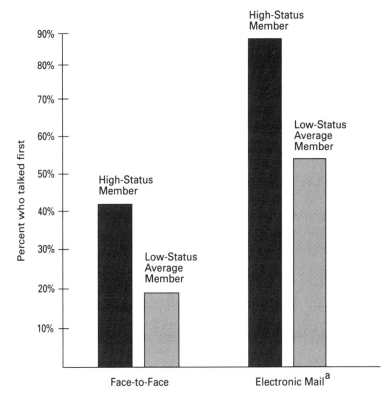

a. Note the overall difference between face-to-face discussion and electronic mail. Whereas in face-to-face discussion, only one person can be the first to advocate a position, in electronic mail, any number of members can be "first." In 38 of 48 electronic discussions summarized above, two or more members sent electronic mail advocating a position before receiving any such messages from others.

Figure 4.3
First advocates in decision-making groups: High-status versus low-status (average) members (source: Dubrovsky, Kiesler, and Sethna in press)

significantly, but when they were "first" advocates in electronic discussion their influence declined (figure 4.4).

Getting to Consensus

One evening in 1980, we asked three students to use a computer conference program for on-line discussion to reach consensus on a type of decision psychologists have studied extensively. Each decision offers two alternatives, one of which is riskier but more attractive than the other. For example, "Would you recommend Mr. Y try to become a concert pianist, a career that is exceedingly risky, or take the less risky path of becoming a physician?" These choices reveal a distinctively group effect: groups usually take a position that is more extreme than the average of the individual positions held by group members before the meeting. While making these decisions using a computer to communicate, the group

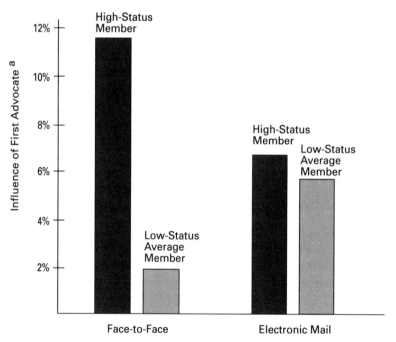

a. Influence is measured by comparing the member's privately preferred position before discussion with the position decided by the group

Figure 4.4
First advocates' influence: High-status versus low-status (average) members (source: Dubrovsky, Kiesler, and Sethna in press)

shifted toward even more extreme positions than face-to-face groups usually do and had enormous difficulty reaching consensus. Group members got so caught up in exchanging arguments, some using violent language, that, at 2 A.M., the experimenter had to halt the study.

This rude, impulsive behavior, dubbed flaming, is more common in electronic communication than in other forums. In one of our experiments, groups made 102 flaming remarks in twenty-four electronic discussions while the same groups made only 12 such remarks in twenty-four face-to-face discussions. Anger in one electronic discussion escalated so much that participants had to be escorted individually out of the building. Flaming was especially extreme when we arranged for group members to talk anonymously. Electronic mail is not the undoing of straightlaced people, but it does increase the emotions people will show in comparison with their face-to-face behavior.

Our observations of flaming have led us to look more closely at how discussion leads to consensus in face-to-face and electronic meetings. One difference is that tendencies to be argumentative and outspoken in electronic discussions sometimes lead to increased group conflict. Suzanne Weisband (in press) found that the pattern of consensus development diverged in face-to-face and electronic discussions. In face-to-face discussions, the second group member to speak up tended to agree with the first member, and the third member even more so. By the time the third member took a position, his or her stand often equalled the final group choice. The electronic mail discussions were different (figure 4.5). The third member's first offer was just as far from the ultimate group decision as the first member's was. This divergence meant that the electronic groups then had to exert more effort trying to reconcile contradictory opinions than the face-to-face groups did. These results suggest that electronic mail reduces conformity and convergence as compared with face-to-face group discussion. If a decision requires consensus, an electronic group has to work harder to get to it than a comparable face-to-face group does.

Decision Quality
In our experiments, every group makes multiple decisions—half face-to-face and half electronically.[3] We have used both real-time computer conferencing and asynchronous electronic mail, with approximately equivalent results. Consistently, we have observed the effects of diminished social information and social deregulation described in chapter 3.[4] When

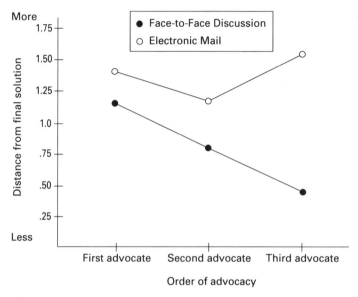

Figure 4.5
How opinions change during discussion (source: Weisband 1989)

the groups decide via computer, people have difficulty discovering how other group members feel. It is hard for them to reach consensus. When they disagree, they engage in deeper conflict. Conventional behavior, such as politeness and acknowledgment of other views, decreases. Group decisions are unpredictable, unconventional, democratic, and less constrained by high-status members.

Sometimes it makes sense for a group to be democratic and to ignore high-status people. In the experiment with M.B.A. students and freshmen, the high-status person was not always the most knowledgeable about the topic yet dominated face-to-face discussions even when the lower-status members had more knowledge. This dominance declined when the group made its decision electronically. When groups should favor expertise over position, then electronic discussion can lead to better-quality decisions. For instance, student pairs who had to choose a project topic electronically were less likely to choose the graduate student's preferred topic than pairs who made the choice face to face. Also, the pairs choosing electronically ultimately produced better projects (Huff and King 1988). In the face-to-face situation, deference to the higher-status student's preference may have obscured problems with the chosen topic that ultimately led to poorer projects, or the lower-status member may have felt railroaded and so had little motivation to be a full contributor. In either case, the face-to-face discussions produced poor decisions when status dominated expertise.

Unconventional and risky behavior sometimes can be valuable. We studied risk taking by asking university administrators and corporate managers, both individually and in three-person groups, to make decisions about investments that varied in riskiness (McGuire, Kiesler, and Siegel 1987). For example, suppose you have a choice between a safe investment and one that is riskier but more attractive. Suppose the first will return $20,000 over two years, whereas the other investment has a 50 percent chance of returning $40,000 and a 50 percent chance of returning nothing. Which would you choose? Most people avoid risk when one alternative is a sure gain; they choose the $20,000 (Kahneman and Tversky 1979). (This option only seems safer; mathematically there is no difference between the two alternatives in the average expected value over two years.) By contrast, when the choice is between a sure loss and a chance of losing nothing, people tend to take risks. For instance, when the choice is between surely losing $20,000 and an investment that has a 50 percent chance of losing nothing and a 50 percent chance of losing $40,000, most people will pick the second investment. They choose the riskier option (although the expected values over two years of the options are mathematically equivalent).

Groups that met face-to-face were risk averse for gain choices and risk seeking for loss choices, just as most individuals are. Yet when the same groups met electronically, they were somewhat risk seeking in all circumstances. (Figure 4.6 shows a screen from one electronic discussion.) The face-to-face discussions produced conventional decisions, whereas the electronic discussions produced unconventional ones that were riskier. Yet the executives were just as confident of their decisions whether they made them through computer-based communication or face-to-face.

"Were the electronic decisions good or poor?" The nature of these decisions makes that question unanswerable. To preserve realism for the managers in our studies, we did not pose technical problems that have a correct answer. Like many others in the world of business, research, and government, our decision tasks cannot be judged by the objective criterion of right or wrong. The value of a risky or cautious choice depends on

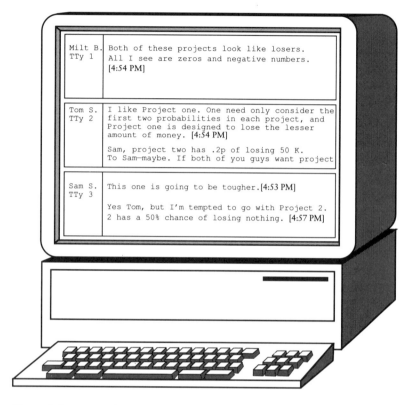

Figure 4.6
Display from an electronic discussion

circumstances. For example, in investment situations, it depends on what the competition is doing and what follow-up resources are available.

Our findings therefore do not bear directly on the accuracy of technical problem solving or the process of finding a correct decision if one exists. Our results do say something about the factors that groups will attend to when they solve problems electronically. As compared with their face-to-face counterparts, electronic groups will consult more people, which will increase the number of alternatives considered. They will more often ignore faulty reasoning promulgated by people who, face-to-face, have good social skills or organizational status. They may experience more conflict in solving problems. Electronic discussions can result in riskier choices, and group members may be unconscious of this. With these factors in mind, managers and group members can decide if their situation is appropriate to on-line discussion. There can be a real value to electronic decision making, but there is a danger, too, of assuming it will be valuable in all circumstances.

How Much Time Does It Take?

In simultaneous discussions, we have found that it takes approximately four times as long for a three-person group to make a decision electronically as face to face and as much as ten times as long in a four-person group. But electronic decision making isn't necessarily slow. Our comparisons consider only the time groups spend in actual discussion to reach consensus—either speaking and listening or reading and typing. They exclude time, like getting to the meeting, that outside the laboratory should be considered in such comparisons. A real problem, though, comes from the lack of social information in electronic discussions. As compared with face-to-face discussion, people communicating electronically have more trouble imagining what others are feeling. It is hard to tell how confident others are and whether they are ready to come to final agreement. We have learned that electronic groups should not be rushed beyond their capacity to exchange all the verbal information they want to exchange. When making decisions under a short deadline, groups reduced the ideas they exchanged electronically by as much as one-half, compounding the problem of diminished social information. Decisions made in rushed electronic discussions were significantly more extreme or polarized than decisions made in electronic discussions in which groups took as much time as they needed. Here, faster is not better.

These experiments do not tell us what happens over the entire life of a group project. Does it take more or less time to do well using computer-based communication technology? We have looked only at how much time people spend communicating with one another. In the software development teams described in chapter 2, teams that used electronic mail communicated in total no more than groups that did not. Total communication was the same because the groups using electronic mail spent less time in meetings, on the telephone, and writing paper memos, yet performance and motivation were better in the groups that used electronic mail. From this, we conclude that electronic communication need not increase the total time groups need to complete a project or to do it well.

Designing and Managing Electronic Groups

Groups are essential in organizations, but people in groups can have difficulty being productive. Designers of computer-based tools to support cooperative work or group work believe that special computer applications can help (DeSanctis and Gallupe 1987; Greif 1988). Managers say that on-line groups can work well (Meyer and Boone 1987). Researchers and developers have recently organized a new field of study, computer-supported cooperative work (CSCW), to reflect these beliefs.

CSCW advocates argue that because group tasks differ from individual tasks, group technology should be different from individual technology. For instance, a computer-based text editor aids individual work. One author uses it to produce a document. If two or more people collaborate to produce a coauthored document, the one-author text editor is less useful. Instead, a collaborative writing tool might be helpful. Suppose, besides text editing, such a tool made it easy for collaborators to distinguish one author's draft from another's and one author's comments from another's, and manage versions by reminding authors of where they are in their outline or production schedule. Collaborative writing tools fall under the rubric of CSCW. So do calendar programs and voting programs that support group management. Other applications filter information to reduce attention demands on group members (Malone et al. 1987). Still others augment face-to-face meetings (see box 4.1). In the future, CSCW tools may streamline and rationalize group work (first-level effect), but second-level changes in group dynamics also will occur.

Box 4.1. What is Groupware?

Among the technologies being developed to help groups is groupware or group decision support systems (GDSS). Many analysts use a simple typology to compare GDSS computer applications (Johansen 1988; Englebart 1989). It assumes there are four environments for group activity: (1) same time and same place (a face-to-face meeting); (2) same time, different places (a telephonic or video conference); (3) different times, same place (group record keeping, such as a project notebook); and (4) different times, different places (dispersed projects and committees).

Type 1 GDSS is software to augment face-to-face meetings. Examples of such software are found in the networked meeting room or classroom where everyone present can type what they want to say into computer terminals (Kraemer and King 1988; Poole, Holmes, and DeSanctis 1988; Dennis et al. 1988; Vogel and

Nunamaker 1990). The group leader or other member can display selected remarks or parts of a report, design, or plan before the entire group. The group might use a voting program. It also might have access to a database system containing relevant data or group records. The system could let group members create, revise, or simply query a database. Other software would allow group members to create or revise graphics designs together. Experimental systems have been used primarily for brainstorming groups and for teaching. One group is trying computer-aided methods for coding aspects of group behavior and then giving the group its own scores as feedback (Losada, Sanchez, and Noble 1990). Some analysts envision wide application in the future to decision making and negotiations, as well as to collaborative design and report writing.

Type 2 meetings are usually audio conference calls; video conferencing is far less common. Video conferencing can be used for teaching or for business presentations, where people need to see pictures, maps, charts, demonstrations with moving parts, or actual products. It also has found a niche for large "town meetings." The camera can focus on anyone who happens to take the floor, giving everyone a chance to be seen and heard. In most cases, either a telephonic or video conference meeting can take place only after someone has used another technology—telephone, fax, or electronic mail—to set up the meeting. New GDSS technology with an open line for spontaneous telephonic or video meetings is still experimental.

Type 3 group activity involves establishing a group record or memory. Suppose members make inputs to the group in the same place but not at the same time. They all need access to the resulting group record. One example of a group record that evolves in this way is a group calendar or PERT document. Another is a laboratory notebook in which project scientists make notations about their experiments. A more casual group record is notes left by shift workers or by project team members as they leave a work site. The notes tell the next shift or team members what was accomplished and what problems remain. Database systems are the new GDSS most people talk about for sequential group record keeping. Databases, especially natural language ones, allow people to create and to share records of their activities dynamically.

Type 4 activities occur at different times and different places. We focus almost exclusively on GDSS for type 4 activities, that is, technology that helps dispersed group members do their work. We do so because we believe computer-based communication technology has the most leverage when people are separated across time and space.

The four-fold typology is supposed to help people think about technology needed to support group meetings and administrative work. Yet the real problem is not figuring out which technology fits which meeting or administrative procedure. It is figuring out which physical and social arrangements need to be made to help groups do their work and make good decisions. Does a group need to meet at the same time to make all of its decisions? Do its records need to be kept in the same place? Should we use some new procedures for brainstorming?

Activities in categories 1, 2, and 3 in the typology make group members dependent on a site, on a time, or both. Often they are also dependent on having a quorum and following normal meeting procedures. With electronic communication, many organizations have found it possible to move group work out of these categories. Even when this isn't possible, tools on an electronic network can be applied interchangeably across all categories. Electronic distribution lists are not dependent on place, time, or membership. Nor are networked databases, calendar programs, voting programs, and collaborative writing and design tools, among others. The same customer database that helps salespeople on the road also can generate reports in their meetings. Throughout this book we give examples of networked GDSS tools that with little effort can be adapted to group work without reference to its previous physical and social arrangement.

When Are Electronic Groups Appropriate?

For any decision situation, managers have three choices: no meeting, an electronic meeting, or a face-to-face meeting. Sometimes no meeting is the right choice. When the task is one of invention and relies on individual inspiration and creativity, meetings are only a distraction to the creator. Beethoven would not have composed better symphonies if he had attended composing meetings.

Physicist Richard Feynmann once explained why he never served on university committees. He said that doing theoretical physics was like building a vast house of cards in his head; it required constant tending. Committee work distracted his attention and allowed pieces of the house to crumble. Certainly organizations should nurture and protect their most creative members, but some meetings are necessary to keep organizations functioning. An apocryphal story from Professor Feynmann's university has it that the members of one division calculated the amount of money wasted during faculty meetings as the sum of the proportion of each salary represented by the length of the meeting, so they decided to abolish all faculty meetings. The result over a year or two was that faculty were uninformed and complained that they had been left out of decisions. Meetings were reinstituted.

Groups often have greater ability to influence their environment and to command resources than does any individual. There is greater force in pooled numbers. Groups are effective when they have a synergistic effect—when the whole is more than the sum of its parts. In group problem solving, people can correct and amplify each other's ideas and then jointly develop a better plan than the plan of any individual. In London's financial houses, the partners often sit together in one room so they can take advantage of one another's judgments. Architects also often do so. In such cases, it is better to create an electronic group when, because of distance, time zones, or organizational or social differences, one would otherwise have no group at all.

It is also better to create an electronic group when an existing group has too little opportunity for face-to-face interaction. Electronic communication can be used to extend this interaction. Electronic communication can prevent dispersed groups from delegating too many decisions to the chairperson or to another group. Delegation can be efficient, but if done merely for convenience, the group may not be using its resources effectively. For decisions like allocating finances or making technical judgments, taking a vote is often better than relying on one person because averaging across people reduces error (Vroom and Yetton 1973; Einhorn, Hogarth, and Klempner 1977; Laughlin and Ellis 1986). If there is chance for discussion before the vote, group members also like the outcome more and feel more responsible for it (Forsyth 1983). The time saved by delegating decisions and not meeting at all may not be worth the disgruntled people who feel disenfranchised.

Given the choice to convene a group, electronic meetings can be more appropriate than face-to-face ones. Group problem solving often falls short because a person with a good solution must convince others to adopt it, difficult in face-to-face meetings if the person with the correct answer has low status. Face-to-face groups do not always ratify an obvious correct answer when only one member proposes it; correct proposals may need to be endorsed by more than one person for the group as a whole to come to recognize their correctness (Maier and Solem 1952; Laughlin 1980). In electronic meetings, which are less influenced by status, support for correct answers might be more easily obtained from lower-status members.

Face-to-face meetings are best when computer-based communication could impede performance or commitment to the group. If a decision requires complex and delicate multiparty negotiations, face-to-face communication is better than electronic communication because it is hard to persuade subtly in electronic communication. Even in these situations, electronic communication may still be useful to gather preliminary information and opinions in a premeeting meeting before a face-to-face meeting takes place. It also may be useful in the future to augment conventional face-to-face meetings with computer support in the meeting room (see box 4.1). Face-to-face meetings are also best for generating commitment to a course of action, for better or for worse. Thus, project teams may hold many face-to-face meetings early in their life to secure commitment to the team's goals and to decompose the task into parts. The individual members can agree to work on the parts by themselves. Teams can then stay in touch largely through electronic communication, thus attaining the simultaneous linking and buffering we described in chapter 2. Finally, some decisions must be symbolically ratified as important ones. Face-to-face meetings permit the laying on of hands in a way no mediated communication can do.

Electronic meetings are not equivalent to face-to-face meetings. When face-to-face meetings are not possible, electronic meetings may be an improvement over no meeting at all. And, when face-to-face meetings are not necessary, electronic meetings may still provide a way to exchange information and keep people up to date. Finally, when face-to-face meetings produce conventional and predictable decisions and what is wanted is something less conventional, electronic meetings offer an alternate forum.

Face-to-face meetings will not disappear, but organizations with extensive electronic communication find their role and character changing. For instance, product designers in one organization report that they still hold face-to-face design review meetings, though designers and reviewers also meet electronically. The face-to-face meetings are now more focused and rigorous because participants exchange information electronically before the meetings to clear up confusions, prune away distractions, and identify the key issues.

General-Purpose vs. Special-Purpose Tools

A face-to-face meeting is a general-purpose tool. People can use it to air differences or come to agreement. They can talk or remain silent, whistle or sing. They can whisper to one neighbor or shout at the whole group. They can say what they mean or lie. They can take notes, doodle, or sign official documents. They can stay or leave the room. Most of the time people just want to talk. Of course, there are times when they need special-purpose tools, such as agendas, blackboards, calendars, or access to databases. They don't want these tools to interfere with discussion. In this respect, electronic groups are not very different from face-to-face groups.

The power of computing tempts people to improve on group discussion by providing tools for structuring and managing it. An example is a foolish attempt we once made to force people in a real-time computer conference to take turns. As we saw in figure 4.6, each conference member had a window that scrolled independently. Because everyone was reading and writing at once, discussion seemed disorderly. To impose more order, we wrote a program that allowed only one member to "talk" at a time. It forced group members to press a special key when they wanted to talk. People not only hated this; they behaved very badly, refusing to relinquish their turn when asked or repeatedly banging the request key. They let us know what they thought of our foray into automated management of group discussion.

As a general principle, we advocate less rather than more external structure for electronic groups. Structuring the group process requires that we anticipate the topics, kinds of social tasks, and strategies people will have to use. If we haven't predicted those topics, social tasks, and strategies very well, people will be frustrated. One example of a group tool that people often resent is the fully automated electronic calendar. The calendar supposedly acts like a good administrative assistant. It arranges group meetings by finding out when everyone is available, choosing the best time, and notifying people of the decision. But the computer version often lacks the flexibility and subtlety of its human counterpart. As March and Sproull (1990) note,

Managers who use them [automatic calendars] have to specify their time constraints, a priority list of people to whom they wish to be accessible, and their bumping rules—their decisions about whom to accommodate if time requests from equal-priority people collide. When this information is made explicit, as these systems require, other people are able to act strategically with respect to a manager's schedule. They can, for example, sign up for large blocks of low priority time, trade time, "sell" their place in the cue, and so forth. "Intelligent" mail filters are subject to the same kind of strategic manipulation. People who want to reach a manager will discover the filtering rules and disguise their mail to slip through the filters. Furthermore, in these systems, sounding out is eliminated. The delicate process by which two people discover (and transform) their mutual importance is inadmissible. Graceful face-saving fictions disappear. "I'd love to see you, but I'm completely booked for the next six weeks . . . " becomes "Schedule X only if someone more important doesn't want to see me. All of the following people are more important than X." (p. 152)

Within a small group that works together closely and has already negotiated all the pecking-order questions, an automatic calendar is a convenience for scheduling meetings that everyone has to attend. It is a tool that cannot be applied gracefully to less routine work. However, electronic communication can still be useful in this situation. A person who needs to schedule a meeting could send a form message to all those who should attend asking them to return the times they are available. The convener could then choose the best time and return a message announcing it. This scheme would certainly increase the efficiency of trying to schedule a meeting by telephone, yet it leaves all of the participants with the autonomy to make their own decisions about when they are available.

Another example of a special-purpose tool is the information filter. At our university, people can organize their incoming electronic mail into separate folders, with a folder for each group to which they belong. Mail passes automatically into its proper folder. Though people do receive a great deal of group mail, only a few of them use these folders. They would prefer to scan one long list of the day's mail than open many folders. Folders remind people of their commitments. They have to be kept up to date.

Yet many groups require some structure, or they never get anything done. People who worked on the Common LISP project using the ARPANET relied on a designated moderator to keep order and to hold votes when people could not reach consensus. The moderator also called several face-to-face meetings when "theological conflict" could not be resolved electronically. (Many fewer people could participate in the face-to-face meetings, however.) The moderator role has proved difficult to automate. The hardest part is to write a program that respects group politics and strategic uses of information. One commercial program lets group members label a message according to its purpose—for example, "Request" when they want to ask a favor and "Promise" when they want to satisfy a request. The program helps manage the group by keeping track of messages and generating reminders when it is time for requests to be met or when promises fall due. The program also permits unlabeled messages. This is wise since often people are more effective when they do not have to advertise their intentions in advance.

Conclusion

A group is an organization with a purpose, structure, and procedures. Because a group is not just a collection of individual people, communications technology can change the whole group's dynamics. The communications of a group are like the nervous system of a person. They decide group functioning, and what is done to one part affects the rest of the system.

Electronic meeting policies and software features can have an impact on group dynamics. Although sophisticated computer software to support group meetings and decision making is being developed and studied, the most widely used group software today is the distribution list, computer conference, or bulletin board. These programs are attractive because they are flexible for different kinds of work and directly controllable by group members. Even so, group dynamics are likely to change as physical and temporal factors become less constraining. Managers can prevent this change by increasing the frequency of face-to-face meetings or by imposing constraints on the use of electronic meetings. Either of these policies will tend to reestablish old group patterns—and in the process preclude some benefits and savings of electronic group communication.

Courtesy of Eldon Dedini

5

Increasing Personal Connections

Not everyone can be the boss, have a big office, make important decisions, be the center of attention. Many employees are geographically and hierarchically distant from the center of things. Whenever an organization has more than two people in it, someone will be out of the center. The larger the organization, the greater the number and proportion of peripheral employees. "Peripheral," however, does not mean unimportant. Peripheral employees in the commercial and service sectors are the first, and often the only, contact that customers have with an organization. Their behavior can make the difference between keeping customers or clients and losing them. Peripheral employees in manufacturing and construction perform and inspect the actual production work. Their behavior can make the difference between acceptable and unacceptable product quality. Yet peripheral workers pose problems for organizations. They may not know what's going on—an information problem—and they may not care—a motivation problem.

Advertisements that encourage us to "reach out and touch someone" reflect the belief that we strengthen relationships when we communicate with others. Every relationship is both informational and emotional. All other things being equal, the more you talk with someone, the more you learn from that person (and vice versa). Additionally, the more you talk with someone, the more you like and feel committed to that person (and vice versa).[1] Participation through communication is an old principle of management. It has recently revived in the United States as managers look to Japan and the industrial democracies of Western Europe for "new" management practices.

Participation plans typically rely on communications initiated from the center and representation of the periphery to the center. Management

initiates most participation plans. Employees receive participation over-
tures rather than initiate them. For instance, management may ask employees
to get more involved through such mechanisms as quality circles, or
employee representatives may be named to various management committees. Much of the internal communications apparatus of modern organizations is designed to "get the word to the troops," to ensure that
employees have current information on policies, procedures, and other
relevant topics. Devices ranging from televised messages from the company
president to routine policy manual updates are intended to reduce the
information distance between peripheral employees and the center. Even
so, peripheral employees may be operating with outdated information,
unaware of new initiatives or policies.

Even if peripheral employees have the information they need to do their
jobs, they may not have any great desire to do so. (Motivation, of course,
can interact with how informed an employee is. Highly motivated employees
will figure out ways to learn what is going on.) Unmotivated employees'
relationship with their employer is strictly letter of the law. Their information
connection may be adequate, but their emotional connection is weak.
Motivation and commitment can affect both work quality and work
satisfaction. When people are "marking time" or "going through the
motions," their behaviors and attitudes are qualitatively different from
those in which people are "gung ho" or "going all out." Episodes of
working to rule, as in, for instance, an air traffic controllers' slowdown,
show the importance of employees who do more than they have to do.
Organizations employ a host of motivating techniques to reduce the
emotional distance between peripheral employees and the center: employee
recognition awards, spirit campaigns, company-sponsored social occasions,
and community events. Like information procedures, the center initiates
most of these for the periphery.

Electronic communication may offer peripheral employees new opportunities to initiate connections within the organization to reduce the
information gap and increase motivation. If connectivity is high, there are
potentially many people accessible via the network. Because of the social
processes described in chapters 3 and 4, employees should feel somewhat
uninhibited about "meeting" new people electronically. If management
policies permit or encourage such interactions, employees can increase
their information and emotional connections. These interactions can

increase both connections between the periphery and the center of the organization and connections among peripheral workers.

In the first section of this chapter, we show how employees can benefit from increasing their electronic connections with other employees. These increasing connections could benefit all employees, but peripheral employees are likely to see a relatively greater benefit than are central employees. We show how both passive and active connections (receiving information and sending it, respectively) can be beneficial. Passive connections offer employees the opportunity not only to learn from other employees but also to discover similarities they share with people who have different jobs and are located in different places. Active connections provide a new opportunity for employees to have a voice in their work group and with their boss. In the second section of the chapter we consider performance implications of having peripheral members increase their connections.

Increasing Information and Commitment Through New Connections

Window on the Corporation

Receiving mail can affect employees' attitudes toward their organization by increasing their informational and emotional connections to other employees. This can be particularly true for peripheral employees who participate in large electronic distribution lists (DLs), bulletin boards, or conferences.

In one Fortune 500 firm, we noted several instances of these benefits. One secretary described several DLs to which she belonged by saying that she liked seeing what people had to say on various topics, including "important people who would never talk to me in person." She said she would never send a message to any of these DLs, but they were her "window on the corporation." Another employee used the mail system to describe his feelings about his employer, which had recently sold one of its subsidiaries. In a message sent to a large DL, the sender explained that another employee had told him: "It's a firm policy that [the corporation] won't make anything that will hurt anyone; they're getting pretty close, and that's probably why we're selling it." The sender then confided (to several hundred people), "That made me feel awfully good." As Martha Feldman (1987) pointed out in analyzing this message, "Though not all people who hear about the reason for selling the operation will agree on whether it is good or bad, the knowledge, by itself, provides organizational members a better understanding of the organization" (p. 97). In a third case, another secretary used the electronic mail system to organize a get well gift for an employee (box 5.1). Tokens of appreciation are common in many organizations. What made this one interesting is that the message went to three hundred people, presumably most of whom had never before heard of Benny, the ailing employee. Probably most people paid little conscious attention to this message. But even with a quick scan and delete, the subliminal message was, "I work for a company with caring people."

Corporate communications offices and human resources offices are in the business of sending employees information designed to increase informational and emotional connections. How could ad hoc communications among employees be any more effective than professionally designed ones? Messages share several characteristics that distinguish them from professional communications and that may make them particularly potent. First, most are from voluntary or discretionary DLs. People choose to belong to these DLs and therefore perceive that they receive messages by their choice, not because they must do so. Second, because these DLs have widespread membership, they can reflect information and feelings from throughout the organization, not just from one communication office. Third, the overt contents of these messages pertain to a variety of topics and

---

Box 5.1. Benny hurt his back

```
Date:   19 May 1983 10:37 am PDT (Thursday)
From:   Sandi Colman
Subject:  Benny Schrinka
To:   [All employees, about 300 people, working in one location]
cc:
Reply To:  Sandi Colman
  Benny Schrinka hurt his back last week and will be unable to
work for at least 3-4 weeks or more.......depends on how he
responds to physical therapy.
  Several of his friends are putting together a surprise
"goodie basket" for him, hoping to cheer him and ease his pain.
We hope to include a ham, some wine, maybe a good book or two
for him to read...suggestions welcome.
If you care to make a contribution toward the basket...I am
collecting $$$; John Devon has volunteered to coordinate
getting the goodies and basket.
I am in "Area 2" of ABC Bldg. 10....x1111; John Devon is in
room 76, same building,
Thanks to you all....Sandi
```

---

interests, not just to official company news or boosterism. These characteristics can make these messages more persuasive than professional ones because of a process psychologists call insufficient justification (Aronson 1966).

When people receive a message, they evaluate the sender's motivation so that they know how to interpret the message. If a recipient knows that the sender was paid for sending the message or was coerced into sending it, the recipient discounts the sender's sincerity. The recipient believes that the sender has "sufficient justification" for sending the message even without sincerely believing its contents. By contrast, if a sender lacks obvious external incentives for sending the message, the recipient does not discount the sender's sincerity. When unsolicited messages appear on large, discretionary distribution lists, readers have little reason to doubt their sincerity. Peripheral employees who frequently receive such messages build information connections over time to other employees of the corporation.

Cognitive processes of everyday inference also can magnify the influence of these messages in the minds of their recipients. Because people commonly ignore base rates and remember singular instances, they overestimate the frequency of rare events (Lichtenstein et al.1978).[2] For instance, people typically overestimate the frequency of death by lightning. (Similarly they tend to underestimate the frequency of death by motor vehicle accidents, which are more frequent and less memorable.) Suppose a person who read the message in box 5.1 were to ask, "How kind to one another are people who work for this company?" The best answer, without any other information, is "About as kind as the people who work for any similar company." The Benny message should carry very little weight in changing that assessment, increasing the kindness score by only 1/nth, where n is the total number of employees. Because the message has memorable features—the ham, the bottle of wine, the books—it is likely to be overweighted (in a statistical sense) in its contribution to the person's assessment.

Reading messages gives employees the opportunity to make connections with other employees who would otherwise be invisible or unknown. Because electronic communication can be independent of geographic and organizational distance, these connections cut across conventional organization boundaries. In this way, employees can learn about people whose experiences are different from theirs because they have different jobs or work in different locations. They also can learn that, despite these differences, they have much in common. Such lessons are reinforced by the nature of the communication—the free exchange of unofficial information. Research on the relationship between electronic connections and feelings of affiliation shows that if you have a choice of face-to-face contact with people exactly like you or meeting via electronic communication, then you will like each other more if you meet in person (Kiesler et al. 1985). The situation is different for meeting people you would otherwise not see in person, whom you might avoid, who are different. Here there is a positive association between electronic connections and affiliation.

It is possible that people communicating electronically could become attached to specific other people or even to favorite bulletin boards or electronic groups without these positive attachments generalizing to the larger organization. No research directly tests the impact of "windows on the corporation" on attachment to the organization. If the process works as it has in other settings, then whether affiliation extends to the larger organization will depend on the orientation of the individuals' communications. If messages about the larger organization are mainly negative, recipients will increase their affiliation with the communicators but decrease it with the larger organization. If the communications are mainly positive toward the larger organization, recipients will increase both affiliations.

A Voice for the Voiceless

Sending messages also can increase information and emotional connections. An experiment conducted by the Rand Corporation demonstrated that peripheral people who communicated electronically became better integrated into the organization (Eveland and Bikson 1988). Two corporation task forces were formed to investigate how employees make the transition to retirement and to develop a set of recommendations about preretirement planning. Each task force had forty members—half recently retired from the company and the other half still employed but eligible for retirement. The only difference between the two groups was that one of them was given electronic communication technology and the other was not. At the outset, the retired people in both task forces were judged by themselves and others to be more peripheral to the group than their employed counterparts. On standard sociometric measures of recognition, knowing, and contact, retirees had lower scores than those who were still employed. Halfway through the year's work, the retired members of the electronic communication group had become intensely involved in the project by electronic mail. They knew more people, had more interactions, belonged to more subgroups, and felt more involved than their retired counterparts in the nonelectronic task force. They even decided to continue meeting after the year's work was completed and the task forces had been officially disbanded.

We found a similar story in a city government (Huff, Sproull, and Kiesler 1989). Over 90 percent of the city employees used electronic mail routinely. We discovered that the more they used it, the more committed they were to their employer—measured by how willing they were to work beyond the requirements and hours of their jobs, how attached they felt to the city government, and how strongly they planned to continue working for the city. The connection between electronic communication and commitment is not explained by employees' total amount of communication across all media, by their technical ability, or by their seniority and hierarchical status (although the later two variables predicted commitment independently). One explanation of our findings is that using electronic mail caused commitment to increase. Another explanation is that already committed people used the modern, symbolically important technology of electronic mail. To compare these alternatives, we proposed that if communicating by electronic mail increased commitment, then the correlation between using electronic mail and commitment should be especially strong among shift workers who are routinely separated from the mainstream of work and decision making in the organization. We reasoned that the technology would be somewhat more useful to them than to employees in the mainstream. By contrast, if commitment caused people to use electronic mail, then shift work should have no differential effect. We found that the relationship between using electronic mail and commitment was much higher for shift workers than for other workers, supporting the idea that electronic mail can increase commitment among those who otherwise might feel somewhat peripheral in an organization.

Once we knew that total volume of an employee's electronic mail predicted that person's level of commitment, we wondered if receiving mail or sending it (or both) contributed to feelings of commitment. It might be that receiving more mail would cause people to feel more informed, as was the case with the large corporation, and therefore more committed. We found, however, that neither the amount of electronic mail received nor a person's reporting that he or she felt "in the know about what is going on in the city" predicted commitment. Rather, the amount of electronic mail a person sent predicted commitment. In this city government, computer communication seems to have increased commitment primarily because it allowed employees to participate actively in the life of the organization by sending messages that they would not otherwise have sent, not primarily because it increased the amount of information they received. One police officer wrote to us, "Working the night shift, it used to be that I would hear about promotions after they happened though I had a right to be included in the discussion. Now I have a say in the decision making." Electronic communication gave peripheral employees the chance to have a voice.

We found a similar relationship between commitment and sending mail in the software development teams that we described in chapter 2. Recall that the teams using electronic mail the most produced the best systems because they could better coordinate their activities than could the teams that relied on more conventional means of communicating. We also looked at how committed each member felt to his or her team. For this analysis, we categorized each person by how much he or she talked in meetings and how much electronic mail he or she sent. We discovered that people who sent much mail were just as committed to their team as were the people who talked a lot in meetings. Also, as is true of the city government, there was no relationship between the amount of mail a team member received and his or her commitment to the team, although receiving mail was related to performance. (See table 5.1.) Thus electronic mail can provide an alternate route to letting people have a voice if they are low contributors to face-to-face meetings.

Face-to-face groups consistently show a positive relationship between how much a person talks and how satisfied that person is with the group and how committed he or she is to it (McGrath 1984; Forsyth 1983). Yet

Table 5.1
Attitudes and performance of individuals as a function of communication behavior

	Performance[a]	Commitment[b]
High communicators[c]	17.4	9.1
High talkers only	17.5	8.7
High mailers only	17.0	8.9
Low communicators[c]	12.3	7.8

a. Performance was measured on a scale from 0-20.
b. Commitment was measured on a scale from 1-10.
c. High or low frequency of both talking and using electronic mail.

air time in meetings is an extremely limited commodity—only one person can talk at a time—and total meeting size is physically constrained. With electronic communication, air time and meeting size are less constrained resources, and so more people can enjoy the benefits of active participation. These benefits may especially accrue to those who, by virtue of geographic or organizational position, would otherwise be peripheral contributors.

Talking to the Boss

Most managers talk more than they listen and issue more directives, make more organizational announcements, and promulgate more policy statements than do lower-level employees. When managers do listen, it's mostly to people close to them. Most talking and listening occurs among people who are physically and hierarchically close to each other. This means managers often don't hear new news; they may be ignorant of information they need that is in the heads or on the desks of lower-level or distant employees—and lower-level employees may feel that no one listens to them.

Giving people a voice is a strong value in our culture. Its embodiment ranges from constitutional principles of freedom of speech and assembly and parliamentary rules of order to public opinion polls, Dale Carnegie's rules for success, and radio call-in shows. Although work organizations are not democracies and free speech does not prevail, giving peripheral people a voice is an important means of binding them to the organization, and it may yield information important for performance.

Managers face three kinds of problems in giving people a voice. One is straightforward logistics problems. By definition, peripheral people are far from the center. Physically collecting their opinions can be time-consuming and expensive. This is one reason that conventional participation mechanisms usually rely on representation rather than direct participation; collecting information from employee representatives is easier than listening to all employees. A second problem is motivational. Although peripheral employees may have a lot to say, they may be reticent, distrustful, or fear recrimination. A third problem is also motivational—but on the receiving end rather than the sending end. Central management may not want to hear what peripheral employees have to say. Given the cultural value we put on being good listeners, this reluctance is not likely to be expressed publicly. Instead it is more likely to be expressed as confidence in the existing ways of hearing from employees and a need to avoid information overload.

Management reluctance may actually stem from confusing a commitment to listen to employees with a commitment to act on what they say.

Electronic communication offers the possibility of increasing the amount of communication from lower to higher levels of the hierarchy and solving the logistics problems of collecting information from distant employees. Workers can send messages at their convenience, without having to wait for an appointment or to catch the manager in the hall. It also can alleviate employee reluctance to talk. Workers feel less intimidated about talking to the boss electronically than they do about talking to him or her face-to-face, particularly if what the worker wants to say is in any way negative. Because there are few reminders of status differences, the fear of evaluation or criticism declines.

In one corporation we studied, people who used electronic communication extensively reported that they preferred this form when communicating up the hierarchy to negotiate or solve problems (Sproull and Kiesler 1986). Box 5.2 displays an example of a message from a first-level manager to a vice-president located four levels above him in the hierarchy. This message

Box 5.2. Talking with the boss

```
DATE:   20 May 89  07:29:24
FROM:   Sam.Marlowe
SUBJECT:  Messages from on high
TO:  Bill.Hargrave  John.East
CC:  Don.Dulane , Bob.Bilk, Sam.Marlowe
This is to inform you of some small personnel problems you have
been causing at lower levels of the organization.  I hope that
being informed, you will do the right thing in the future. I
have made a suggestion at the end.

I like your (electronic) open-door policy; anyone can send you
a message on anything, and you will read (and maybe respond to)
it. I hope that we do not misuse this policy by sending you so
many messages that you will have to close the door, and I would
ask that you not misuse this policy by running the organization
with it.

There are many good ideas floating around this organization.
We do not have enough resources to work on all of them, so
managers have to allocate their resources to the most important
one (which sometimes are not the most ingenious ones).  When a
person has a good idea, and it is not worked on, that person
tends to be disappointed.  Usually, he understands the situa-
```

```
tion, and respects the decision of his boss(s).  sometimes when
he thinks a mistake is being made, or when he is just plain
angry, he uses your open-door policy to sell his good idea.
This is just what the policy is for, and I see no harm done.

The problems arise when you, with all your weight and author-
ity, endorse the good idea to the point where the originator
believes he now has your blessing to start work on it.  He
believes that you have/will over-rule his boss, and [the
organization] will implement his idea because you think it is
so good.

SUGGESTION

When someone sends you an idea, and you are willing/want to
respond, please continue to give your opinion (for/against) of
the idea, but please make sure that you indicate that the
decision to work on the idea will be made by the normal pro-
cesses in the organization (like release planning or chain of
command).  I am not suggesting that you stop responding alto-
gether.
```

illustrates how status imbalance can be reduced in computer communication both in the style of communication from subordinate to superior and in the behavior about which the subordinate is complaining. Although both had offices in the same building, the sender almost never talked with the vice-president directly; most of the occasions on which they were in the same room were formal or ceremonial ones in which the vice-president was making a speech or conducting a large meeting. Yet the sender felt he could send this frank complaint electronically. Notice that the topic of the message is electronic mail behavior. The sender liked the vice-president's electronic open-door policy but did not like what he saw as an electronic endorsement policy.

Managers notice that the nature of the conversation often changes when they walk in the room.[3] One manager calls this the "social Heisenberg effect." "With electronic communication people can forget that I'm their manager when they talk to me," he told us. The manager did not mean this literally, but in our terms many cues to status differences disappear with electronic communication. For this manager, that produced benefits. The cliché is that the boss is always the last to hear the bad news. Electronic communication may convey it sooner.

Why should managers want to encourage more communication from their subordinates, particularly if it's likely to be bad news, negative opinions, or complaints? Obviously, smart managers may prefer to know sooner, rather than later, that all is not well. That justification assumes a view of managers as problem finders and problem solvers. Another view of managers as involvement increasers also suggests benefits from encouraging more communication from lower-level employees. In this view, managers elicit communication because they believe it increases involvement and improves morale. High morale may be sought for its own sake, because it has some direct link with performance, or both. It may turn out that what is most important is letting people talk, not acting on what they say. In the city government we described, we have no evidence that anyone acted on the messages sent by the shift workers, but the electronic communication gave peripheral employees the opportunity to communicate more actively with the boss.

Electronic Discussion Groups

Electronic discussion groups offer the opportunity to consolidate and magnify the effects of passive and active electronic participation. Most employees belong to few groups at work—a primary work group, perhaps a committee or two, and perhaps a social group. (Group membership is positively associated with hierarchical position; high-level managers belong to many more groups than do lower-level employees.) Except for committee assignments, these memberships are relatively stable and enduring, and they lead to important benefits for their members. Electronic group communication makes it possible for more people to belong to many groups and to tailor their group memberships to their changing interests. The groups are not constrained by physical location or fixed-length meetings and can enroll anyone who wants to participate, either actively or passively.

Employees in one Fortune 500 firm received an average of twenty-one DL messages per day from over seven hundred DLs (Finholt and Sproull 1990). The majority of the average person's DL mail came from strangers (company employees unknown to the recipient), and a high percentage came from remote locations. Thus DLs represented a way for people to receive information and make connections that otherwise would have been difficult or impossible. About half the DLs were required ones: an employee's name was placed on a required DL as a function of his or her job or work location. The employee had no choice about belonging to required DLs, which ranged from ten-person DLs for subunit groups to six-hundred-person site lists for all employees working in a particular city. The discretionary DLs, which people joined by choice, covered a wide spectrum of topics, some about work and some extracurricular. They ranged from the exotic to the mundane: Oenologists for wine fanciers, NetSpecs for computer network designers, GoPlayers for students of the Japanese strategy game Go, Classifieds for selling things, and ChildCare for locating babysitters.

Some discretionary DLs, such as Classifieds and ChildCare, merely served as a convenient way to broadcast information; others functioned as interacting discussion groups. (See box 5.3 for descriptions of three electronic discussion groups and sample messages from each of them.) The discretionary discussion groups were large and geographically dispersed, averaging 260 members located in seven different cities, and they interacted regularly. Four days out of five, messages went to these groups, week after week—an average of four messages a day. Messages were sent by an average of 41 different people in each discussion group over a two-week to one-month period. Although most of these members were not personally known to one another and had no common tasks, most messages were not simply disconnected broadcasts unrelated to one another but explicit replies to previous messages. These groups sustained involving discussions over distance and time among strangers. Each discretionary group also worked at being a group. They sent messages discussing the purpose and procedures of the group and membership criteria for it. Although group members were physically invisible and unknown to one another, the groups took on personalities and lives of their own.

Membership in any group confers informational and emotional benefits to the member, including increased information resources, emotional resources, and the opportunity to take on different roles and identities. These processes are so powerful that peoples' mental health status is positively associated with the number of groups they belong to (Thoits 1983). It is plausible, although only a hypothesis at this point, that membership in multiple electronic groups has similar beneficial effects, particularly for people who belong to few face-to-face groups. For those who belong to a great many face-to-face groups, we would expect much less effect; the costs in demands on their time and energy might well outweigh the benefits.

Box 5.3. Electronic discussion groups

UserFeatureForum

UserFeatureForum was a work-related discretionary DL for employees interested in discussing interface features of company products. UFF had 125 members and received a mean of 2 messages a day (max = 8, min = 0). Many of the messages on UFF were mildly pedantic, as people demonstrated their technical opinions or virtuosity.

```
Regarding contention resolution in Graphics:  I like meaning 1
(option 2) of the next key (next item in the contenders list).
Meaning 2 would seem to me to be very unpredictable from a
user's point of view.  The internal sibling structure could not
in general be predicted from the image they see whereas the
next contender would be much more natural.  Regarding how
frames behave during pagination:  both alternatives have
undesirable qualities.  Data should never be intentionally
thrown away (as in alt1).  And alt2 would more than likely
result in an unacceptable positioning of the frame.  Given the
current of document structure in [product], I don't see any
better pagination heuristic that what we do now.  One possibil-
ity might be to post a message when one of these guys is
encountered and let the user decide what to do such as abort
pagination.  then the user could change the page props of the
problem page and repaginate.
/Joe
```

Still, UFF was not all bland discourse on "contention resolution problems" or "multinational user interfaces." Personal rivalries sometimes surfaced. For example, toward the end of one particularly arcane exchange, one member pointedly observed in a message that "some people" on UFF spent more time talking about user interfaces than building them. On the whole, though, talking about interfaces was the raison d'être of UFF. It had no identity outside the mail system. UFF was an arena for people to display their knowledge before their superiors and peers—although this knowledge was rarely acted upon (in our sample of messages, only two UFF communications resulted in actual changes to an interface). In the words of one UFFer:

```
To paraphrase a famous saying about economists, which pretty
much summarizes my feeling about all this endless user-inter-
face niggling that's been going on for the last six years, and
shows every indication of continuing out to eternity:

If all the user interface experts in the world were laid end to
end, they wouldn't reach a conclusion.
```

In response to this complaint, though, another member responded with a hoary mail system adage: "If you don't like talking about user features, drop out of UserFeatureForum."

Cinema

Cinema was an extracurricular discretionary DL, with over 500 members—managers, professionals, technicians, and secretaries. Cinema members received a mean of 4 messages a day from this DL (max = 31, min = 0). Messages were related to movie reviews—highly subjective commentaries on everything related to the movie, including the ambiance in the theater and the quality of the popcorn.

```
John,
I just saw flashDance, you were very right.  I stopped by Tower
Records on the way home and picked up the sound track.  I am
taping it now.  I am not a big movie goer and I am at odds with
Mann and AMC theaters but this film was well worth the trip to
my local corporate theater.  Fortunately I was spared the
newspaper ads by arriving 5 minutes late.

Well, I did not start this as a flame about corporate theaters.
I wanted to say that FlashDance is a clever, well filmed,
moving musical that runs around your head for a long time after
leaving the theater.  Go see it and check out the sound track
on Casablanca Records.  It's a Polygram Record with a few built
in flaws.
Later...
/PRL

V was a mashed-up composite of about twenty science-fiction
stories.  Not a single original idea in it.  And besides
that,it wasn't very good.
Save Joe-Bob!
```

Rowdies

Rowdies, a discretionary extracurricular DL, had 98 members, 73 percent of them male technicians or professionals. Typically Rowdies was the source of over 20 "RowdieMail" messages per day (max = 50, min = 0). Although some work issues occasionally crept into Rowdies discussions, most messages concerned gossip (mostly about other Rowdies), group activities (such as organizing softball teams or writing electronic novels), and crude humor.

```
Sounds to me like you have quit while you were ahead!!
Has anyone else noticed that we've actually been getting
messages from 666 lately, and most of them have times on  them
like 3:05 a.m.-5:42 a.m., etc., etc.  Do you think he's trying
to impress us with his devotion to duty?  I'll bet his boss
gets a message every day at that time as well....even if 666
```

has nothing much to say to him. He also lets us know that he
is working a 13 hour day — he has stated that more than once.

I mean, we enjoy your messages 666, but, really, impressing us
isn't going to change the fact that there are no merit increases this year — unless, of course, they change their mind
in June or July after re-evaluating this situation.

And by the way, 3:00 a.m. to 12:30 p.m. is only a 9-1/2 hour
day.........
2
GeezSomePeople

Rowdies regularly sent messages to organize afternoon beer busts, which were
the focus of elaborate preparation. These outings were documented in full, and
their histories were carefully indexed and archived for future reference in secure
Rowdie disk space.

John and Phil,
     I have room for both of you in my car plus one more
RowdieLuncher. I'm pretty sure the luncheon is still on
for 12:30 pm.
44

.....zzzzzzzzzzzzzzzzzz.Hmmph. Burp...huh? who me....what
column? miss a deadline...what day is it? ohmygod it's
wednesday already. What? somebody wrote it? Joe, who? Oh
yes, JOE! — he's the one I had always thought was bald.
zR722

Was a great party, in fact I'm still smiling.
....that whipped cream was good stuff

Rowdies messages displayed complex stylistic conventions, including closing
messages with a Rowdy number and a run-on commentary that often took the form
of sarcastic observations on previous messages or continued observations from
other messages. Rowdies sometimes referred to fellow Rowdies by using Rowdy
"handles," such as "Colt45" or "Mr. Toon-toon," an important part of Rowdy
identity. Periodically Rowdies issued a membership list indicating numbers,
handles, birthdates, and favorite "RowdieDrinks." During our observation, the
membership list contained the names of honorary Rowdies, including several
waitresses at Rowdy hangouts, and Divine, the transvestite star of *Pink Flamingos*
and *Polyester*.

Rowdies messages expressed clear opinions about Rowdies and the larger
electronic community. On one occasion a prominent Rowdy noted, after three new
Rowdies members dropped out after only two days, "They weren't Rowdy
material. Keep up the good work!"

Source: Adapted from Finholt and Sproull (1990).

Performance Implications

This chapter emphasizes the information and motivation benefits of increasing peripheral employee participation through electronic communication. Do these connections also differentially benefit the performance of peripheral workers? There are almost no data to help us answer this question; we can only lay out the basic reasoning underlying why we might expect to see a differential benefit and report some tantalizing bits of evidence.

Differential Performance Benefits for Peripheral Employees

The basic argument suggests that peripheral employees have more to gain from electronic communication than do more central employees. We assume that peripheral employees start out at an information disadvantage. In principle, both groups of employees could benefit equally, illustrated as "equivalent benefits" in figure 5.1. But central employees are likely to experience ceiling effects on their communication. That is, each new communication benefits them relatively less because they already know a great deal and are already active contributors. Peripheral employees, by contrast, derive more benefit from each additional communication both because they know less and because they have fewer other opportunities to participate actively. This relationship is illustrated as the "decreasing gap hypothesis" in figure 5.1: peripheral employees' performance increases more than central employees' performance does, closing the gap between the two groups. Of course, there could be other relationships as well. Both groups could be equivalently harmed by electronic communication. This outcome could be produced by a simple information overload process in which each new communication distracts attention or confuses the recipient. Or central employees could benefit much more than peripheral employees. This "gap-increasing" benefit (shown at the bottom of figure 5.1) could most plausibly occur if central employees had better access to computer-based information resources, or if they communicated only with one another or communicated entirely different kinds of information. We believe, however, that when access is open the effects are mainly positive, with differential benefit to peripheral workers.

We have found evidence of differential benefits to peripheral workers in an investigation of how physical oceanographers use computer networks (Hesse et al. 1990). We examined how the use of electronic communication

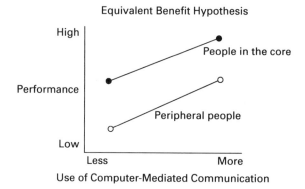

Equivalent Benefit Hypothesis

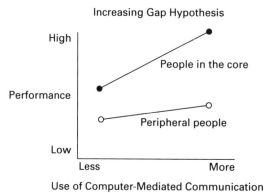

Figure 5.1
Some hypothetical relationships between computer-mediated communication and employee performance

affected the relationship between age and professional recognition (scientific awards, appointment to editorial boards, professional committees, and advisory committees). In this kind of analysis, younger scientists are considered more peripheral than older scientists. We found that while older scientists generally received more professional recognition than younger scientists (and scientists who used electronic communication more received more professional recognition), electronic communication benefited younger scientists more than it did older scientists in receiving professional recognition.

John Earls has discovered a similar pattern of advantage for people with physical handicaps. He directed a multiyear program for participants in a rehabilitation program designed to teach confidence and positive attitudes toward the disabled among both disabled people and human service professionals. He compared a control group with an equivalent experimental group that used a computer bulletin board for communication over several years. Each group had thirty members: ten disabled people, ten therapists, and ten university students. The experimental group did not differ from the control after six months in the program, but after two years there were highly significant differences. By then the experimental group was more positive in its attitudes about disability and the disabled than the control group was. The disabled members were even more positive in their attitudes than other experimental group members were. Also, the disabled people in the experimental group participated more actively. They logged onto the network and read and sent more messages than the professionals or students did (box 5.4.)

Box 5.4. Differential benefits of computer-based communication

T is a 30-year-old man whose disability is cerebral palsy. He works in the office area at Centrecraft Industries, a sheltered employment facility. In the last year he has been nominated as a representative of the disabled people working at his work facility.

T states that one of the personal benefits of his participation in the Bulletin Board project has been the opportunity to resume communication with people with whom he had lost contact. In addition, he sees that being able to talk to other people with disabilities about work issues as well as his own thoughts and feelings as being a great strength of the Bulletin Board. The fact that he is able to talk to individuals using their private mail box is particularly good; especially when he wants to discuss a problem at work and wants to be assured of privacy. Its use as a public forum, allowing the discussion of issues relevant to the disabled consumer group, has been very helpful in his role as a consumer representative. It has enabled him to get different people's ideas, discuss matters with them and report them to the consumer group at Industries.

In T's opinion, his involvement in the Bulletin Board has enabled him to better express his thoughts and opinions. In effect, it has made him more confident in talking to groups both via the Bulletin Board and also face to face. In addition, it has made him more willing to consider other people's viewpoints. He reported that prior to his use of the Bulletin Board, he was probably "one sided" in his attitudes. Now, he is more able and prepared to consider the attitudes and feelings of the group as a whole. In addition, T feels that his involvement with the Bulletin Board has resulted in staff looking at him "in a much more positive light."

During his participation in the Bulletin Board project, T was initially loaned a computer, modem and communications software by the organisation. He has subsequently purchased his own computer and equipment and reports that this is a direct consequence of his involvement with the Bulletin Board. He uses the computer not only for communication purposes but also for word processing. He is currently writing a book and has begun to see other possible uses for his computer.

T is now accessing a community bulletin board as well as that run by the organisation. T reported that this board extends his information capability and there is more opportunity to communicate with people you do not know. It also has a variety of different interest areas covering topics such as sports, politics and hobbies. Although T has not yet communicated with people in these areas, he enjoys reading the comments of others and feels that one day he will want to share his own thoughts on some of the different areas.

Source: Earls (1990: 204–205).

Short-run versus Long-run Implications

Even if increasing affiliation and commitment through increasing electronic connections is feasible, the direct link between increased commitment and increased performance has not been demonstrated. Happy workers are not necessarily more productive workers.[4] Nor are more informed workers necessarily more productive workers. Charles O'Reilly (1980) looked at the relationship between employees' attitudes toward and use of information and the quality of their job performance as rated by their supervisors. He found a positive association between how much information people had to do their jobs and their satisfaction with the amount of information they had. That is, people who reported they had more information were also more satisfied with the amount of information they had. But he also found a negative association between how much information people had to do their jobs and the quality of their actual performance. The more information people had, the worse was their performance. These findings are consonant with the view of economists who point out that people often overinvest in information; they acquire more information or more costly information than they need to do their work. In this view any strategy that seeks to increase information and motivation connections among employees should be viewed with suspicion. This view is typically characterized by an extremely short-run perspective, considering the relationship between performance and amount of information or amount of satisfaction at only one time. Companies or managers that have primarily a short-run orientation can use similar reasoning to forbid or minimize widespread use of a computer-based communication system.

Companies and managers with a longer view, however, may think of increasing employee participation by electronic communication as a capacity-building strategy with implications for long-term performance. They might consider three components of such a strategy: creating connections among employees, building new skills, and increasing employees' ability to absorb new ideas. Increasing employee participation increases links among employees. Although most of the time these links are irrelevant to routine performance, they are available when needed, in times of crisis or opportunity. A case from Manufacturer's Hanover Trust (MHT) illustrates the point. Several years ago, MHT launched a new financial product in the Far East under extremely tight time deadlines governed by impending regulatory changes. MHT lawyers in Washington, corporate officers in New York, and marketing personnel in California used the MHT electronic mail system to coordinate their activities with one another and with the Hong Kong office to bring out the product under the deadline. Employees told us this story to illustrate how much they depend on their mail system. It also illustrates a capacity-building strategy. At the time of this opportunity, MHT personnel already "knew" many employees through communicating with them electronically. They could use these connections because they already existed.

Research on teaching and learning shows that people don't learn new ideas or skills just by being exposed to them.[5] Learners must be prepared to learn; they must have the mental scaffolding and requisite skills to understand and master new ideas (Cohen and Levinthal 1990). Listening to network discussions may help produce this "absorptive capacity" in employees, both old-timers and newcomers. It is easier to join and be socialized to electronic groups than to face-to-face ones (Moreland and Levine 1982). When group members are physically invisible, as is true with electronic interaction, the high salience and potential stress associated with the newcomer identity decline. Putting new employees on the mail system, especially if they can join large discretionary distribution lists, can help bring them quickly up to speed on how and what their fellow employees are thinking. It can get them more oriented toward the organization.

What about Extracurricular Mail?
Although some companies discourage any electronic discussions, many permit or encourage discussions related to company business for the reasons noted. Extracurricular messages and groups are a more difficult issue. It is easy to dismiss them as a waste of company resources—both network resources and employee time. The question of extracurricular mail is not one to be settled in a vacuum. It is simply an instance of a much more general view of human resource management. Some companies subsidize extracurricular benefits for their employees. Exercise facilities, discount entertainment tickets, office celebrations, softball teams—all could be viewed as a waste of resources. Companies that invest in them do so as a way of building employee enthusiasm, loyalty, or commitment. A recent study of employees in a high-technology service sector firm showed that "socializing with coworkers and supervisors, either on or off the job or both" was correlated with positive organizational attitudes (Kaufman et al. 1988). Allowing extracurricular messages and groups may serve a similar function. Where we have systematic data, it seems lower-level employees rather than managers more often send and receive extracurricular messages and participate in extracurricular electronic groups.

Allowing extracurricular mail also can contribute to a capacity-building strategy. A steely-eyed controller might frown on a company DL called ChocolateLovers. Yet that DL might be just the means to get peripheral employees motivated to increase their network connections and skills. In the accounting department of one large organization, a new employee was enrolled in a ChocolateLovers DL by another employee as a friendly orientation gesture. (She was also enrolled in all of the DLs required for her job and location.) After reading ChocolateLovers for a month or so, the new employee decided she wanted to print out some recipes she had read, so she had to learn various commands for manipulating and printing text. She then decided that she would compile recipes from the DL into a book to give as a Christmas present. To illustrate the book, she learned color desktop graphics by experimenting during her lunch hour. Over an eighteen-month period, this accounts payable supervisor became the office guru on desktop publishing and color graphics because she had joined ChocolateLovers. These skills were not directly applicable to accounts payable supervision, but they represented an increase in her skill repertoire and an increase in the skill capacity of the entire office.

Conclusion

It may seem paradoxical that computers, stereotyped as cold and impersonal, can be used to increase personal connections and affiliation. Electronic communication is not a substitute for face-to-face relationships, but for many peripheral employees, satisfying face-to-face relationships are hard to come by in the workplace. Electronic communication can increase the informational and emotional connections of these employees. The benefits to individual employees are immediate. The organization can additionally benefit by increasing employee capacity to work beyond the letter of the employment contract.

From the organization's perspective, giving a voice to the voiceless and opening a window on the corporation can produce bad effects as well as good ones. If the previously voiceless employees use the mail system to complain or to mobilize protest, managers might prefer that they had remained mute. And even if increasing participation by electronic means does not lead to riot or revolution, it still costs money. Some managers may be unwilling to support communication services that are not directly tied to task performance even if they do increase employee motivation and commitment. That decision, however, is one that should be taken in the light of more general human resource strategies.

Reprinted by permission of NEA, Inc.

6

Control and Influence

Those who control information derive power and influence over others from their position of control.[1] New communications technology can change the balance of information control in organizations. A city manager told us that electronic mail causes too much "upward delegation." "I love it," he said, "but employees send me their problems. I want to give them assignments, not the other way around." Before the network was installed, people who wanted to meet with the city manager left a telephone message, made an appointment with his secretary, or waited for his open office hours. Procedural and human gatekeepers buffered the city manager from problems he didn't want. Computer-based communication technology made it possible to bypass traditional information gatekeepers, thereby leading to a change in who had influence.

In this chapter we examine patterns of power and influence that can result from computer-based communication. Any technology, if it is a valuable resource, can become an instrument of power. Computer-based communication technology differs from many other workplace technologies because it has more potential to support upward influence and lateral influence, not just downward management control. The first part of this chapter briefly describes the development of communications technology as a controlling element in modern business organizations. Next, we consider how electronic communications can change the balance of information control—and people's power and influence over one another. We look at responses to these changes and how management can alter policies or technology design to reassert its control. Then we consider some complications of increases in information control. Finally, we apply these ideas to an increasingly important phenomenon in organizational life: the remote worker.

Information Control and Systematic Management

Before the middle of the nineteenth century, information and power in organizations were right at hand. Because firms were small and run by a single individual or family, people got their information—and their influence—by just talking with others. Beginning about 1850, the spread of manufacturing, transportation, and communication technologies expanded markets, leading to a growth in the size of firms and to organizational differentiation. Experience soon showed that informal conversation was inadequate for larger organizations run by managerial hierarchies and competing in expanded markets. A theory of management, later called systematic management, developed in response (Litterer 1961). The theory advocated formal, standardized, and impersonal procedures. System was supposed to substitute for ad hoc decision making and incidental oral communication. Formal communication methods, such as the printed circular and weekly performance report, and new technologies, such as the typewriter, stencil copier, and vertical filing cabinet, played a big part in systematic management. Each was designed and operated to control workers, materials, and production processes on behalf of management (Beniger 1986; Yates 1989).

E. I du Pont de Nemours and Company exemplifies this rise of system and information control (Yates 1989:201-270). Du Pont manufactured only one product, gun powder, during the nineteenth century. Beginning in 1902, the du Pont family took over most of the explosives industry and rapidly expanded the firm, devising at the same time a complex and extensive formal internal communication system, mainly based on writing. Management communicated down the hierarchy through circulars, manuals, and memoranda to give instructions and impart policies. It required upward communication through regular reports and performance statistics to monitor and evaluate employees. It used lateral communication through memoranda, and also telephone and telegraph, to coordinate and document interactions. (By 1919, the mail department handled 5,500 pieces of interdepartmental mail daily within the Wilmington headquarters.) Meetings formalized and documented conversation to gain cooperation and maintain morale. Written documentation, kept in filing cabinets, formed an organizational memory to ensure consistency across time and units. The company developed statistical analysis and graphing techniques to aid data compression and analysis; treasurer F. Donaldson Brown devised the return-on-investment (ROI) formula for using financial statistics. In time, so much information came to the executive committee that it became overburdened with information and analyses. One response was du Pont's chart room, equipped for displaying graphs from huge metal racks hung from the ceiling (Yates 1989:266). All of these procedures, arrangements, and technologies had the purpose and effect of tightening management control over operations and interactions among du Pont employees. Even the employee newsletter, meant to humanize the workplace, was crafted to reinforce managerial values and aims.

The design and use of communication technology at du Pont was not atypical. From ancient times to the present, new communication technologies have served the status quo and have been administered under the authority of elite gatekeepers.[2] Egyptian scribes wanted to keep writing for themselves as an elite skill. The first printed books were versions of existing manuscripts selected by Christian gatekeepers. The French telephone system initially was accessible only to municipal officials and other elites. Limited accessibility is still true of communication technologies in China and the Soviet Union (box 6.1). Not surprisingly, people often resist changes in information control that diminish their position. At du Pont, routine reports meant to monitor and control operations were a constant source of conflict (Yates 1989:245-246). Headquarters complained about the inaccuracy and lateness of reports. Superintendents in the plants saw the reports as so much red tape. More important, reports took away power

---

Box 6.1. Bread and circuits

Technological innovation can thrive only in an environment that invites, or at least tolerates, dissent. Technological innovation is largely a process of imagining radical alternatives to what is currently accepted and sharing these new possibilities with others. Problems must be openly recognized and ferment must be generated among creative minds to find solutions. But these are, in effect, acts of subversion. They almost invariably stir things up. And no clear boundaries exist between different categories of imagination, between different realms of subversion. The scientific, the managerial, the economic, the philosophical, the cultural, the political: they have a way of running into each other. It is no accident, as the Marxists used to say, that many of the Soviet Union's most brilliant scientists and artists are also political dissidents.

Moreover, many of the new technologies are themselves subversive. Computers, word processors, and telecommunications equipment not only incite unorthodox ideas, they also allow them to be exchanged instantly. They inspire communities of dissent. Totalitarian regimes understand this; they monopolize the technologies of communication—the press, radio and television, telephones, and now the computer. Nothing threatens a police state's legitimacy more than private and robust debate; nothing assures its survival more than the isolation and fragmentation of the citizenry.

. . . These ironies lie at the core of [Mikhail] Gorbachev's dilemma. For more than a half century, the Soviet police state has maintained tight control over communications among Soviet citizens. Even today, senior scholars and scientists are loath to use copying machines: in most enterprises and universities, copying departments are staffed by the KGB. How, then, can the Soviet Union be expected to adapt technologies that will unleash so much communication? How could the Soviets embellish and improve upon the new technologies without simultaneously inviting political and social dissent? To gain technological sophistication, Soviet economics and politics would have to be transformed. This the Soviet bureaucracy will not allow. Technological sophistication is essential to the Soviet Union's economic and political survival. Technological backwardness is essential to the Soviet Union's system of government.

Source: Robert B. Reich (1987). Bread and circuits. *New Republic, 197* (5), (August 3, pp. 32–33). Review of Marshall I. Goldman (1987), *Gorbachev's Challenge: Economic Reform in the Age of High Technology.*

---

from the superintendents since plants could be compared against each other, and executive decisions about resource allocation could be made on the basis of this information. As Yates noted, "The upward reports, like downward communication, shifted power from the superintendents to the main office. It gave the main office the information necessary to evaluate the efficiency of one plant against another and to make decisions about where to locate production. And indeed, the efficiency of the plants was improving, so the systematic management that headquarters was imposing in part through these reports was paying off" (p. 246).

Computers and Information Control

If we had visited du Pont forty years later, the by-now-giant chemical company might have evidenced similar frictions over computer technologies. In the 1960s and 1970s, mainframe-based computer technologies were intended to reinforce managerial control. The special units that managed information technology put barriers between people and corporate information. Information technology personnel seemed more interested in their computers than in the needs of employees (Danziger 1979). The emphasis on standardized, numeric data reinforced performance measures chosen by management (Ridgway 1956; Markus and Pfeffer 1983).

But not all technologies reinforce managerial standards and control. The telephone initially began as a technology for businessmen to give orders and monitor performance, but it also made possible lateral communications among coworkers, which changed interpersonal relationships and control patterns. Computer networks also were viewed initially as a way to increase centralized control; with computer networks, managers could extend their authority across time and space. This view changed, however, as personal computers enabled people to control their own work and analyses. People realized how easy it was to talk informally or share data with anyone (or with everyone) on the networks. In this respect, computer-mediated communication seemed much like the telephone, which to a degree also permits open, informal interaction. So far computer networks have allowed broader access to information and a decrease in the power of traditional gatekeepers. The process can lead to conflict, though, as people who have power seek to protect their position. This conflict is apparent today in some computer-based communication systems and helps explain some second-level reactions to these systems.

Who's In Charge Here?

•A brokerage firm introduced electronic mail between customers and their brokers to speed up the transmission of information that otherwise would be done in more time-consuming, conventional ways. Customers felt more comfortable asking questions electronically because they knew they weren't interrupting the broker with a telephone call. They felt their access to the broker grew by this technology and they became more active participants in the relationship. Brokers, in turn, felt they could process customer questions more efficiently and used the "saved" time to sell new accounts (Hirschhorn 1985).

•The Social Security Administration introduced an interactive claims processing system to reduce the amount of time necessary to decide if a client's claim was authorizable. With the new system, clients provided information to case workers, who immediately entered it into the networked system. The system analyzed that information fast enough so that case workers could learn the determination and pass it on to clients while they waited (Turner 1984).

•Police officers who previously radioed their dispatcher for information on suspicious persons or vehicles now use a terminal in their patrol cars to interrogate databases directly. They get information much more rapidly with this technology, an important benefit when trying to decide if a suspicious person or vehicle should be stopped for interrogation (Palys, Boyanowsky, and Dutton 1984).

In each case, the designer's intention to increase the speed of information transfer—a first-level technology effect—succeeded. Unnoticed and unintended by the decision makers who authorized the new systems, each also changed the balance of information control among the parties who used the systems, a second-level social effect. Network-based communication technology can change patterns of information control by allowing people to bypass gatekeepers and access information sources directly. Typically this results in not only a faster flow of information but also changes in the relative power of the parties in the transaction.

In the brokerage firm, both brokers and clients apparently benefited from faster information exchange with the new technology. But there is more to the story. Network communication changed the relative balance of control over information by giving customers a greater relative share of access to important information. Because information about their accounts' activity was on-line, customers could now assess their broker's performance in a detailed way. Brokers felt more vulnerable to customer scrutiny, knowing that their daily performance could be compared against that of the market as a whole. Because the firm's on-line research bulletin was also accessible by customers, brokers no longer were the sole gatekeepers for research information.

In the old social security claims system, a client provided the claims information and had to return days later to learn if the agency had authorized the claim. Officials assumed that everyone would like the new system better. It was easier to use and provided information much more rapidly than did the old system. In reality, case workers did not like the new system at all. They made more errors and reported that they felt much more stress with the new system. The new computer system degraded the nature of the social relationship between claimant and case worker. In the old system, case workers did not have to confront claimants directly with the news that they were denying (or accepting) the claim. Often claimants did not hear the dispensation of their case from the same worker who recorded the initial information. Even if the same worker both recorded the initial information and later gave the returning client bad news, enough time had intervened that the interaction could be dispassionate, at least for the worker. With the new system, the case worker had to record information and then immediately tell the claimant that the claim had been denied (or accepted). What officials saw as time delays in the old social relationship were really time buffers that allowed case workers and claimants to interact with little stress. The increase in stress emerged from the changed social relationship between case worker and claimant, not from some property inherent in the new technology. In this situation, technology fixes, such as improving the command language, the user interface, the documentation, or the training, would not change the new social relationship. They therefore would not eliminate the stress.

The police officers who no longer had to depend on dispatchers for information were happy with their new system because it gave them more control over information access. Under the old system, all radio calls to the dispatcher could be heard by all other police radios. Thus a patrol officer's peers always knew where he or she was and what kinds of information he or she was asking for. Dubious requests were often the butt of jokes from other officers. The requests were also audible to the dispatcher, of course, who might challenge dubious ones or keep the officer waiting before filling them. The police officers liked the new system because it gave them more control over information; the dispatchers disliked it intensely, for it reduced their control.

In each of these cases, a technology introduced simply to speed up the transmission of information led to changes in who had control over information and expertise. These changes made old social relationships much more fragile and problematic. Changes in control over information led to changes in job performance. Those who lost control over information became dissatisfied but were unable to demand the abolition of the new systems because of demonstrable performance gains. Also the "losers," while generally of higher status than the "winners," were only mid-level employees, without the hierarchical power to abolish such systems. In other cases, when electronic communication changes the relative power over access to information, the potential "losers" have been senior management. When hierarchical control of information is strong and information exchange follows strict channels, computer networks and widespread electronic communication have the potential to undermine long-established patterns of management control. The predictable reaction of top management under these conditions is to reassert control.

Zuboff (1988) describes such a case in a large pharmaceuticals company known for its narrow, highly structured channels of communication. As an internal report from the company said, "Specific information about the

way the company and each division are organized is carefully controlled so
that employees in one division may not have a clear picture of other
divisions or the company in its entirety. Official communication is handled
hierarchically . . . There are periodic warnings about only sharing information on a 'need-to-know' basis" (pp. 366-367). This company installed a
computer-based conferencing system that, by 1982, had 2,400 participants. In 1983 employees began a conference titled "Women's Professional
Improvement," which described its purpose as "helping professional
women cope with life in a male-dominated corporation" (p. 382). It
quickly became very popular, with 130 members sharing information and
advice electronically. But members of the management hierarchy began to
feel threatened. The personnel department feared that women employees
might use the conference to organize a union. The legal department feared
that the conference might become a vehicle for initiating affirmative action
suits. In each case, a hierarchical unit that previously controlled access to
information saw its control slipping away. After management complaints,
leaders of the conference were cautioned to rein in the discussion and focus
it only on "legitimate business issues," that is, ones that did not threaten
the hierarchy. The complaints and cautions had a chilling effect on the
conference: membership declined, and free exchange of information de-
creased. Hierarchical responses like this one ultimately led to a refashioned
computer-based communication system. According to Zuboff, "everyone
involved agreed that the new emphasis was one of formality, self-con-
sciousness, and self-protection" (p. 384).

In the pharmaceutical company, executives clamped down on communication in the name of legitimate business practice. But the women's
discussions were not bad business. Officials were more concerned about
control. Suppose they had let the group prosper? An electronic interest
group of women might decide that women would fare better in the firm if
they mobilized as a group. They might use the network to solicit support
from disaffected individuals and try to influence management policies.
Other groups might see this and become encouraged to also try to influence
policy. Any of these behaviors could threaten management control.

A World Worth Talking About

Open communication leads to unsupervised information sharing. In
electronic conversations employees might discover more about company
policies and practices than management intends them to know. For

example, if salaries are kept secret, connected employees can compare salaries; they can compare the size of their offices; or they can ask who has and has not been consulted on a major decision. Organizational authorities often try to keep staff content by convincing them their share of resources or influence compares well with that of others, even if it doesn't. To succeed in this, they have to control access to the information that might be used to make comparisons among people or subunits. For instance, a large engineering firm forbids its professionals working on different projects to talk across the network about anything other than specific technical information used for their projects; project teams are not allowed to discuss and compare performance evaluations received by each team, for example. The justification for this policy is that it protects everyone and permits impartial treatment. In another case, a financial services company installed a separate local area network for each of several functional subunits. Electronic mail does not move between the networks. The company's justification for this design is that confidential information must not go inadvertently to inappropriate people.

Restricting communication and secrecy are control strategies in these companies (Pfeffer 1978). In the case of the engineering firm, project members develop a notion of how much commitment management should make to their projects in terms of expertise, funds, time, and other resources. If comparative information about how management is treating other projects is unavailable because of project secrecy, then the employees can't make a good evaluation of their treatment. They must test the organization's commitment either by looking outside the organization or relying on the judgment of the organization. Secrecy allows the organization to discriminate more in its distribution of resources and rewards to different projects than it could otherwise do; it permits concentrating resources in some projects and giving only minimum resources to others.

In the case of the financial services company, compartmentalizing the networks helps protect the integrity and confidentiality of data. It prevents employees in different units from trading data and discourages formation of electronic groups across physically separated units. Security officers have an easier time preventing illicit communications when networks are compartmentalized; an interconnected open network is full of headaches for them. In the ideal world of the security officer, nobody talks with anybody. In such a world, however, no one does much worth talking about.

Social Control

As the women's interest group in the pharmaceutical company illustrates, open communication among employees usually does not threaten management's direct control over performance. It can threaten management's social control of the workplace. Social control is a more subtle way of controlling behavior than the reporting requirements, formal communications, and other systematic management techniques used in performance control. Social control entails imbuing workers with a sense of "the way we do things around here" and a desire to excel. It also entails maintaining appropriate relationships among people, fostering the feeling that "we are the company" and should work as a team. Organizational culture can promote social control through such devices as company rituals and war stories (Martin 1982; O'Reilly 1989). Electronic communication can promulgate cultural values. But if people communicate openly across the organization and management has little control over what they say or how they organize these communications, social control tends to divide more unpredictably between workers and management. Electronic communication does not change the total amount of social control but can be used to change who has social control and the kinds of behavior regulated by social control.

Social control in electronic mail is illustrated by this message from an electronic interest group called SportsFanatics:

```
Hey fellow Fanaticists,
Working here at Corporate Headquarters is no picnic with all of
the political "bs" and red tape that sometimes goes around.
However, I am occasionally privy to some information that y'all
may not hear. For one, there is a process underway that would
do away with all of the nonbusiness electronic groups that
currently reside on our net. The folks involved seem to think
that these groups tie up mail servers. Not to mention the point
they make about the time spent corresponding over these types
of groups not being very productive. I think all we
SportsFanatics can agree that we enjoy most of the topics
discussed here and we don't want someone "upstairs" to pull the
plug. If you don't think the threat is serious, it is. It's
been elevated to a VP level, and they're looking for more
justification and a practical method for deleting these
groups...... Big Brother is definitely watching...believe
it! . . .
```

Although this message complains about top-down control in the organization, it reflects social control at the employee level. The person who sent this message was part of a large group that had nothing to do with the hierarchical structure or with the work of the company. The topic was not business. Yet the sender had a claim on the attention of many other employees. In this message he exhorted his group to forgo "petty bickering" and "cheap personal shots" in electronic mail group messages. "Let yourself cool down before answering that mailnote that put down your favorite team," he urged. "If we act like responsible people and not like a bunch of goons, we may be allowed to keep this electronic group going a little longer." In other words, if the group behaved itself, it would retain some control.

Alliances are the primary vehicle of social control. Employees frequently find they have experiences, anxieties, and attitudes in common, a discovery that leads to the development of reference groups, that is, groups whose opinions people respect. Employees conform to the norms of these groups and reject people who don't conform. Group rewards are conferred on those who achieve according to the group's criteria of excellence (Kiesler and Kiesler 1969; Weick 1979). It is no wonder management would like to control reference groups and the cultures they promulgate. Unintended social control is exemplified by the emergence of "gripenet" at IBM. When that firm initially introduced the computer network, VNET, lower-level managers and staff used it to publish an underground electronic newsletter. They discovered they shared many concerns and problems and used the newsletter to argue about management policies. Top management became alarmed and instituted a new policy restricting access and content in the network, and it even began monitoring network communications (Emmett 1982).

Social control is intimately connected with participation. The more people participate in organizational affairs, the happier they seem to be, and the more they feel they can influence others. In chapter 5 we described how city employees on shift schedules used electronic mail to increase their participation in city government. For example, by making it possible for a police officer to advance her views of a promotion even though she was on the night shift, her potential influence on her department was improved, and she felt more solidarity with her coworkers. This would have increased their potential influence on her too, of course.

Yet there is also potential for more friction as social control increases at lower levels. One study showed that in software development teams, the more participation and influence staff professionals had, the more disputes there were over policies and practices (Robey, Farrow, and Franz,1989). At our university, the administration once proposed a new policy governing the ownership of intellectual property. The news spread on the computer network, leading to the following message:

```
I cannot resist fanning the flames of discontent. Under the
kindest interpretation, the motives of the administration were
to view the intellectual properties issue as an adversary
conflict, and send up a trial balloon taking an extreme
hardline stance. Then, any amount of yield gives a false
appearance of conciliation....regardless of whether their next
proposal is almost as ludicrous as the present one. It is also
possible that the administration actually means to ram through
their policy with minimal notice or comment....I propose we
draft a statement ....
```

This message elicited answers from thirty-five people in two days, mobilizing an effective opposition to the administration's policy.

Electronic groups greatly extend the possibilities of upward and lateral social influence. The messages to the SportsFanatics group and to the group of professors at CMU are not very different from similar messages that could be given in person, but each was sent to hundreds of people, most of whom the writers had never met. Ordinarily we pay little attention to people we don't know and know little about; however, by virtue of their membership in the network community, the writers had legitimacy. Many readers responded who would never have heard about the problem without the network. Participants in electronic communities report that on occasion the network erupts in flaming and public debate over a matter that would have received no attention in the past. An inflammatory remark or gossip receives wide electronic distribution, fanning discontent or even collective action by employees (Emmett 1982; Stoll 1989). In some high-technology organizations, employee-initiated and highly participative debates ensue over issues ranging from what computers to buy to what reorganization plan is best to what is a proper C.E.O. salary. The labor market in high technology is such that valuable employees can demand participation as their right (Sitkin forthcoming; Hybels and Barley 1990).

Complications of Information Control

Changing patterns of information control can result in second-level complications that cannot necessarily be solved by better technology designs or policies. Control leads to fundamental organizational conflicts. Technology design and policy can affect the conflicts but not eliminate them. How a company views the legitimacy of information exemplifies one basic pattern. Organizations value what they measure (Pfeffer 1978; Kiesler and Sproull 1982). For instance, standardized financial information that bears on profit-making objectives can dominate attention to the exclusion of equally essential but less legitimate information such as information about employee morale. If computer-based communication technology were used periodically to collect and distribute data on employee job satisfaction, it would not change the organization's response to legitimate information. Yet it might lead to a new basis of legitimacy for data about morale.

Information Overload
One unintended effect of widespread information control is information overload. If members of a large unit send their progress reports not just to their supervisors but also to coworkers, and those readers reply to the writer and forward comments to other employees in the unit, interpersonal influence increases. So do the demands on people's attention (Hannaway 1989). Because who gets attention has symbolic and task importance, people in an overloaded system may escalate their requests to be noticed, thereby increasing overload even more (Thorngate 1988).

Often information overload is really an argument about control. Complaints about information overload usually come from recipients rather than senders of messages and apply to burdens unwelcomed by recipients. Recipients reject information they do not want by claiming they are overloaded. Typically the problem is not too much information literally but lack of control over information exchange. People usually prefer communications they initiate themselves, and they prefer to have choice in the content and format of information they send and receive (Thompson 1981). Choosing what to learn can produce a better match of information to task than can be accomplished when information is selected by others. Also, if information is valuable, then people want the freedom to negotiate its exchange. Elites usually have more control over their communications than do other organizational participants. Yet the sheer amount of communications they engage in voluntarily is larger, belying overload as simply a problem of volume. Some electronic mail systems let people build filters for their mail so they can control what they see (Malone et al. 1987). Such systems typically let people specify what should come through the filters (all mail from the boss, all mail with "URGENT" in the subject field).

The filters delete all other messages or place them in a lower-priority folder. If such filtering systems are useful, it probably is because they give people a sense of more control over their mail. The difficulty with such systems is that they can greatly reduce the amount of new information (some of it worthless, to be sure) and new contacts (some of them useless, to be sure) that people will encounter electronically. (One way around this dilemma is to establish a filter that lets through a certain fraction of the low-priority mail every day.)

Illusions of Control
In principle, physically dispersed organizations with good communication links can delegate responsibility widely (Kraut 1987; Becker 1986). One reason is that there are fewer physical limitations on the number of people a supervisor can handle. Yet good communication links also provide an occasion for superiors to exert control. A complication of information control is that it can give distant superiors the illusion that they know enough to act at a distance, though they cannot capture all of the knowledge available to those on the scene (Fischhoff and Johnson 1990). Before the invention of the telegraph, diplomats had considerable autonomy once they landed in a foreign country. With the installation of the international telegraph, officials in the home country monitored and gave orders to nineteenth century diplomats well beyond the actual information they received. Military command-and-control systems are said to provide commanders with six-thousand-mile screwdrivers. The counterargument is that the canny distant actor can use technology to manage what the home commander knows (Metcalf 1986).

Misinformation
Communication is partly a strategic exercise through which people define, protect, and pursue their interests. They misrepresent and disbelieve information in ways that are advantageous to themselves and their groups. Beau Sheil (1983) describes his attempts to describe precisely the office procedures used in a branch sales office of his company as a preliminary step to designing an automated system. It turned out that the procedures were precise and rational only on the surface. Office workers would give different people different information according to the different impressions they wanted to give. By controlling the impressions they gave, office

workers caused others to interact with them in ways they found advantageous. For example, sales representatives were told about a phantom procedure in their head office that took much longer than the actual one did. The purpose of the phantom procedure was to justify requiring the sales representatives to begin their interactions with the office workers well before their actual deadlines. Sheil argues that the office workers' distorted descriptions of their procedures were not a sign of stupidity or resistance; the office workers were controlling the procedures that affected the rest of their work lives.

Technology and technology policies that assume everyone shares or wants to share accurate information can generate new problems that did not arise with more organizational ignorance. Other things equal, if groups send and receive accurate and complete information, they potentially compromise their strategic positions and threaten the balance of control in the organization. Senders, knowing this, misrepresent information. Recipients, knowing this, discount information. Simply increasing the rate and scope of information sharing might only increase the number of misleading and discounted communications.

Controlling Remote Workers

All remote workers—traveling salespeople, forest rangers in the wilderness, professionals working at home, and others—pose problems of control for employers. If the outcome of remote work can be measured unambiguously, then control of performance can be attained by establishing quotas, such as sales volume or new accounts landed. Agreed-upon quotas influence behavior and control performance while the employee is operating remotely. When employers cannot measure performance outcomes easily or unambiguously, they may try to establish standard behaviors. For instance, are predator-sighting reports up to date? Are fire-watch towers properly supplied? Here behavioral standards control performance while the employee is operating alone. For many workers, particularly professional or white-collar workers, both outcomes and behaviors are hard to specify. Then employers must rely on social control, employees' understanding of "how we do things around here," and commitment to "what it takes to do a good job." Organizations instill these internal beliefs formally through training programs, policy manuals, and supervision, and informally through social interaction—watching other people, exchanging war stories, and general conversation.

Network communication makes it possible to increase the efficiency of remote work, both on the road and at home. With portable or personal computers and dial-up connections, remote workers can be in immediate touch with the office, whether to access up-to-date databases, to submit orders and reports in a timely fashion, or to send and read electronic mail. While all remote work benefits in principle from electronic communication, portable computers on the road are much more popular than is computer-supported work at home. Differences in control, we think, explain part of the difference in popularity. Before they used computers, employees such as sales personnel or off-site auditors had only tenuous connections with their colleagues and managers back at the office. Computer networks can increase those connections dramatically. By contrast, people working in an office setting decrease their connections with others if they stay at home and work only via computer. Social control and influence increase both for managers and for workers who use computer networks on the road and decrease when office workers use computer networks to work at home (figure 6.1).

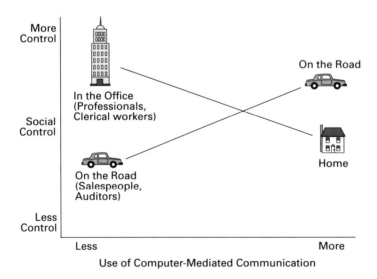

Figure 6.1
Relationship between computerization and social control of work

On the Road

About 2 million portable computers were sold between 1986 and 1989. As one analyst noted, they process information about everything from "corn niblets, multiple vitamins, frozen fish, dead moose, gasoline supplies and prices, corporate profit and loss statements, [to] Alka Seltzer" (Halper 1988). As stand-alone machines for small amounts of data entry they are very useful, but their real power comes from using them to connect to mainframe databases and through electronic mail to other people. The two largest groups of people who use these machines are sales workers and auditing and accounting personnel. Sales workers appreciate the convenience of using a portable computer instead of having to haul around heavy notebooks of product information and paperwork. Using telephone lines, they can access and download up-to-date databases while they are at customers' sites. Miles Laboratories' consumer health care division, for instance, equips its sales force with portables that let the salespeople access electronic mail, customer files, sales progress reports, and order status information and forms for reporting assessment of sales calls. Accounting and auditing personnel who work at client sites also appreciate having access to standard forms, analysis packages, and up-to-date regulations without having to carry around heavy volumes. In each case, the first-level or efficiency effects are obviously positive. Also in each case, formerly isolated workers can now talk directly with one another and with colleagues back in the office via electronic mail. This gives them the opportunity to share in informal conversations and exchanges of information that help build commitment to the organization and foster social control.

At the same time, computer links between the office and employees on the road can increase supervisors' performance control (Rule and Brantley 1990). For example, a burglar alarm company used data from each alarm call to check whether the field inspector assigned to a machine had given it its periodic manual servicing. Computerized analyses of sales are a common vehicle for increased control by managers. In the Rule and Brantley study, one employee said of a firm that fabricated steel parts and entered every order into the computer:

The President gets a copy of every order and the order lists the profit margin and dollar profit for every order. Before computers, he simply got the dollar total made on the order (and he got it much later). Now, he is much tougher on the sales people when he sees a low margin. Since he often sees this before the bill has gone out, he will often change the price. He usually gets the customer to pay that price. Before computers, by the time he saw the dollar profit on each order, the invoice had probably gone out already. He didn't want to issue an additional bill because the customer wouldn't pay it. Also, since he only saw total dollar profit, he might think an order that made $1,000 was a good order without realizing that the profit margin was only 3%. Now, he sees both dollar and percentage and this leads to keeping better tabs on the sales and salesmen. (p. 11)

Here management control extends to areas where it had been desired but was infeasible without the new technology. By enabling the president to gain access to performance data through the computer, he gained the means to exact more control.

When communication technologies increase the control connections between workers on the road and supervisors in the office the effects need not be positive. Fischhoff and Johnson (1990) give an example of negative effects in the abortive attempt to rescue American hostages in Iran during the Carter presidency. With their modern communication systems, Washington military officials believed that they could control operations at a distance and thus did not give field personnel full authority to act on their own. When they heard that the number of disabled helicopters exceeded the prespecified number necessary for safe operations, officials in Washington stopped the rescue plan. Later it was learned that military personnel on the scene, using local resources and their intimate knowledge of extant conditions, probably could have conducted the rescue with far fewer helicopters.

Working at Home

Although an eight-hour office workday is the rule, eight productive hours at the office are the exception. White-collar workers are particularly susceptible to unproductive time at the office. Constance Perin (in press) notes, "As employees and managers often see it, putting in an appearance at the office is bound to *lower* their productivity and their job satisfaction." She quotes a manager of authors of in-house training courses who says, "I send my people home to get their work done." Also a financial analyst says, "With fewer interruptions I'm more productive at home—I also save the commute time."

Electronic communication and computing technologies now make it possible for many people to work mostly at home, a practice known as telework. The best candidates for telework are clerical employees who do large amounts of routine transaction processing and relatively autonomous professionals such as writers or designers. Analysts have estimated that up to 50 percent of white-collar workers, or roughly 26 million workers, could work at home with computer support at least part time (Harkness 1977). They advertise telework as a magic nostrum for organizations, with some predicting that in the 1990s up to 40 percent of work will be telework (Kelly and Carpenter, cited by Kraut 1987). The claimed benefits include great economic savings for both employers and employees. Employers should save through lowered facilities costs. Workers should save through lowered commuting and child care costs. The claimed benefits also include higher-quality work—achieved by reducing the distractions of the office and letting people work during their peak performance hours instead of during an arbitrary office schedule. Worker satisfaction is supposed to increase because employees have more time with their families or the opportunity to live in desirable locations far from the workplace. Despite the hyperbole, the actual number of full-time teleworkers remains small. A consulting firm specializing in telework estimated that there were only about ten thousand full-time teleworkers in the United States in 1984 (Electronic Services Unlimited 1987). More commonly, professionals use telework to augment office hours, not to substitute for them (Kraut 1987:121; Perin in press). That is, people first put in a full day at the office and then do telework in the evenings and weekends from home. Home work for professionals is not new; electronic communication simply makes it possible to increase the kinds of work professionals do at home.

With all the apparent benefits of telework, why is it not more popular? On the employer's side, the big problem is control—both performance and social control. Security, or protecting the integrity of company files and data, seems not to be so big an issue. For clerical workers, performance control can be accomplished straightforwardly by monitoring the rate and quality of output in files transmitted back to the employer. Monitoring performance is more difficult for professional workers working at home. Often professional work has long-term projects with few explicit benchmarks. When progress is difficult to measure hourly, managers may feel uneasy if they can't literally see their people at work. All stay-at-homes pose problems of social control for employers. Home-based workers see fewer reminders of larger corporate goals and identity than do workers physically present in the workplace. They can learn less from more experienced or successful workers. They are less likely to pick up on subtle cues about company culture. They are less easily managed because they encounter none of the subtle, implicit, and indirect mechanisms in the physical workplace that influence employees' behavior. Attributes of electronic communication that allow people to feel freer in their communication, while a benefit to open communication, can become a drawback to social control. The relative lack of status cues in electronic communication means that supervisors who want or need to invoke their authority to influence employees must do so explicitly. This can be distasteful to supervisors who would prefer to rely on implicit means to remind others of their position.

For the stay-at-homes, work entails less direct supervision, greater informality, greater ability to set hours, and more flexibility in combining personal errands and work. In other words, there are looser connections between employer and worker (Becker 1986). However, people may have romanticized the expected homelife benefits and underestimated the career costs. For some parents the workplace may represent a welcome refuge from the demands of small children. This is probably true more for clerical workers than for professional workers. When the latter work at home, they more often have a separate home office and child care help. Internal career mobility is lower among people who are unable to participate in the informal contact networks that operate in the workplace. Further, for professionals in our society, work provides a substantial measure of self-identity. Going to the office is an important component of that identity. It takes a strong person to sustain that identity in isolation from peers and the social context of work. One teleworker, a professional writer, described his deep chagrin when he went in to the editorial office, something he did about once a month. A coworker greeted him and asked seriously, "Didn't you used to work here?"

Conclusion

Computer-based communication technology increases control for some remote workers but decreases it for others. In neither case is communication between office and worker a simple matter of information exchange. Communication can't be separated from who is in charge of the giving, receiving, content, and use of what is communicated. Information control is tied to other forms of power and influence. When we change information control using technology, we also change the conditions for other control relationships in the organization.

Computer networks give people access, in principle, to ever increasing information about others. The potential for access can be abused by people who snoop in others' mail files or access databases containing personal information. Computer-based communications technology could be used to collect data automatically and provide statistical reports on how employees spend their time away from the office, when and where they travel, who they talk to, what they read, how they spent their money, and how healthy they are. Current laws and regulations do not cover all the possibilities because lawmakers must continually try to catch up to advances in computer and communication capabilities.[3]

Most policy analyses of computer-based technology ignore the politics of information exchange that influence the control dimension of communication in comparison with a narrowly task-oriented one (National Research Council 1989). As we have seen, information has strategic significance that can influence the choice of communication technology—its design, policies governing its use, and its actual use (Pfeffer 1978; Burns 1989). These strategic choices affect control over information, performance, and social influence.

7

Designing Information Procedures

It is said of a former president of Harvard that he ran the whole place with the aid of a secretary and a little black book in which he kept the names of the faculty, the subjects they taught, and their salaries. That was all the information he needed to make sensible educational policies. Most organizations today are larger, more complicated, and more diversified than the college of sixty years ago. No one person with a notebook can manage the information necessary to make intelligent decisions for an entire organization. When information exchanges in organizations are routine and repetitive, information procedures can help regularize them. Computers can help in this process. An even more interesting possibility is to design information procedures for nonroutine information exchange. In this chapter we take up routine and nonroutine information exchange in turn. While some would consider electronic data interchange (EDI) an important example of electronic routine behaviors, we defer its discussion until chapter 8 because we emphasize its contribution to changing organizational structures.

Information Procedures

One hundred years ago, a lieutenant newly assigned to the U.S. Bureau of Pensions found that congressmen who asked for information about the war service of constituents had to wait six months for an answer. One year after Lieutenant Ainsworth's arrival, congressmen had their answers within twenty-four hours. The instrument of this revolution was the card indexing procedure that Lieutenant Ainsworth devised (Morison 1966:45-66). Lieutenant Ainsworth summarized each man's service record on a card having specific categories for information about men, places, time, and money. The cards had a standard format that could be read and sorted easily. They could be alphabetized by name, ordered chronologically by beginning or length of service, or categorized by state. With the card index, the bureau could store the information it received from many places, organize it, file it accessibly, and retrieve it as needed. Sources and recipients of information communicated easily and efficiently. It was a scheme within which the government community could act sensibly and cooperatively.

Information procedures make it possible to summarize, synthesize, and share vast amounts of information. Suppose A and B are a source and recipient of information, respectively. For situations that are repetitive and explicit, reporting and requesting procedures—progress reports, financial statements, tax forms, invoices, library book requests, purchase orders, billings, credit checks—move information efficiently and reliably from A to B. In each case, A and B are specified in advance; sources and recipients know each others' identities. The information they exchange is abstracted and organized in categories that are also specified in advance. In Lieutenant Ainsworth's time, these information procedures were carried out on paper. Paper has many advantages over talk alone. With paper, people don't have to remember information; it resides in external memory and remains accessible over time. It can be passed from A to B, or from A through various other people to B. Also paper triggers activity. When paper arrives on their desks, A and B are supposed to act. By controlling paper, people control information and behavior. Today the information and the control may be in a computer rather than on paper. For the navy, today the equivalent of Lieutenant Ainsworth's card index is 26 million lines of Cobol code (Patrick Larkey, personal communication, April 3, 1989).

Routines via Computer

Automating information procedures with computers can improve the coordination of people and organizational units. For instance, manually scheduling work loads for people such as pilots, police officers, and nurses is an awkward and slow task. Administrators have to juggle organizational requirements (such as covering holidays and factoring in seniority privileges) and unusual circumstances (such as unexpected illness or equipment breakdown), while also treating employees fairly. Scheduling procedures are notorious for inflexibility and for the disputes they provoke. Computer-based scheduling can be even more infuriating, since clerks can blame "the computer" for inequities or bad outcomes. On the other hand, a computer can be programmed to collect detailed work preferences from employees, to match these preferences with administrative requirements, and to propose schedules that best meet everyone's wishes.

A hospital in Pittsburgh is developing a scheduling program for nursing staff that allows nurses to touch a calendar on a computer screen to indicate which hours and days they want to work and do not want to work. The program collates the preferences and calculates and reports to the nurse administrator a schedule that best fits both hospital requirements and nurse preferences. The report also lists the nurses and graphically shows the administrator how well the schedule meets each nurse's preferences. This procedure could be carried out manually. Airlines, for example, have a manual system for pilots that works on a principle similar to the nursing system; however, the procedure is costly and inefficient. British Airways is developing a computer network and set of programs that will collect bids from pilots as to when they want to fly or fill a vacancy in the schedule (Benson, Ciborra, and Proffitt 1990). With a networked system, pilots are free to bid for slots regardless of their physical location and to trade slots with other pilots even if they don't know them personally.

Computer-based information procedures also can increase efficiency in coordinating large project groups such as large software systems projects. Unlike small committees or formal organizational units, large project groups often experience formidable coordination difficulties stemming from their size, complexity, and unpredictable or uncertain task. The task cannot be decomposed with parts of the project proceeding independently; each piece of the system must mesh perfectly with the others (Curtis, Krasner, and Iscoe 1988; Kraut and Streeter 1990). A recent major disruption of the AT&T long-distance network shows how interactions among modules introduced while updating a software system to give it more capabilities can have disastrous, unanticipated consequences (Travis 1990). The combination of size, uncertainty, and required integration requires special coordination techniques that may not be necessary in smaller or more standardized manufacturing or office situations.

Routine information procedures have been developed to alleviate coordination problems in software development: written documentation, data flow modeling languages, requirements specification languages, and formal project management to track and monitor the development process. In formal project management, each stage of development is specified in advance, has well-defined products and milestones, and requires tests to ensure that the pieces do what they are supposed to do. All code and documents are under change control. Nothing can be written without design reviews; code can't be tested before code walk-throughs; changes or error corrections can't be made without issuing modification requests; no piece of code goes to system test without an integration test. The general manager of IBM's Federal Systems Center, reviewing the Houston Manned Space Center, reports being "appalled" by the "sheer bureaucracy" of a formal development system until he visited other sites where the process was less formal and the projects were "out of control" (Fox 1982). Formal procedures are necessary, but they impose an extra burden: increased staff, increased communication, and increased project information. Fox estimates that 50 percent of the cost of large projects is for planning, checking, scheduling, management, and control. Many software systems projects have begun to use computer-based communications to reduce these costs.

Some projects use computer-based communications to store and process change orders; the computer not only automates the changes needed but also the documentation and reporting of change (Reddy 1990). With computer-based communication, some kinds of errors are harder to overlook. It is harder to forget to notify people of changes affecting them. Networked databases can be constructed that keep track of project schedules and specifications over time. There are also on-line electronic forms for documenting code, ordering supplies, and so forth. People can run automated consistency checks on a formal specification document or use a modification request tracking system to trigger management intervention when a project schedule slips. There are also new electronic project services. The "expert locator" queries documents in the corporate database to find experts for people on the topics that concern them. An alerting service can monitor project information such as changing requirements and can send messages automatically to the subunits that should know about the changes. Alerting messages can be made to trigger communication of other information, such as new documents, promotions and reorganizations, travel reservations, meeting notices, and results of customer or market tests (Kraut and Streeter 1990).

Robert Kraut and Lynn Streeter at Bell Communications Research, who are studying the effects of manual and electronic information procedures in over 150 different software systems groups, have confirmed that both large project size and task uncertainty are significant barriers to coordination. They have found that projects that use routine information procedures such as change control significantly reduce the negative effects of large size on coordination.

Limitations of Routine Information Procedures

Despite their power and ubiquity and even when they are intended to be individualized, as are the new nursing staff and pilot scheduling systems, routine reporting and requesting information procedures have some shortcomings. Sometimes A and B cannot be specified in advance. B may not know that A has potentially useful information, or A may not know that B needs it. If either knew of the other's need or capability, he or she would gladly exchange the information. Organizations do have some procedures for these situations. For instance, routine scanning procedures such as reading a company newsletter allow B to look for ill-specified information from possible sources (Mintzberg 1973; Keegan 1974). Routine distribution procedures such as posting notices on bulletin boards allow A to announce information to anyone who might be interested. Still, these procedures typically are less reliable than reporting and requesting procedures. A variant of the unknown sources and recipients shortcoming occurs when A and B are unwilling to share information. Perhaps the information is personally valuable, sensitive, or strategic. Sometimes it is in the interests of both parties to leave a situation as fuzzy, amorphous, and undefined as possible. In his report on military avionics repair facilities, Kmetz (1984) provides an example of unwillingness to share information that is widespread in manufacturing. Because parts are frequently unavailable at the time they are needed, repair people keep unofficial stockpiles of them. They hide these parts so employees from the parts department can't demand their return. Meanwhile, people in the parts department don't tell repair people about expected shortages because that would provoke repair people to stockpile even more. Unwillingness to share information is prevalent in culturally sensitive or personally taboo areas involving prejudices and preconceptions, and when the area is merely a new one that could be seriously distorted by using old definitions and old solutions.

A second shortcoming in routine information sharing procedures occurs when categories for describing and abstracting information cannot be specified in advance. This state characterizes novel, puzzling, and ambiguous situations (Suchman 1988). In these cases, simply coming to understand what the question is often is the most important step. James March gives an example:

[It] began with a broadside request from a scientist to his colleagues. He was seeking a copy of a book that he had found unavailable in the library. Shortly, several people responded indicating where he could find a copy of the book. One reply was different, however. It came from a librarian who complained that the original request was badly formulated. What he sought was not a specific book but some information that was known to be contained in the book. Had the scientist asked the librarian (information retrieval specialist) for the information, he would have been directed to several other sources, available in the library, that contained the specific information he desired. A trivial exchange, to be sure, but a reminder that our search for information is heavily influenced by our views of the structure of information; and several centuries of a book-based information system have influenced our ways of thinking about knowledge and obtaining access to it. (March 1987:25)

Kraut and Streeter say that the same principle applies to large software systems projects. That is, routine information procedures tend to reinforce existing information categories. They are appropriate and helpful for coordination problems involving expected, usual information. They are inappropriate for coordination problems caused by uncertainty of task, changing requirements and pressures, disputes among people, and other nonroutine events. When categories cannot be specified in advance, people have to "talk things out" using their own words and their own experiences to come to understand what information they need or can share.

One hope for computer networked databases has been that exposing more people to organizational information would broaden their base of knowledge. More knowledge would lead to thinking more broadly. Networked databases can be made accessible to many people and can offer them more hard information than meetings or written documents can. More people can contribute to the shared information pool. Problems of size may be partly overcome through efficient coding and search mechanisms. Yet most database systems resemble routine paper reporting and requesting procedures. They "know" only the information the organization wanted to collect, collect only what can be measured, and measure only what can be defined.[1] Therefore they tend to focus attention on old rather than new kinds of information and ideas.

A third shortcoming of routine information procedures is that they can become too important. Reputations, careers, and organizational battles can revolve around procedures. Following the rules can become more important than getting the job done. Morison (1966) gives an example from the nineteenth-century British Navy. In those days all ships at sea were required to conduct firing practice at least once a year and send a report of this practice to London. No seamen liked this regulation. It took up a whole day, dirtied the guns, and so forth. One ship delayed until the last day, when the men discovered that water leaking through the hatches of the ammunition storehouse had ruined the powder supply. What to do about the report due at the Admiralty? First, the gunnery officer ordered the deteriorated powder to be jettisoned. Then he filled in the Admiralty forms with some imaginary scores for the various guns. He tore the report in little pieces, put them into an Admiralty dispatch box with six cockroaches, and sent the box to the Admiralty headquarters. A year later the ship received a dispatch from London requesting another copy of the target practice report because cockroaches had destroyed the original. Back to London, eventually, went word that the gunnery officer had been transferred to another ship and apparently had taken the report with him.

Carried to an extreme, procedures can become an autonomous world, a world in which there is no gunnery report, not because sailors neglected gunnery practice, but because there were cockroaches. All organizations need routine information procedures to ensure efficiency and coordination. Procedures create a consistent information environment, a stable culture, and stable roles. But they also can create too much emphasis on efficiency, responsiveness, and consistency. Organizations are loosely coupled systems that have two essential aspects: the connections among the individuals and subunits—the ways they work as an interdependent whole—and the individual people and subunits that have unique contributions to make (Thompson 1967; Weick 1976; Orton and Weick 1990). Information procedures like scheduling programs and formal management procedures in software projects standardize, routinize, and smooth information exchange. They reinforce the connectivity aspect of organizations; they contribute to the responsiveness of people and departments to one another rather than to their uniqueness. To preserve the unique contributions individuals can make, and also to attract and keep valuable employees who desire autonomy, organizations also need to maintain their "looseness." This may be especially true of organizations facing rapidly changing competitive environments; they must reinforce initiative and adaptivity (Meyer and Rowan 1977; Manning 1979).

Encouraging Information Sharing

In dealing with uncertain situations—that is, in much of life and work—people exchange information through informal communication (Ouchi 1980; Stohl and Redding 1987; Kraut et al. in press). Informal communication happens in hallway conversations, business meetings, lunch, and squash games. It is spontaneous and interactive; it takes place with the participants who happen to be present and talk about whatever occupies them at the time. None of these is scheduled in advance. The communication lacks prespecified categories and sources or recipients of information. People do not execute courses of action without modification. They work out courses of action that fit the circumstances. Also, they can express emotion more readily than they can in most routine, formal communications.

Informal communication is the primary way that new information flows into and through organizations. It is particularly valuable in large projects and research and development, enterprises marked by uncertainty (Pelz and Andrews 1976; Adams 1976; Allen 1977; Tushman 1977; Von Hippel 1987). Recently researchers from the Harvard Business School compared automobile development projects in Japan, the United States, and Western Europe (Clark, Chew, and Fujimoto 1987). Their study revealed several factors accounting for why Japan leads the United States and Europe in its ability to get products to market efficiently. Two of the most important factors were leadership and communication. The most efficient development teams, which were mainly Japanese, showed a pattern of strong project leadership and intense communication throughout the development process. One advantage of intense communication was that different aspects of a project could be carried out in parallel rather than sequentially. Overlapping, parallel activities allow a project to proceed rapidly. But without ongoing communication and information transfer, overlapping activities lead to mistakes and pursuit of poor alternatives and to more work hours to correct problems. Japanese projects were highly overlapping, but the teams used intense formal and informal information transfer both within R&D and between R&D and production. This allowed for coordination while preventing too many surprises that could delay the project. U.S. projects were somewhat overlapping, and the teams did hold formal meetings, but they did not communicate much informally. European teams communicated informally but did not overlap activities. Perhaps as a result, Japanese delays were one-sixth of the planned introduction date compared to the one-half and one-third delays of the U.S. and European teams, respectively.

Informal communication, at least in the sense of the hallway conversation, isn't always feasible. It becomes more feasible if some of the burden of informal communication can be shifted to the same electronic networks used for routine, formal information transfer. Potentially the computer-based communication technologies we have discussed in this book support procedures that permit and encourage informal communication. Despite the loss of management control this may represent, some organizations have devised procedures to leverage electronic mail technologies in this direction.

Does Anybody Know?

"Does anybody know . . . ?" is a common phrase in organizations—typically heard in informal encounters in office hallways, before meetings begin, at the water cooler, coffeepot, and lunchrooms. In the terms of the general information procedure, one person asks a search question that may be vague or ambiguous. Usually the asker is seeking a piece of current or arcane information, not easily found in official documents. The audience for such questions usually knows the asker and is sympathetic or at least tolerant because the behavior is conventional, the questions are not onerous, and answerers themselves may one day need to ask a question.

In the conventional world, if the asker's acquaintances cannot provide an answer, the asker is stymied. But with electronic communication, the asker has access to a much broader pool of information sources. An oceanographer broadcast a message to an electronic network of oceanographers: "Is it safe and reasonable to clamp equipment onto a [particular type of insulating] wire?" The official instructions said, "Do not clamp." Right away the sender got several messages from other places saying, "Yes, we do it all the time, but you have to use the following type of clamp." The oceanographer did not know the people who responded and would never have encountered them in a face-to-face setting, but through electronic communication, he benefited from their knowledge and experience. Folklore is an important part of science and technology, consisting of idiosyncratic information about how equipment really works and what tricks you have to know to get the experiment to come out right. It never appears in journal articles or manuals, and it is typically conveyed by word of mouth. With electronic communication, folklore can be more broadly accessible.

We described in chapter 2 the product developer with a new idea for a product who received 150 replies from people he had never met. He did not have to know in advance who would have helpful information nor did they have to know in advance that their advice would be wanted. The electronic version of the does-anybody-know procedure is common on extensively used networks. In the general reporting and requesting procedure, it means that any B has potential access to an extremely large number of A's. With a small amount of organizational effort, it is possible to leverage the does-anybody-know procedure to increase its utility. One potential difficulty comes from readers who don't know answers or don't want to read questions. These readers can be alienated if they continually confront unwanted questions. Some organizations remedy this potential problem by asking people to identify their does-anybody-know questions with a "??" signal in the subject field of the message. Then those who want to ignore (or peruse) such questions have an easy way of identifying them.

Often more than one person wants to know the answer to the question asked by B. Instead of having each person ask the question or ask B for the answer, B can create a reply file of all of the answers received to a query. A common variant on the does-anybody-know question is to ask the question and then say that replies will be available in a file on the network named "<something>." Anyone who is interested can read the reply file. By means of this procedure, more than one person can benefit from the query procedure.

What if someone new joins the network or did not see B's original query and has the same question that B had? That person might broadcast the same question. Redundant questions discourage potential readers by cluttering up the network with duplicate questions and discourage people who provide answers by asking them to repeat themselves. Some organizations mitigate this problem and further leverage answers by creating electronic archives on the network where reply files can be stored. Then before a person asks a does-anybody-know question, he or she can check the archive for recent replies to similar questions. In this way people can share knowledge across time as well as across space. In contrast to standard database systems that contain only answers, the archives of reply files contain questions as well as answers and thus provide information on what people want to know as well as what they do know. We have described an extremely simple three-part procedure that can increase the effectiveness of the broadcast query: (1) mark queries with an identifying symbol, (2) create reply files of useful answers, and (3) make reply files accessible in public archives.

Employees of Tandem use the supplementary procedures we have described to leverage broadcast queries. These procedures are available to all employees but are used most by sales and service representatives. A sales representative might describe a potential customer's situation and ask if any other sales representatives had dealt with similar situations. Or a service representative might ask if anyone had encountered a technical configuration similar to one he or she was trying to debug. Box 7.1 displays some sample questions from the Tandem network. Based on a study conducted by David Constant, we estimate that employees broadcast about six questions a day that elicit about eight replies apiece. About half of the question askers create reply files that can be read by all other Tandem employees. According to a study conducted by Tom Finholt, the archive of reply files is accessed over a thousand times a month. Through the computer network, the does-anybody-know query, and some simple supplementary procedures, Tandem employees can learn from their colleagues no matter where they are located.

Box 7.1. Does anybody know? questions.

```
Sent: 88-02-18
From: Kent Larson (Washington State)
To: All Tandem
Subject:  2: ?Dial-up SNAX/EXCHANGE RJE?

Hi All Tandem,
Does anyone out there know of a customer that uses DIAL-UP  RJE
(SNAX/EXCHANGE) to/from an IBM?

Checked the Archive and didn't see anything like this.
Thank  you!
Kent
```

Kent says that without electronic mail, he would have submitted this question as a technical product report to headquarters and that it would have been answered within several weeks. Kent received three answers to his message within a few days, each of which he placed in a public reply file. He was able to give a detailed answer to his customer.

```
Sent: 88-02-18
From: Dolly Hendricks (North Carolina)
To: All Tandem
Subject: 2:?? MIIS, MEES (COUSIN TO MUMPS)??

Howdy,
Anybody ever heard of this thing which I cannot spell?

Thanks!
Dolly
```

Dolly received eleven replies, six of which she put in a reply file.

One can imagine that the electronic does-anybody-know procedure could generate a flood of questions and no answers, thereby completely defeating its purpose. Suppose you are a busy employee and you see a request for information you can supply. Why should you take time and effort to answer? The benefits to the asker and to your organization are likely to be much greater than the benefits to you. Theories and studies of this problem indicate that you will not supply as many answers as might be most beneficial to the organization as a whole (Marwell and Ames 1979; Messick and Brewer 1983; Thorn and Connolly 1987). Still, we have observed several networks where this procedure seems to work reasonably well. Enough people voluntarily answer such questions that people find it worthwhile to ask them. But it is important to realize that the procedure depends fundamentally on the goodwill of people who are willing to provide answers voluntarily when they see a question they can answer. Supplementary procedures can help support goodwill.

Digests and Reviews

Another kind of electronic information-sharing procedure that relies on voluntary participation is the digest or review. In this procedure a moderator or coordinator announces a topic and then collates and perhaps edits messages sent in on this topic. The collated material is then broadcast to all interested parties.

The Forest Service, an organization long concerned with internal communication, is using such a system in which rangers send to Washington, D.C., observations and ideas on topics ranging from pesticide use and seedlings to grizzly bears and marijuana growers. Each ranger sends electronic mail about what is locally important, using his or her own words to describe the topic. Federal issues coordinators organize this information, make it available to rangers on-line, and use it to identify and develop interpretations of emerging issues. Political trends, such as opposition to below-cost timber sales or forest fire policies, can be identified and evaluated before they become disruptive. When a congressional inquiry arises, the Forest Service has already gathered the information, verified and analyzed it, and developed an interpretation (Stasz and Bikson 1989). This procedure resembles the use of Lieutenant Ainsworth's card index because it allows a federal agency to respond rapidly to congressional inquiry. The fundamental difference is that the information in this system does not consist of fixed-format responses in prespecified categories. Rather it consists of dynamic, evolving information identified and described by the rangers in their own words.

Filters and Forums

As people find electronic communication helpful for exchanging information, participating in groups, meeting new people, and learning, the volume of mail traffic will increase substantially. While sheer volume of messages is not necessarily a problem, procedures for managing that volume do become important. Four quite different philosophies for managing message volume are developing in organizations today: prohibition, pricing policies, software filters, and social forums. Each results in different consequences for information exchange.

Prohibition confronts an increasing message volume by denying people access to the mail system, to group membership, or to readers. This philosophy may be imposed by officials on groups of employees or by individual employees who choose to drop out of the mail system. This strategy certainly confronts the volume "problem," but it also eliminates the benefits that can derive from electronic communication.

Pricing policies can be devised such that the system automatically charges sources or recipients of information, or both, for sending more or longer messages. (It need not be a money-based system; for instance, people can be given some limited number of communication units that they can then distribute among messages as they wish.) Pricing policies are "rational" in the sense that consumers and producers of information can decide if receiving, or sending, longer or more frequent communications is worth the price. If there is no adjustment for assets, this policy will penalize employees who have fewer resources to pay for communications. It will also penalize those who have more useful things to say or who can make best use of information.

Software solutions typically operate on the receiver's end of message traffic. People can specify filters to sort their incoming mail into various categories before they read it, based on who sent it or its topic (Malone et al. 1987). For instance, messages from the boss might go in the urgent folder and want ads messages in the junk mail folder. A variant of this approach for the future envisions intelligent software agents that will roam the network looking for publicly readable messages with characteristics specified as interesting by the agent's owner. They would be placed in the "interesting messages on the network" folder. Software filters are based on the philosophy that people receiving mail are in the best position to anticipate what they want to see.

Several characteristics of filtering systems are noteworthy. Filters depend on people's being able to anticipate what they want to read in their mail traffic. This is often a reasonable assumption. Surely employees will want to read mail from their boss, for instance. Furthermore, filtering systems assume that the message environment contains relatively few surprises. That is, people can anticipate what they want to see and write filters to highlight that information. Messages that they cannot anticipate are not likely to be interesting to them. These assumptions may hold for some employees in some situations, but they certainly are not true for everyone and, furthermore, run counter to the general trend in electronic communication of discovering new people and new information. One study of such a mail filtering system found that some people who used it preferred to filter mail after they had read it rather than before (Mackay 1989). For them, filters became a useful filing system after they had read messages. But first they had to read the messages in order to know how to categorize them. Finally, filtering systems do little to promote a sense of community. They are oriented to people who extract benefit from the mail community by receiving information, not to people who provide benefit to the mail community by giving information.

An alternative philosophy on procedures for managing the volume of mail focuses on establishing social expectations about appropriate forums for various kinds of messages. Distribution lists and bulletin boards are one kind of forum. People are expected to send messages relevant to the topic of the particular list, and anyone interested in that topic can expect to find relevant material there. People join or visit these forums because they are interested in their topics. Because members are motivated by the topic, they are also motivated to keep the forum interesting. Therefore, such forums usually display self-policing of message behavior. That is, if a person sends an inappropriate message, other forum members are likely to respond by pointing out the inappropriateness.

The difference between an individual focus in filtering systems and a community focus in social forums is highlighted by considering how people respond to inappropriate behavior. In a filtering system, people can write a rule to filter out messages sent by a person who is known to send inappropriate mail (Mackay et al. 1989). Then those using filters no longer have to see the offending messages. The person whose behavior is offensive, however, gets no feedback on that behavior; he or she does not know that his or her messages are being filtered out and continues to behave inappropriately. Carried to an extreme, this could produce a distribution list in which no message was read by any person because every member had designed filters to screen them out. But people kept sending messages to the list because no one knew that no one was reading them. By contrast, in a social forum, people are motivated to help others participate appropriately.

Another way of designating forums has been established at Tandem. Their mail system is organized in three classes: first, second, and third. First-class mail is designated for one-to-one messages between named recipients and for conversations inside groups whose members are named and known to one another. Second-class mail is designated for company-related broadcast messages that go to the entire organization or to everyone in a particular region—for instance, announcements of personnel openings, new training programs, cafeteria menus, and summaries of industry news. The does-anybody-know messages are second-class messages that are broadcast worldwide. Third-class mail is designated for extracurricular messages. For instance, these may be restaurant or movie reviews or want ads sent to everyone who lives in the same geographical region as the sender. The message sender designates its mail class, thereby acknowledging the sender's responsibility in contributing to a social forum. The system helps with this process. A message sent to a named person is automatically classified as first class unless the sender requests otherwise. A message sent from within a class folder automatically takes on the class designation of the folder unless the sender requests otherwise. Also, to avoid distracting people, extracurricular messages are not delivered until 5 P.M. Everyone has three mail folders for incoming mail (one for each mail class). Incoming messages are automatically sorted into their designated class folders. Within such a system of class-based social forums, people can further customize their mailboxes by writing additional personal filters if they choose to. Tandem's first-class mail, mirroring mail systems in many places, puts identified sources in touch with one another. Its second-class and third-class mail bring together people who do not know one another and often put people in touch with information they did not know existed. The separation of electronic mail into classes shelters the forums for strangers to meet and allows them to interact without interfering with first-class communications among known coworkers.

If computer-based communication systems do more than simply speed up old ways of transmitting old information, they will generate large volumes of messages. Procedures for managing messages will come to be increasingly important. It is fairly easy to imagine building software to help people filter their incoming mail, and these projects are useful. It is more challenging and just as important to imagine building social forums to encourage people who send mail to do so as a social contribution.

Mandatory Procedures
While all of the previous procedures described rely on voluntary participation, it is also possible to require participation in a variety of ways.

Procedures for Group Mail   Project groups can use electronic mail to coordinate their work by simultaneously linking and buffering group members. When members use electronic distribution lists to send mail simultaneously to all group members, they can be reminded of group goals and member activity even between meetings (Wasby 1989; Eveland and Bikson 1988; Finholt, Sproull, and Kiesler 1990). Managers can capitalize on this behavior by establishing a procedure requiring that every group member both read group mail regularly and contribute by sending regular electronic progress reports to other group members.

Designated Experts   Organizations can designate people or groups as official experts on particular topics whose job is to field electronic questions on those topics. This procedure increases the efficiency of access to these known experts and allows experts to prepare standard answers to often-asked questions and to monitor the occurrence of classes of problems. Experts can maintain publicly accessible files of questions they have received and answers they have provided. In this way people with questions can first check the archives to see if their question has already been asked by someone else and answered by an expert.

Tandem maintains archives of reply files from both does-anybody-know? questions and questions directed to experts. While each archive is equally and easily accessible to everyone, people access the does-anybody-know? archive much more frequently than they access the experts' archive. We doubt if this behavior means that Tandem employees generally do not value formal expertise. Rather we think it means that they have many procedures for accessing formal expertise, whereas they have no other easy way to access the experiences of anybody—employees worldwide who answer a does-anybody-know? question. This archive does not represent authoritative or authorized answers. It represents a slice of experience or opinions that employees could sample in no other way.

Conclusion

Many people would argue that if you implement the kinds of procedures described in this chapter, you can wind up with more communications, more impositions on people, and more unfocused projects initiated that go unfinished. Any time there is intense communication, there also will be more information than people can use and, in the short term for the individual, some wasted time and effort. The evidence thus far suggests some valuable compensations for the individual and for the organization. Electronic communication can make routine procedures more efficient and more humane, reducing the need for redundant information exchange. It also can expand the scale and scope of informal communication, which is necessary for coordination and for maintaining ties among disparate people and subunits.

There is another advantage. An old Chinese proverb says, "If we don't change direction, we'll end up where we're headed." Information procedures using paper technology typically move prespecified categories of information among preidentified groups of people. Computers can improve the efficiency of these old procedures as demonstrated in transaction processing systems, database systems, and management information systems. They also make it possible to have procedures for exchanging unspecified kinds of information among unspecified people. These new procedures are especially appropriate when organizations and activities within them are large and internally diversified, when internal or external change is great, and whenever nonroutine events create a need for new ways of thinking, acting, and organizing.

8

New Ways of Organizing

In the 1960s people speculated that large time-sharing computer systems would overturn familiar organizational structures or patterned relationships among people and subunits. Conventional channels of authority and processes of decision making would be replaced by something else. Relationships among subunits would change. Jobs would be transformed. Technophiles dreamed about increased rationality and efficiency. Technophobes had nightmares about Big Brother. As it turned out, neither the dreams nor the nightmares were realized (Simon 1973; Weizenbaum 1976; March and Sproull 1990). Mainframe computerization did lead to the creation of computer centers and information systems departments (McFarlan and McKenney 1983; King 1983). There may have been small reductions in the number of clerical workers and a slight decrease in centralization associated with increasing computerization (Whisler 1970; Pfeffer and Leblebici 1977), but by and large, computing technology has not yet led to widespread changes in how work is organized.

By contrast, three other technologies have had profound effects on the structure of modern organizations: the telephone, the railroad, and office paperwork technologies. It is useful to keep them in mind as a standard of comparison when thinking about the potential for computing technology to change organizational structure.

Managers must be in touch with the production process. Before telephony, they worked at production sites. With telephony, managers could locate their offices several miles away from a production site and still be in immediate touch with it. In a place like Pittsburgh, this meant that managers no longer had to work at the mills. They could move their offices downtown (and upwind), away from the dirt and noise of the factory or mill. The telephone made possible the (literally) white-collar manager and the separation between production and administration. At the same time long-distance telephony made possible the creation of national markets in stocks and commodities (Aronson 1971).

The railroad led to the vertical integration of asset-specific firms. Consider the meat packing industry. With long-distance railroads and refrigerated railroad cars, local butchers in Chicago could expand and consolidate their operations. They built new organizational structures with livestock ranches in the West and Southwest, slaughter houses in the Midwest, and retailers in the East. The railroad also made possible the mass distribution of commodities and consumer goods supported by particular administrative structures. As Alfred Chandler (1977:209) noted, "All these mass marketing enterprises had the same internal administrative structure. Their buying and selling organizations, by using the railroads, the telegraph, the steamship, and improved postal services, coordinated the flow of agricultural crops and finished goods from a great number of individual producers to an even larger number of individual consumers. By means of such administrative coordination, the new mass marketers reduced the number of transactions involved in the flow of goods, increased the speed and regularity of that flow, and so lowered costs and improved the productivity of the American distribution system."

Office paperwork technologies enabled the growth of administrative systems and the back office. Until the end of the nineteenth century, organizations stored their correspondence in piles, laying one piece of paper on top of the previous one until the pile got too high and then beginning a new pile. Some organizations stored these piles in stackable letter boxes, perhaps stipulating separate boxes for internal documents and external correspondence or giving very large customers their own box. Finding something that had been stored was difficult and inefficient (Yates 1982). The introduction of vertical filing systems made it possible to store and access efficiently much larger volumes of paperwork. This development combined with new copying technology, such as carbon paper and mimeograph, to enable the growth of back office support for transactions.

The telephone, railroad, and office paperwork technologies enabled sweeping changes in the number and nature of communication links that organizations and their employees had with one another. These linkages then could become formalized and regularized in new patterned relationships or structures. Compared to these large-scale technologically supported changes, structural changes associated with computing up to now have been puny indeed. Recent developments in computer networks and computer-mediated communication suggest that more substantial structural change may be possible. The foundation will be computer networks: telecommunications transport and data networks that reach throughout the organization and beyond it to customers or clients and suppliers. (Voice and video networks are additional components of network infrastructure, but they are beyond the scope of this book.) Computer networks will let organizations create new organizational structures or links between processes and groups and will let organizations rapidly reconfigure structures. Some links will be relatively formalized as in electronic data interchange for fixed-format data on such matters as order processing or engineering designs. And others will be relatively informal and personalized as in electronic mail. Computer networks will let organizations experiment with new structures in ways heretofore impossible.

This chapter reviews three such possibilities. One is increasing organizational interdependence; the second is solving the out-of-sight, out-of-mind problem; the third is creating dynamic structures. The first focuses on relationships between organizations and the second and third on relationships within organizations. The general process of creating links by regularizing communication is common across all three topics. The evidence in this chapter comes almost entirely from case experiences. There has been almost no systematic empirical research on changing organizational structures through electronic communication because the processes are just beginning.

Increasing Organizational Interdependence

To extend John Donne, no organization is an island. Every organization is interdependent with others. Manufacturing organizations depend on suppliers for raw materials and completed subassemblies. Sales and service organizations depend on customers or clients to buy their products or services. From any one organization's perspective (organization A), the best relationship is one in which it can have a continual presence in the other organization (organization B). A would like to capture B's attention and form mutually interdependent relationships with B. A would like to see B's employees behave as though they were employees of A without, of course, expecting a paycheck from A. With electronic communication, these conditions can be approximated.

Although this book emphasizes relatively unstructured human communication via computer, we begin by considering more stylized communications via electronic data interchange (EDI). Using network communications and precise formatting rules, organizations can exchange routine information rapidly and efficiently. EDI is widely used in order processing in various industries. A customer can transmit an order for goods through EDI from the customer's computer into a supplier's computer. There the order triggers other computer programs to generate one or more of the following: packing list, shipping order, invoice, inventory charge, or customer profile. The shipping order and invoice may be transmitted by EDI back to the customer and, when coupled with receipt of goods notification, may trigger payment authorization within the customer's computer system.

EDI, like many other computer-based communications technologies, was originally envisioned and is still often thought of as a way to speed up preexisting manual processes. It eliminates duplicate keypunching of the same information into both customer and supplier computers. It substantially reduces the transmission delays of sending order information via postal mail. American Hospital Supply (AHS), an early exemplar of EDI, demonstrates how the process can work. AHS distributes medical supplies to hospitals around the country. A few years ago it began installing direct-order terminals in hospital medical supply rooms. When hospital employees noticed that supplies of particular items were dwindling, they could enter restocking orders directly into the AHS system, which guaranteed 24-hour order delivery. In effect, hospital employees became part-time sales and order clerks for AHS using electronic communication.

Manufacturers also are now coming to rely on EDI. Just-in-time (JIT) manufacturing reduces the lead time required to obtain components from suppliers by, in part, increasing the communications bandwidth between a manufacturer (organization A) and its suppliers (organization B). An automobile assembly plant procures components, such as tires, upholstered seats, and windshields, from other organizations. With JIT, components for the day's assembly run are ordered through EDI a day or two in advance. Organization A uses a direct terminal connection into organization B to print out the orders for B to fill. Organization B's employees take those orders off the screen or printer and begin filling them, either through drawing down their own stock or through producing then and there what is needed.

We have seen that electronic mail does more than simply speed up existing work; so too does EDI. The second-order effects are more related to changing patterns of attention, social contact, and interdependencies than they are to speeding up information flow. EDI can cause organizations to focus attention on their internal procedures in new ways. For example, when Gillette opened EDI links with some of its biggest customers in the retail food distribution industry, it discovered anomalies in its internal pricing procedures.[1] Prior to EDI, Gillette sales representatives were able to offer promotional pricing discounts with some degree of discretion to their favored customers. With EDI, all price allocations were made by a centralized pricing routine. When formerly favored customers began complaining about missing their discounts, the company discovered that EDI meant more than accelerating information flow. It meant changing the social relationships between sales representatives and customers, and it led the company to rethink its entire discount pricing policy.

EDI can also help companies discover new businesses. Foremost-McKesson pharmaceuticals, like AHS, uses terminals located in their customers' pharmacies to maintain on-line inventories of customers' stock. They provide automatic stock replenishing when stock drops below a certain level. The employees of organization B (the pharmacists) become, in effect, sales and order clerks for organization A (Foremost-McKesson). But Foremost-McKesson uses the electronic connection for another purpose as well. Many pharmacy customers apply for third-party reimbursement of prescription costs. Foremost-McKesson uses information keyed in by its customers (pharmacists) at the time of a sale not only to maintain inventory records but also to prepare and submit third-party reimbursement requests for its customers' customers. It expanded its focus of attention from pharmaceutical supply information to third-party reimbursement information. Pharmacists can offer reimbursement requests as an attractive benefit to their customers and Foremost-McKesson gets into a new business. In terms of interdependence, the customers of organization B are encouraging it to buy from organization A.

The value of computer-supported connections in changing the focus of attention and creating new relationships between companies can be assessed by the concept of switching costs. If electronic connections between A and B would make it more expensive for B to obtain the identical product by switching to a different supplier, then A has increased the switching costs for B. Increased switching costs are a sign that free market relationships between organizations have been replaced by different relationships or different structures. But isn't this an unstable situation? Won't company A's competitors also find ways to increase switching costs?

American Airlines offers a case in point. The first on-line airline reservations system, which was run by American, always displayed American flights as a first response to any query. Travel agents using this system effectively became part-time reservations clerks for that airline. But other airlines recognized the inherent competitive advantage the system gave American, and forced an end to that practice. Tom Malone, a professor at MIT, suggests that strategies like these for organizational interpenetration are fundamentally unstable (Malone 1987). Competitors of organization A will argue, as in the case of the American reservation system, that the interpenetration induced by the technology offers an unfair competitive advantage and operates in restraint of trade. It is too soon to tell if Malone's analysis is correct. If so, we may still see organizations using computer-based communication systems to catch the attention of potential customers or suppliers. If not, and in the meantime, computer-based communication is creating new means of organization interpenetration.

The concept of switching costs typically employs an economic perspective. Unfair competitive advantage and restraint of trade are measured in economic terms. The remedy is to make economic switching costs equal for all by allowing all equal access to the technology. But switching costs can also be assessed in psychological terms, particularly when EDI is coupled with electronic mail to provide links among people, as well as links among computer processes. In this view, even if economic costs are equivalent, if people from different organizations have developed satisfying personalized relationships with one another, they will be reluctant to forego those relationships by switching to another supplier.

E. I. du Pont de Nemours and Co. understands the concept of psychological switching costs. It offers electronic connections to over eight hundred of its customers and suppliers, links for both data and electronic mail. As vice-president R.E. Cairns, Jr., sees it:

If you're a company that we're dealing with and we have your engineers dealing with our engineers on electronic mail and they've established a relationship and they know each other, it's different than just working through the purchasing agents. If John [our competitor, figuratively speaking] comes in with a penny a pound decrease in price or a nickel a pound, okay? The cost for you to switch to him in the past would have been just that. Now you have to switch your engineers.

Who are they going to contact? How is the relationship going to be developed? How are the partnerships going to be enhanced? Because we're really talking about greater partnerships between companies these days. And so by doing that, switching costs will increase. (Mead 1990:68)

The psychological links can also be strengthened by pleasurable interactions that have nothing ostensibly to do with work. In the travel industry, hotels and car rental companies are continually trying to catch the attention of travel agents so that the agents will recommend and use their services rather than those of their competitors. Within the on-line reservations systems, heavily used by travel agencies, there are few obvious cues to differentiate one company and its services from another. Some hotels and car rental firms, recognizing this, have added popular extracurricular messages to their system files. Thus, for instance, a travel agent who wants to read his or her horoscope or the daily soap opera summary selects a particular hotel chain from the system and within that hotel chain's directory pulls up the daily horoscope or soap opera file. The transaction has nothing overtly to do with work, but it keeps the name of one hotel chain (rather than its competitors) on the agent's screen. (And it suggests an additional function for extracurricular messages beyond those discussed in chapter 5.)

Psychological links can also be strengthened by the perception of receiving special treatment. The strength of EDI is in regularizing relationships. But even in such regularized interactions as order processing, exceptions occur. A customer, for instance, may need to return ordered goods. Black and Decker illustrates how electronic order processing can be coupled with electronic mail to give customers special assistance. Black and Decker's power tools division sells a wide range of construction and home maintenance products to hardware distributors and retailers. At times, a customer in California might have a surplus of a certain product and return it to Black and Decker for credit. Meanwhile in New York another customer might require that product. If buyer and seller can be matched, the goods are shipped directly from California to New York rather than being reprocessed through Black and Decker's inventories. In the past, sales representatives and managers depended on postal mail to try to engineer such swaps. Only 10 percent of the requests for buyers were satisfied in this way, with the remaining 90 percent of excess goods returned to inventory.

Black and Decker recently installed a computer-based communication system for its 260 sales representatives and managers used for order entry, product line shortage reports, and managerial communications (Meyer and Boone 1987:84-86). The system also has an on-line swap shop. When a customer wants to return goods, an electronic message is sent to the swap shop coordinator. If the request cannot be matched with a buyer, an electronic notice is sent to the entire sales force. Requests are now resolved in fewer than 48 hours, and the swap rate has risen from 10 percent to 80 percent. Local governments in western Pennsylvania use a similar electronic swap shop to exchange information about such items as needed fire engines or surplus snow plows.

In a highly competitive market, insufficient buffering against regional fluctuations in customer requests represented a significant loss of profits and a significant opportunity for computer-based communications technology. Black and Decker could have improved its own inventory system, but given its manufacturing realities, the savings would have been small. Instead it gained a significant marketing advantage by helping remote customers manage their inventories at the same time it helped its remote sales managers manage theirs.

Electronic linkages between organizations will substantially increase in the future. They will undoubtedly reduce processing time and cost for many routine transactions. Their more important effects, however, are likely to be found in how they change the focus of attention, social contact patterns, and interdependencies among organizations. We cannot predict the particular form that these changes will take, but organizations that see more than efficiency benefits will be best positioned to capitalize on them.

Solving the "Out of Sight, Out of Mind" Problem

We're All in This Together
In large organizations, geographically separated subunits may need to work together. If left to their own devices, however, each experiences subunit drift, the tendency to develop parochial views and to drift in idiosyncratic directions. From the organization's perspective, the best situation is one in which subunits A and B keep each other continually in mind. But with geographic separation, it is difficult for each unit to keep the other continually in mind and therefore also to keep their common goals in mind. People naturally attend to what is close at hand and ignore what isn't (Kiesler and Sproull 1982). Importance isn't perfectly correlated with proximity, though, and remote communications are essential even in

highly decentralized organizations. Yet they can be difficult. For instance, the director of European operations for an automated testing equipment firm claims that if he were to stay in touch by telephone with his firm's U.S. divisions, corporate headquarters, and subsidiaries, he would be on the telephone constantly. Because he can't do this and because of time zone and language differences, it is easy to lose touch with physically distant people and operations.

Organizations use a variety of ways to keep people in touch. Members of one subunit may travel extensively to the other. They may schedule routine conference calls. Some organizations have experimented with video conferencing.[2] All of these methods are better than nothing, but none includes informal mundane contact—the exchange of everyday experiences that people in the same setting can't help but do. In fact, the unnaturalness of these methods may exacerbate differences across subunits rather than reduce them. The coffee pot, the telephone, and electronic mail share the advantage of encouraging informal conversation and gossip about ongoing events, but electronic mail is the only one of these three to allow such conversations to take place both asynchronously and at a distance.[3]

Computer-based communication technology alleviates some of the routine communication problems, but it also has a more subtle impact on what is in the manager's mind. In a neighborhood, people recognize one another and share common context and mundane events on a frequent basis. As a result of this interchange, people come to identify with the collective group and find common interests with other group members. The telephone extended peoples' psychological neighborhood in the first half of the twentieth century by letting people share common context and mundane events independent of physical proximity (Aronson 1971). Computer-based communication may allow people to extend their organizational neighborhood in much the same way.[4] As the European manager described above noted, "Japan is now on electronic mail and it's like we found them again!" (Meyer and Boone 1987:220).

Austek, a small custom computer chip manufacturer, has its main offices in Adelaide, Australia, and a substantial sales organization located in Silicon Valley, California. The president of Austek commutes between Adelaide and California, spending two or three weeks in each location before returning to the other. He is not fond of travel but takes on this schedule because his presence in both locations reminds employees that they're all working for the same company. Austek uses electronic mail to the same end. In addition to one-to-one mail and group mail, Austek uses one electronic bulletin board for the company's daily events that people in both sites read. On any day, in addition to announcements of seminars, special meetings, or visitors, it might include a message that strawberries will be served with tea in the commons room at 4 P.M. or nachos will be served with beer in the courtyard at 5 P.M. A newcomer to the organization thought he could save money by forbidding the cross-posting of "irrelevant" messages, arguing that no one in California would want to know what was being served with tea in Australia and no one in Australia would want to know what was being served with beer in California. The president of Austek disagreed with this analysis, arguing that it was important for people in each site to be reminded every day of the existence of the other site. "Irrelevant" messages, which took only a few seconds to scan, were an almost subliminal reminder of the other site.

Even more extreme subunit separation exists when one company (A) acquires another (B), which is to continue its own business. In this case the acquired company must retain enough autonomy to continue doing well what it did before it was acquired. At the same time, each firm must begin exchanging information with the other, and each must come to believe B is part of A. When Tandem acquired three smaller companies in 1988, its first postacquisition act was to put each of the three companies on the Tandem electronic mail system. Electronic mail provided easy information access between Tandem and each of its acquisitions, which were located in different parts of the country. In the terms of chapter 2, electronic mail reduced the transaction time for exchanging information between Tandem and its acquisitions. And it did more than that. It helped employees in each company begin to "meet" people in the other company—to know their names and what they do. With this information, employees in each company could develop a sense of whom to contact for specific information to solve a particular problem. Furthermore, by joining electronic distribution lists or special interest groups, employees of the acquired companies could "watch" Tandem employees by reading group messages. The president of Tandem hoped this would serve as a socialization experience, helping the acquired employees learn about Tandem employees and norms. Precisely what they learned was never measured, but surely any acquired employee who read group mail did begin to learn the "Tandem way." In most acquisitions, formal mechanisms are established to educate each company about the other. Ordinary employees are likely to be a bit skeptical of information disseminated by these mechanisms. They are likely to take more seriously information that they glean from "ordinary" people—regular mail system participants—who are not paid to convey that information. It is the process of attributing greater sincerity to people who have insufficient external justification for their actions.

Computer-based communication can usefully counter the tendencies of subunit drift, exhibited when subunits are not closely linked to one another. Although it does not substitute for face-to-face communication, it can keep people reminded of one another so that every new face-to-face meeting is not a meeting of strangers but a meeting of neighbors.

Connections through Copying

Drift can occur not only when people or groups are geographically separated but also when they are too busy with their own concerns to inform and keep informed about others. A product marketing manager for Telecom Canada had to interact with his staff of eight people, along with the engineering department building the product, public relations, the legal staff, and others. Although he could not be everywhere, he had good insight into what everyone was doing because he was being copied on communications that, without electronic mail, would have taken place in private telephone calls or face-to-face meetings that he could not attend. Were it not for the electronic mail system, he would have found out about these communications only when his staff reported to him—if they had time and remembered to do so (Caswell 1988).

Electronic mail not only increased what the manager knew about his subordinates' doings, but it also increased his knowledgeability about related activities in other departments. The manager was responsible for marketing the new product, but his engineering counterpart was responsible for building it. Each had staffs of equal size, along with responsibilities and problems of similar magnitude. The two managers had to coordinate their work closely but had to spend most of their time on their separate tasks. Yet both were kept apprised of the other's doings through electronic mail. Both parties were copied on messages that related to anything associated with joint coordination and were often included on marginally related problems. Instead of communications flowing only up the hierarchy, they often flowed from subordinates of one manager to both higher-level managers simultaneously. This increased the probability that the two managers would talk about problems or capitalize on opportunities that involved both of them.

Connections through copying can create problems as well as opportunities. Subordinates who habitually copy their superiors on messages may "copy up" problems they should resolve themselves. In one company with an active electronic mail system, mid-level managers complained that they were sucked into everybody else's problems by being copied on irrelevant messages. A trivial message might be copied to more than one manager or could be sent by more than one subordinate or might even be sent to many people, perhaps to the entire company via a broadcast message. It is much harder to ignore problems that have been publicized than problems that are kept private.

The desirability of copying up depends on how close to the firing line management wants to be (McLaren 1982). If people know about only their assigned tasks, they will be less distracted by outside events. On the other hand, they may miss opportunities to become better informed about and contribute to the larger context in which their tasks are situated. Other considerations equal, our choice would be for more connections through copying, but ultimately it is a dilemma with no single right answer.

Dynamic Structures

All organizations have some form of hierarchy, but all hierarchies are not created equal. Some organizations, such as those in some R&D firms, are so fluid that it is not even obvious which hierarchical level is the superior one. Other organizations, often disparagingly termed bureaucracies, have clear lines of control and a firm sense of which subunit is responsible for which activity. Two merits of bureaucracy are that work and job responsibilities are rationalized and that behavior is buffered from the whims and idiosyncrasies of individuals. The same features are its demerits. When activities are rigidly specified, how does the organization do something new? How does a manager exert leadership? One way to allow for flexibility without eliminating stability is to create temporary dynamic structures, such as ad hoc groups and teams. These can be thought of as soft structures, sets of systematic and patterned relationships that emerge, evolve, and disappear over time.

Electronic Groups at Work

Modern organizations are generally structured to locate routinely interdependent activities in close proximity. While this strategy increases the efficiency of routine behavior, it can disadvantage organizations facing nonroutine problems and opportunities that cut across conventional structures and boundaries. Electronic groups may help organizations create more flexible structures so that the experience and expertise of employees can be mustered wherever it is needed.

Electronic task groups can have larger, more complex, and more fluid structures than their face-to-face counterparts. The Rand experiment on electronic task forces showed that both retiree task forces created subcommittees, but the task force with electronic communication created more of them. Both task forces assigned members to subcommittees: the task force without electronic communication assigned each person to only one subcommittee; the task force with electronic communication had people on more than one subcommittee. Not only were there more subcommittees in the task force with electronic communication, but also they were organized more complexly in an overlapping matrix structure. New subcommittees were added during the course of that task force's work. And indeed the group decided to continue meeting even after the official one-year life span of the committee had ended. Electronic communication helped the structure of the one task force to grow and change as its task evolved.

The software development teams first described in chapter 2 also used electronic communication to create useful subgroup structures. Using one-to-one mail, project managers and chief programmers created two-person crisis management groups that kept on top of the ever-changing project requirements and personnel shifts. Using the all-group distribution lists, project managers and chief programmers kept all other team members informed of changes. In this fashion electronic communication technology helped the teams create in-groups without out-groups.

All complex organizations experience conflicts between organizational subunits. For instance, it is not uncommon for marketing departments to vie with R&D departments over control of projects. The department that has less control exhibits hostility toward the favored group, which acts defensively. This divisiveness could be reduced by the multiple group memberships that electronic mail technology permits. Members of the marketing and development departments who belong to DLs that span interests in both places—Consumer Research, for instance—act as "link pins" who can promote cooperation and solidarity between the separate departments.

A Structure for Every Task

Organizations have formal subunit structures—blunt instruments for delicate and complex tasks. General-purpose structures are not often the best for any particular task, but over many tasks, they are good enough. One conceivable alternative—designing a separate special-purpose structure for every task—is infeasible in most cases. Computer-based communication may make it more feasible for some tasks by allowing people who are physically located at one place to participate in multiple electronic task groups.

When a complex organizational task involves more than one subunit, a change made by one subunit can have ramifications for others. Consider the design task for a new automobile. Subassemblies, such as window handles or chassis, are designed by different teams and are subject to common design goals and constraints. Once component designs have been set, any further change in one of them must be accompanied by proper notification to those in charge of all other component designs that could be affected by the change. That is the process in theory. In practice people or units can be inadvertently dropped out of the loop or not notified of changes that affect them. Such oversights then lead to delays downstream when incompatibilities or conflicts are discovered. This problem could be eased if all the relevant parties spent all their time watching for changes in other components that might affect their own. If they did that, though, they wouldn't have the time to do their own jobs.

All the relevant parties do attend to some common stimuli, however. The most important are the design document and the project budget. We can envision an "intelligent document" in the future—one that knows, whenever a change is made to it, which other people need to see that change. The document thus has embedded within it a representation of the organization structure relevant to that task. Whenever a change is made to the document by one party, all the affected parties are automatically notified of the change via electronic communication. If necessary, all recipients could be required to return an electronic acknowledgment of the change. Every document may have a slightly different structure associated with it, but that is fine. In this view, employees no longer work in one structure and carry out a variety of tasks. Instead they work in as many different structures as they have tasks.

Conclusion

Organizations are just beginning to experiment with using computer-based communication technology to create new interorganizational linkages, to solve the out-of-sight, out-of-mind problem, and to create dynamic structures. Organizations first need to gain experience with and be comfortable with electronic groups and changing information procedures before they attempt electronic restructuring. We have very little evidence about electronic restructuring because such attempts are just getting underway. Their long-term effects, though, may be profound.

So will be the management challenges. Imagine the difficulty of trying to hire someone who will work in ten different soft structures. How do you manage and evaluate such a person? Where will such a person's loyalties be? How do you think about the organization chart when it may look different for every employee and for every day of the week? The bookkeeping won't be too complicated. If the structures are electronic, there can be computer support for allocating effort to different budgets and maintaining running records of progress across structures. Organization charts can be displayed dynamically on-line. The real challenge will be to the human imagination to envision and invent new ways of working in these structures.

9

Making Connections

An organization making new connections does not merely add new behaviors to an unchanging base. Rather, the process is a transforming one, leading to and reinforcing fundamental changes in how people work, interact, and think. We have documented some of the potentially transforming changes in interaction and work. Here we briefly suggest how people in networked organizations can come to think in transformed ways about three important topics: the relationship of an employee to his or her organization, the nature of organizational structure, and the nature of management.

In conventional organizations employees typically work within one discrete and identifiable work unit. Their relationship to that unit is strong, whereas their relationship to the larger organization is weak. In our vision of a networked organization, employees can come to be thought of and think of themselves as employees of the larger organization. When they share information with unknown colleagues located in distant places and work in electronic groups whose members are drawn from many subunits, their mental maps of the organization become more elaborate and well informed. Their identities and loyalties also are likely to be more influenced by the larger organization. In the past, organizational cosmopolitanism— a broad view of an organization's goals and processes—has been mostly the province of senior management. Our vision makes it possible to think of extending cosmopolitanism throughout the networked organization.

The organization chart is a useful way to display patterned relationships among subunits in conventional organizations. It reflects two properties that define conventional views of structure: stability of relationships over time and hierarchical decomposition of goals and tasks. In our vision of a networked organization, people are simultaneously linked to and buffered from numerous others in multiple groups; groups or subunits are also simultaneously linked to and buffered from one another. The concept of structure as a static, or even stable, set of relationships gives way to a concept of soft structures, as dynamic and flexible relationships emerge and evolve. In our vision of a networked organization, an organization chart would be obsolete before it could be printed and distributed. Moreover, even if it were theoretically possible to capture a picture of structure at any point in time, to record it would require an enormously wide piece of paper because hierarchical decomposition gives way to distributed latices of interconnections.

In conventional organizations managers know whom they manage and manage whom they know. The concept of management will require substantial revision when people work in multiple groups, when groups are composed of members who collaborate only electronically, and when soft structures emerge without management directive. We do not prophesy the demise of management, but our ideas about management will certainly change. Rather than know intimately each worker and each job under their personal supervision, managers will become strategists who coordinate a variety of workers and situations. The morale of some managers will be much higher because of their varied responsibilities and experience. The morale of others will suffer. Hence one cannot just impose new structuring arrangements and new kinds of management without considering the qualities and attributes of the employees one has or can have.

A recent event in mathematical research suggests some of the challenges. Two mathematicians employed by Bell Communications Research and Digital Equipment Corporation used electronic mail to recruit several hundred researchers from companies, universities, and government labs around the world. They asked them to work on solving a large and important mathematical problem, one with practical implications for cryptography. Researchers who volunteered to help were sent a piece of the problem and returned their solutions by electronic mail. All of the partial solutions were then used to construct the final solution. The electronic message announcing the final results contained a charming admission: the two mathematicians who organized the work and constructed the final solution from the pieces returned to them did not even know the names of all of the people who helped them:

```
We'd like to thank everyone who contributed computing cycles to
this project, but I can't: we only have records of the person
```

at each site who installed and managed the code. If you helped
us, we'd be delighted to hear from you; please send us your
name as you would like it to appear in the final version of the
paper. (Manasse 1990)

Although the world of computational number theory is far removed
from the daily concerns of managers, this case highlights some of the
limitations in conventional thinking about organization and management
when networked organizations become more common. Typically managers influence their subordinates in large measure by allocating resources to
their projects and allocating credit (or blame) to their accomplishments.
How will the manager's role in resource allocation change when people can
reach out across the network and directly solicit resources from others to
help them with their work? How will the manager's role in allocating credit
or blame change when managers do not know, and perhaps cannot know,
who contributed in what ways to accomplishments?

If our first message is that making and managing new connections is what
is important, our second message is that technology by itself does not impel
these connections. They do not happen just by installing a network and
distributing electronic mailboxes. For connections such as the ones we have
described to arise, decision makers and employees should be guided by a
vision of a particular kind of organization or a particular way of working.
A vision can help in evaluating experience (are we moving toward or away
from where we want to go?). It can offer guidance in dealing with
unanticipated situations (should we think of this as a problem or an
opportunity?). And it can help in making choices within constraints (given
limited resources, what should we do first?). Our vision of a networked
organization is one in which all employees participate fully in the information
life of the organization, independent of their geographic, organizational, or
social location. They share information in dynamic and flexible ways that
evolve with organizational issues and opportunities. Not all organizations
will be comfortable with the kinds of electronic connections described in
this book. New connections will be most attractive to organizations
committed to employee competence and involvement and to organizational flexibility as ways to achieve and sustain success. Without such
commitments, analyses of electronic communication will be dominated by
first-level efficiency thinking.

Our vision is supported by four principles: (1) a view of people as people,
not users; (2) open access to people and information; (3) diverse forums

through which people can work together; and (4) policies and incentives that encourage information exchange. Our vision does not include advice about particular hardware or software systems because such advice rapidly becomes obsolete. Nor does it entail separate sections of advice for "managers" and "technologists." Such separation leads to separation of responsibility; a vision should be shared by all.

The first principle of our vision is to design a networked environment for people, not users. In the early days of computing technology, the term "users" distinguished those who worked with technology from those who did not ("nonusers"). In our vision of a networked organization, everyone communicates through the network; thus the old distinction between those who do and those who do not is meaningless. Furthermore, the concept of user focuses attention on the relationship between a person and technology. Our vision focuses attention on the relationship between a person and other people. The concept of user also implies a view of technology as a discrete commodity whose attributes and functions can be specified by the designer. Synonyms are "operator" or "consumer." In our vision people want to talk to people, and they want to do so for many reasons. Technology is a facilitator.

The second principle, open access to people and information, follows from the assumption that every employee has something to offer on an electronic network, and every employee has something to gain from it. Therefore every employee should have access to the network. Furthermore, every employee should have access to the same network. If sales and engineering people use different networks, they cannot benefit from one another; they do not have open access to one another. Open access implies the same network for all employees. And it implies software and management policies that make it easy to share information over the network. Software can make it easy (or difficult) to find people and other resources on the network. It can make it easy (or difficult) to contribute information. Management policies about access to the network are just as important. Much of the value of electronic communication comes from informal, quick exchanges. If a person has to walk down the hall, share a terminal, or pay by the message, the value will be reduced. The most extensively used computer-based communication systems are ones in which communicators see no message charges; the costs are allocated as overhead. Electronic mail traffic decreases when people are charged for use. Group communication decreases substantially. As overall traffic decreases, its distribution changes.

Who uses the system begins to depend more on who can pay rather than on whose job can benefit.

While we advocate open access, we strongly distinguish between open access and invasion of privacy. Open access to people—the ability to contact them via electronic mail, is different from open access to data about people—the ability to access files containing information about them. Managers can unreservedly promote the former while offering clear guidance about the latter. This guidance must help employees distinguish between sharing information and snooping.

The third principle, building and maintaining diverse forums, follows from the assumptions that people need to work collectively and that collective work is of different kinds. Hence, group communication is necessary, but it is not generic. The forums in which groups work must match the kinds of communication needed. (Of course, they will differ across organizations. Box 9.1 gives an example of some developed in a school system. Box 9.2 gives an example of some developed in a scientific community.) Many forums cannot and should not be specified in advance but will emerge and evolve dynamically as organizational problems and opportunities change. Software can make it easy for people to know about, join, and participate in multiple groups.

Box 9.1. A vision and diverse forums at Central Kitsap

Just after northern California's 1989 earthquakes, the librarian at Cougar Valley Elementary School sent electronic mail to each of the school's eighteen teachers, telling them about a parent who had experienced several earthquakes in Guatemala. Less than five minutes later had come back the first request for the parent to give students a firsthand account of earthquakes. Cougar Valley is part of the Central Kitsap school system, which decided in 1985 to install computers in its schools. The planning . . ."involved 150 teachers, parents and other volunteers who laid out the educational principles for the two new schools. Strategy 2020's vision of these schools of the future took the form of "paradigm shifts"—new ways of doing things." Among them were the following:

• Administrative and educational decisions should be made at the lowest level, preferably by teachers and students.

• Teachers should become managers of instruction, not presenters of information.

• "My classroom is my castle" must be discarded as a guiding principle. Teachers should function as teams of professionals, sharing ideas and communicating frequently.

• Students should become more actively involved in their own learning, both individually and in groups.

•Technology should be employed to manage learning as well as diagnose, present, and evaluate it.

Central Kitsap's implementation has two key parts. One is small-group instruction. The other part is . . ."a tool of cultural transformation . . . one that turned out to be surprisingly important, has been the local area network linking all the computers in the school. Teachers and administrators use its electronic mail feature to take attendance, assemble lunch orders, schedule meetings, and exchange information on items such as assignments for particular students. 'Not only does it free teachers from busywork, but they are no longer isolated from each other' [the superintendent's administrative assistant said]. Even if they go through a whole day without seeing each other, teachers can work together. Education has become a collective enterprise."

Source: Edward B. Fiske, "Reform by High-Tech," New York Times, January 7, 1990. Sect. 4A, 48–49.

Box 9.2. Example of SCIENCEnet features for oceanographers

Examples of Electronic Services

Omnet.fax: To send a fax anywhere in the world.
Papermail: To have hard copy mailed in the United States or Canada.
OCE.review: To submit a proposal review to the National Science Foundation Ocean Division.
Sonic: Gateway to data services at Ocean Network Information Center.
ECS: Gateway to satellite data services at National Climatic Data Center.

Examples of Electronic Bulletin Boards

Enso.info: El Nino southern oscillation information.
FIC.status: Information for Fleet Improvement Committee.
Grad.students: Information of interest to oceanography graduate students.
Mizex: Marginal ice zone experiment.
Products.services: Advertisements by members of SCIENCEnet.
Ship.sched90: University National Oceanographic Laboratory System research vessel information for 1990.

Examples of Electronic Discussion Groups and Projects

Arctic environmental drifting buoy experiment.
Gulfstream experiments planning committee.
National Research Council panel on physical oceanography.
South Atlantic ventilation experiment.
Warm core rings principal investigators.

Source: SCIENCEnet Subscribers/Catalog of Services, Fall 1988. Omnet, Inc., 137 Tonawanda St., Boston MA 02124.

Management policies should encourage people to take responsibility for their electronic groups. Managers can forbid all forms of extracurricular interaction, require supervisors to approve messages before they are sent to a group, or reprimand people who circulate controversial or distasteful ideas. Elaborate rules and restrictions can save managers from some embarrassments, but they discourage people from taking responsibility for their own behavior.

Making it easy to exchange information through providing open access and diverse forums is a necessary but not sufficient condition for communication to occur. Additionally, people must want to contribute to and benefit from coworkers and other resources on the network. By way of illustrating the distinction, consider a network in which anyone can send the C.E.O. a message. Being able to send messages to the boss often typifies an open access network. If the C.E.O. actually responds to received messages, then the network also embodies incentives to communicate. Motivating people to communicate via the network can be accomplished through both technical and human means. Software can motivate beneficial information exchange through, for instance, automatically notifying a contributor when someone reads his or her contribution or through filtering and organizing messages. Incentives for beneficial exchange can be conveyed through modeling (high-status people communicate via the network), evaluation feedback (rewarding electronic contributions to others), and norms (expecting people to communicate via the network routinely).

In one organization, half of the employees used electronic mail routinely and the other half did not, despite easy access to the technology. This meant that all communications that were intended for everyone had to be sent two ways: via electronic mail and via hard copies distributed to mailboxes. This situation changed, however, as a result of the "King Tut caper." The organization had purchased tickets for a very popular museum exhibit, "The Treasures of Tutankhamen," to be distributed on a first-come, first-serve basis to its employees. By the time employees found the hard-copy announcements in their mailboxes, the employees who read the electronic announcement had already signed up for all the tickets. Apparently when relatives heard they had missed out on King Tut because their spouse or parent didn't read electronic mail, they applied strong pressure to make sure they wouldn't be left out again in the future. Even independent of family pressure, the left-out employees had a vivid demonstration of the utility of electronic mail for routine communication.

Getting Started

Organizations can decide to have a network, but the process of acquiring, installing, and adapting or designing forms of computer-based communications can be expensive and time-consuming. As some organizations are beginning to demonstrate, the long-term process is made less burdensome if employees know they come before technology and organizational effects are considered along with the efficiency ones (see National Research Council 1986; Bikson, Gutek, and Mankin 1987). For organizations new to networking, we advocate a "plain vanilla" system that everybody can use over a fancy system that only some people can use. Simplicity and ease help make people feel comfortable in the networked environment and spend their time doing their work. They should be able to connect to the network easily, retrieve their computer files easily, and find their electronic mail easily.[1]

In the same vein, connecting everyone early—with modems, for example— is preferable to connecting only a few through fiber optics that may take months or years to install. By this, we do not deny the value of more advanced technology. (We would not have wanted our forefathers to widen the Erie Canal instead of building railroads.) But connecting everyone with something simple from the start and more gradually introducing expensive, special equipment and asking employees to learn more difficult skills gives a correct signal. People see that what they do counts more than what technology and a few technology enthusiasts can do. Getting everyone connected early also provides valuable organizational experience. It gives employees experience with new connections and new ways of working and thinking. It gives management experience with changed behavior and responsibilities. It allows for experiments in organizational design.

Connecting everyone also provides a built-in stimulus to behavior change. As the past twenty years of experience with facsimile machines has shown, if few people can use a new form of communication, they are driven away; they do not know if others will get their messages and thus have less reason to send them. When many people can use a form of communication, they believe others will see their messages and thus have more reason to send them. A critical mass of people communicating in the same way therefore tends to increase the per person frequency of communications (Markus 1987). That in turn increases the fraction of people's daily communications met by communicating in that way, reduces the personal cost of using the system, and encourages even further use. Nonetheless some networks, although they connect large numbers of people, are too specialized to meet many of a person's communication needs. For instance, employees using a parts order system may be connected with customers and suppliers but not with their coworkers. Here, the critical mass for parts ordering exists, but the critical mass for each person's beneficial communications does not. Such a system is unlikely to change behavior or to have broad second-level effects.

Unfortunately, introducing even a modest electronic communication network usually involves an additional cost to the start-up burden imposed by stand-alone technologies. Installation may require rewiring or construction, new telephone connections, and interaction with new and multiple vendors. Employees must adjust to disruption, unexpected patterns of use, and unforeseen problems. Problems in interconnected systems often spread to the entire organization rather than being isolated on one person's desk or in one person's machine. Management can pass through many of these costs to employees by insisting they weather these crises without help, or it can buffer employees from confusion and technical complexities by offering services to help. For instance, if there is no on-line directory of names and electronic addresses, management can give employees a paper directory. The paper directory doesn't obviate the value of developing an automated on-line directory later; meanwhile people can find most of the people and information they need.

Many organizations employ people who provide technical advice and help others get started. In some organizations, these jobs are oriented toward the technical components of nodes, pathways, and packets. They emphasize such matters as registering accounts, verifying passwords, and setting switches. In other organizations, these jobs are oriented toward the human network—people, forums, and resources. They emphasize helping people join groups, helping them create and manage groups, and helping them locate and acquire services. People especially may need expert humans to help them administer electronic groups. Piling technological start-up costs on top of group management and coordination costs can create a burden that potential groups cannot or will not assume. As a panel of the Commission on Science, Engineering, and Public Policy reported about its own attempt to create an electronic group, there was no "access to service support (comparable to telephone system operators) . . . Panel members had to rely on their own resources to remedy any system inefficiencies . . . Analyses of a sample of messages received by Panel staff indicate that approximately 10 percent contained some complaint about delays, losses of material in transmission, or unavailability of the group mail system" (National Research Council 1989:27). If group development and support is an organizational function, then it makes sense for the organization to facilitate groups rather than expecting them to operate their own technical services.

In some cases, one organization can provide services for many organizational clients. In the sciences, for instance, OMNET™ provides electronic mail services for many disciplines. Started by an oceanographer, OMNET staff know what its subscribers actually do in their daily scientific work, so they can tailor services for their scientists. OMNET has a telephone hot line to answer questions ranging from how to hook up a printer to how to connect to other scientific networks. No one's equipment is too primitive; no one's requests are too silly. OMNET distributes electronic and hard-copy directories listing all subscribers and a newsletter telling about improvements to the network. It also encourages subscriber exchanges through electronic bulletin boards. (See box 9.2.) Encouraging subscribers to discuss resources, problems, and ideas helps to foster independence and learning. Yet a human buffer remains between the technology and the people whose job is science, not communication technology.

Costs and Predicaments

Introducing computer-based communication can entail considerable direct costs for equipment, installation, programming, routine maintenance, and upgrades. Other costs arise from choices that managers make to introduce organizational changes, and the predicaments, or dilemmas, that involve giving up one goal in pursuit of another. For example, is our goal to supervise work more closely or to decentralize authority? Reaching one goal necessarily sacrifices the other. Electronic communication is transforming the nature of some organizational predicaments, but predicaments, and the choices they require, cannot be avoided.[2]

Managers emphasizing different costs will approach a new technology differently. For a new business telephone and voice mail system, manager A concerns herself with direct costs, such as those that arise from delivery delays and usability flaws. Manager B sees new system costs as opportunities to be leveraged. She proposes to use the system to deliver new services to customers, such as a 24-hour-service help line. She wants to use system training as a testbed for a bigger program in employee education. Manager C concerns herself with predicaments. Other things equal, the new telephone system tends to emphasize the marketing function, by, for instance, allowing each customer to order a custom-made product. But this strategy is in conflict with a productivity strategy that lowers costs through standardized production. It is difficult, if not impossible, to optimize both simultaneously. The new system also has cost-reduction objectives. By routing calls to most offices directly, the system saves the expense of having telephone receptionists, but that obviates the objective of pleasantly buffering employees from unwanted interruptions. These predicaments are not unique. Home builders in the postwar period who changed from high-quality, handmade homes to lower quality, assembly-line developments had to trade cost-reduction objectives for custom service objectives. So did bankers who installed electronic banking machines rather than hire more trained tellers. In the case of manager C, she must fashion policies in which marketing dominates production, or vice versa. She must decide if direct calling will dominate receptionist-channeled calls, or vice versa.

Computer-based communication amplifies some predicaments, poses some new predicaments, and makes some obsolete. We alluded to a predicament amplified by electronic communication in chapter 6, when discussing information overload. While more connections can bring peripheral or distant employees beneficial information or influence they would have lacked otherwise, it also will bring undesirable information and influence. We noted that information overload is more of a problem for visible or top employees, when they lose control over their own communications. One solution is to ignore all distribution list messages and messages from unknown people or to use automatic filters that accept only known names and desired messages. Yet this solution poses an opportunity cost by cutting off unexpected information from unexpected sources. Another solution is to compromise by accepting a random but small set of unanticipated messages each day along with all prespecified ones. This reduces the opportunity cost of not using the technology to get unexpected information.

Still, no matter what solution one chooses for information overload, a predicament is unavoidable. It is impossible to seek valuable information without encountering valueless information. More information also increases the complexity of people's view of the organization. While having a complex perspective makes employees "smarter," it also increases the likelihood of conflict as employees become more involved in more affairs of more parts of the organization (Robey, Farrow, and Franz 1989). Some firms restrict communication with "irrelevant" people, or they restrict communication on "irrelevant" topics, but these attempts at control do not resolve the predicament. Because organizations and their environments change continually, an ideal structure of relevant and irrelevant people and topics may look smart at one moment and stupid the next. There may be inequity as some people have more access to valuable communications and contacts than others do. And in the end, some people will get "too much" information while others get "too little." The only answer is to choose broad information access or narrow controlled access and live with the strengths and weaknesses of one's choice.

A new predicament brought about by modern communication technologies, including computer-based communication, is entailed in the increased speed and access of communication that they make possible. When people can communicate instantly, they start expecting instant communications. For example, employees who use their electronic mail system to send requests for information or publications to their library press the pace of library search, retrieval, and copying. They also push library administrators to make faster decisions about acquisitions, databases, and services. The predicament comes from the fact that when events change quickly, they can't happen slowly. Yet sometimes a slower, more deliberate pace is preferable.

Direct access contributes to direct communication. In a big company, employees in the field can connect directly with the offices at headquarters whose advice they need, and people at headquarters can connect directly with the regions where they have business. Why use the field office coordination department? But direct communication has costs. For example, without a filtering structure at headquarters, who will coordinate all the individual decisions, proposals, and activities that take place? Suppose many offices at headquarters decide at once to implement new programs, overloading the field personnel. Suppose the field personnel bombard one office with requests. Intermediaries slow decision making and even garble communications, but they aid coordination, consistency, and control from the center. Again, the predicament entails a choice with both benefits and costs.

Electronic communication is making some organizational predicaments obsolete or changing the way people have thought about them. We have alluded to some of these changes: simultaneous linking and buffering, in-groups without out-groups, big groups that seem small, and long-distance supervision. One dilemma that may disappear in its present form is between external and internal modes of accountability. In the past, managers have had to choose either to allow supervisors to monitor and evaluate their units or to have specialized staff do evaluations. When supervisors evaluate their groups, there is little assurance that they will do so rigorously. When outsiders evaluate groups, there is little assurance they will do so sympathetically. They may not understand fully the problems the groups face, and the groups may pay little attention to the evaluations. But with databases, on-line performance statistics, electronic notebooks, and computer conference transcripts, the relationship between insiders and outsiders can change. Both can have access to some of the same information. This could make it possible for supervisors and outside staff to do evaluations in parallel or even together (McLaren 1982:83-84). Despite these changes, better technology and management policies cannot solve all predicaments. Dilemmas are built into organizational structures and processes. Technology designs and policies can affect responses to these dilemmas but not change them fundamentally.

The Future

Technology advances continue to increase the variety of electronic communication tools available. While many of the arguments we have advanced will hold true no matter what the particular technology details are, at least three changes may substantially affect some of our predictions. The first change is increasing bandwidth in computer-based communication. Soon electronic mail may include graphics, pictures, sound, and video. These advances are under development today and in early use in some settings.[3] Increasing bandwidth is likely to reintroduce some of the social context cues that current electronic communication lacks. For instance, when you read a colleague's message, you may be able to look at his or her image or perhaps you'll prefer to see a representation of his or her facial expressions when he or she wrote the message.

Many think that if technological improvements can reintroduce such social context cues, then electronic communication will resemble face-to-face communication. But this conclusion probably is incorrect. Adding social context cues will not make electronic communication identical to face-to-face communication. Electronic communication has a qualitatively different temporal, social, and structural rhythm (McGrath and Hollingshead 1990). For instance, suppose people could use electronic mail with video at their convenience—in the office, on the road, or at home. Meeting with the boss electronically while wearing a bathrobe at home will not replicate the face-to-face business meeting in the office.

In addition to increases in bandwidth, the number of gateways connecting networks of different organizations and interorganizational networks will increase. In this book we have emphasized intraorganizational communication—connections among employees, departments, or businesses within the same organization. Interorganizational computer networks connect different organizations, such as firms within an industry, school systems, and government agencies. These networks allow for the rapid exchange of information across organizational boundaries and underlie, for instance, just-in-time inventory links between suppliers and producers and reorder links between distributors and consumers. In Sweden, interorganizational communication enables national trade union representatives to meet remotely. Interorganizational communication is important in its own right but raises a different set of issues from intraorganizational communication. For example, it is highly sensitive to legal and regulatory institutions. In the future, it will undoubtedly become more important, but because its legal, regulatory, and economic implications are likely to run counter to the principles of open access and diverse forums, we cannot make substantial predictions about its course in this book.

A third change to come is public electronic communication: commercial access networks will connect households with one another and with retail firms and community services. The United States is actually behind other industrial countries, notably France, where millions of telephones have small screens attached, and services from the telephone book to on-line news, from classified ads to pornography, are available (Kinsley 1989). Currently in the United States, newspapers, cable TV companies, and long-distance and local telephone companies are warring over which of them will dominate commercial electronic communication. When these battles are settled, we should see a vast increase in public electronic communications, along with stronger incentives to improve services and convenience. There will also be more incentives for companies to offer portable communication technologies, such as computers you can read in bed, wall hangings that turn into movie screens, and eyeglasses that turn into computer and television displays. "Letters by telephone" may mean the demise of postal services as we know them today. Even more than bandwidth and interorganizational communication, public electronic communication opens up many new questions not addressed by our current research within organizations and closely associated groups of people.

Monitoring Change
Although no one can predict and prepare for all the changes that will occur, decision makers and citizens can systematically monitor these changes and learn from early experiences with them. This is necessary because profound technological change is accompanied by new skills, new knowledge, and new ways of thinking (Tushman and Anderson 1986; Barley and Williams 1985; Hirschhorn 1985). Such changes can destroy cherished competencies and traditions. Diesel locomotives required new skills and knowledge that steam engine manufacturers did not typically possess. Typewriters created new occupational roles and changed the organization of the office. Automatically controlled machine tools required wholesale changes in engineering, mechanical, and data processing skills. Organizations that do not understand how and why such changes are taking place can neither exploit nor adapt effectively to them.

Learning about the organizational and social components of technological change is part of the more general job of organizational learning. People often have difficulty with this task because their own organization's experience is limited, and their access to others' experiences is constrained (March, Sproull, and Tamuz in press). Suppose you wanted to compare the effectiveness of the information system you purchased with the systems you almost purchased or with a different type of system that came on the market later. Assembling good comparison information involving other technologies and organizations would not be simple.

One way people in organizations learn is by carrying out thought experiments and simulations—comparing the organization's experience with what might have happened or could happen in slightly different circumstances. Near catastrophes sometimes stimulate this behavior. People in the airline industry monitor near-collisions of aircraft to help them understand, anticipate, and forestall real crashes (Tamuz 1987). Recently a Cornell graduate student propagated a computer virus through many computer networks, causing breakdowns in hundreds of systems. Although previously people were aware that computer security could be compromised, the incident prompted them to analyze weaknesses in their computer systems and in how employees and institutions were organized to deal with such events.

Another way to learn is by doing systematic research and planning. A predicament connected with doing research is that if it is left for employees to do on their own, their everyday, routine activities tend to drive out the special, nonroutine research tasks. As a result, many organizations establish separate research or planning units, or they employ professional research consultants or support research by outside laboratories. Yet whereas professionals may do excellent research, they may have limited access to the organization and limited credibility, with no way to ensure that their findings and recommendations will be heeded. Because of these limitations, outside researchers may be best suited to helping top-level managers or other employees understand their problems and options and compare them with those in other organizations.

Most learning about technological change in organizations takes place through people's varied experiences and contacts with others. For people to exploit new methods and ideas, they must have a prior mental scaffolding—broad knowledge and experience—that may not have much to do with current job requirements. Organizations expand the flexibility and knowledge of their employees through such vehicles as research laboratories, visits with outside experts, sabbaticals for employees, and cross-organizational forums. These internal procedures for learning in order to learn increase the absorptive capacity of the organization (Cohen and Levinthal 1990).

Organizations best realize benefits from new technology when they make complementary changes in organization and management (National Research Council 1986). Often there is no argument here; new technology is viewed as an opportunity to make other organizational changes, and the only question is what changes to make. New computer-based communication technology has prompted some managers to invoke the following organizational objectives: a clear chain of command reinforced by routing all network messages through the hierarchy; rationalization and control of information exchange by blocking certain channels of communication; reduced inefficiency and waste by forbidding extracurricular messages or work messages outside a person's responsibilities; and improved security by surveilling message files.

The same technology has prompted other managers to initiate or intensify a different set of objectives: a flexible, internally motivated, continuously learning work force; a strong internal culture to support information sharing and participation in problem solving; delegation or shared responsibility in recognition that dispersed activity requires local action and flexibility and that employees have or can locate salient information; and creation of dynamic procedures, structures, and groupings to amplify expertise and technology. These two sets of objectives are contradictory but together make a point: computer-based communication allows people to work somewhat more efficiently, but the realized benefits depend ultimately on the policies, designs, and vision of people who want to organize work in new ways.

Appendix

A Lesson in Electronic Mail

By Robert F. Sproull

Electronic communication technology uses computer text processing and communication tools to provide a high-speed information exchange service. Anyone with a computer account can create and send information to anyone who has a mailbox on that computer or on any other computer to which it is connected through a computer network. The networked computers might be physically proximate and connected to a local area network, or they might be in different states, countries, or continents and connected via long-distance telecommunications that form a permanent network or a transient dial-up link. Depending on software sophistication, the mailed information can be a message, a document, a computer program, statistical data, or even a collection of organized messages—a computer discussion—forwarded from some other mailbox. At the recipient's convenience, he or she can read the information, edit it, save it, delete it, move it to another computer file, and/or reply to the sender.

Access

The utility of an electronic mail system depends heavily on who has access to it and how convenient the access is. If only a few people have access to the system, it won't serve an appreciable fraction of anyone's communication needs and may become an unused curiosity. Barriers to use arise if people have to share computer terminals, or walk "to the computer room" to get access, or learn a complex set of instructions to send and receive mail. Electronic mail can be as convenient and uninhibiting as picking up the telephone, or it can be one more piece of office drudgery.

For people who already have terminals on their desks, electronic mail can be offered as one of the services available on the terminal. Whether these terminals connect to large computers or are part of personal computers, they can all deliver the mail.

An initial implementation of electronic mail often identifies clusters of users who already have computer access for another purpose and equips their computers with sufficient software and communication capabilities to send and receive mail. This user group can then be grown by offering mailboxes to new users, perhaps with incentives for joining. Deciding on a rate of growth and corresponding expense is one of the key parts of designing an organization's electronic mail system.

Naming

Each electronic mail message must name precisely the mailbox to which it is destined. It would be nice to use names like "John Smith," but names are rarely unique, and the electronic mail system has insufficient information to resolve ambiguities properly. Some systems assign a unique number to each mailbox, just as a unique number is assigned to each telephone line, but this technique forces each sender to remember or look up mailbox numbers in a directory and gives people the impression they are just numbers to a computer—hardly conducive to smooth communication. A better solution is to add addresses to names, much the way addresses are placed on envelopes, so that the name and address together identify a unique mailbox. For example, "John Smith at Computer Science at Carnegie Mellon University" may suffice to identify a unique mailbox and to give the electronic mail system enough information to transport the message from the sender to the recipient. (Issues surrounding naming and addressing in electronic mail are much more complex than this discussion implies. Devising a scheme that can gracefully handle worldwide use by millions of people has taxed the committees setting electronic mail standards. Supporting "white pages" directory services for millions of users is especially challenging.)

Transport

How is electronic mail delivered from a sender to one or more receivers? There are two basic methods and combinations of them.

At one extreme, all electronic mail terminals communicate with a single computer, where the electronic mail software runs. A person signs on to the computer and uses the software to compose a message or to read messages from a disk file that serves as a mailbox. For delivery, the text of the message is simply copied into the recipient's mailbox file. Because all mailboxes are on the same computer, a message can be routed to anyone just by copying it to the proper mailbox. If the users of such a system are geographically distant, telecommunications must be used to link the terminal to the single "mail computer." Commercial electronic mail systems, such as CompuServe, operate essentially in this way.

At the other extreme, each person operates a separate computer, which runs electronic mail software and holds on its disk a single mailbox file for its user. To send a message to another person, the computer uses a computer-to-computer communications network and an associated electronic mail protocol to transport the message text from the sender's computer to the receiver's computer and thence into the receiver's mailbox. Alternatives to a network are also possible, such as dedicated communications links between computers used only for electronic mail traffic or dial-up links that are used only when mail transmission is required.

In practice, electronic mail systems usually operate between the two extremes. A local group of users will all have mailboxes on one computer and can send mail to each other by simply copying messages directly into mailboxes. Messages for distant users are transported through the computer network to the computer where the recipient's mailbox is located. Each local site has such a computer, holding mailboxes for all local users. These computers are linked via a network in order to transport mail from one local site to another. If a site's computer becomes overloaded, a new computer can be added to the network to share the load at the site.

Today electronic mail systems cannot always send mail to other electronic mail systems because software from different vendors uses different formats and conventions. Dissimilar systems can sometimes be connected by mail gateways, whereby one computer's mail system can format and deliver messages to a foreign system. For example, Digital's All-In-One mail system can send mail to a gateway that in turn sends the mail to IBM's SNADS mail system. Eventually the need for gateways will be obviated by using standard electronic mail protocols, a single set of rules for formatting messages that flow between computers, so that all computers use one format. A worldwide standard for this purpose, called X.400, *Recommendations for Message Handling Systems*, has been defined and is beginning to be implemented.

Different electronic mail systems also provide different facilities for ensuring privacy and security. The transport and storage of electronic mail messages can be as secure as sensitive military communications or as public as waving a banner at a football game. Encryption can be used to obtain security so that a message can be read only by the sender and receiver who know a secret code that scrambles and unscrambles the message. Today very few electronic mail systems will encrypt messages. A computer system's access controls, such as log-in procedures and passwords, may help ensure that a mailbox and other computer data are not accessed by other people. But many personal computers lack these controls; a night visitor can read anyone's mail. Facsimile machines also have poor security: the telephonic transmission is not secure, and the receiving machine may be accessible to many people. The rather poor state of electronic mail security is likely to improve only slowly; for now, people are concentrating on making mail easier to use for wider audiences.

Group Communication

Electronic mail transmits messages to individuals by copying messages to their personal electronic mailboxes. A single message will be copied to several mailboxes if the sender lists the name of each recipient explicitly. One message may also be delivered simultaneously to many mailboxes by sending the message to a group name or distribution list (DL)—for example, PC Users, Strategy Group, or Movie Reviews. The sender does not specify, or need to know, the names and addresses of group members. The computer automatically mails a copy of the communication, which is addressed to the group as a whole, to the personal mailbox of each group member. Electronic bulletin boards (bboards) and conferences transmit messages to a single named mailbox that is accessible to more than one person. The distinction between these forms of group communication is that in DLs, messages come to recipients' own mailboxes, intermixed with personal communications, whereas in bboards and conferences, people have to take a bit more initiative to find messages. Bboards and conferences differ from one another in that bboards simply display messages in chronological order as they are received; conferences group messages by topic and display grouped messages together.

Interface

A person sends and receives electronic mail by using a computer program designed to manage mail. These mail programs may provide only primitive mechanisms for sending and receiving mail, or they may offer a rich set of facilities. Here is a list of features sometimes found in these programs:

• Composing a message using a word processor or text editor. Other text files can be copied into the message. The mail program may check the names and addresses of recipients to detect typographical errors. The mail program dispatches the message.

• Extracting incoming mail from a mailbox and displaying a short summary of each message.

• Selecting one or more messages and displaying them on the terminal or printing them on a printer.

• Searching a mailbox or a set of saved messages by date, keyword, or sender's name.

• Deleting a message.

• Copying a message to a computer file for permanent storage or some other use.

• Replying to a message, using conventional message-preparation tools, but without having to specify the name of the recipient. Some systems allow one to reply by annotating the original message, distinguishing original and reply text.

• Displaying messages by category, such as name of sender or subject.

• Determining whether a message has been read by its recipient—a form of "return receipt requested."

• Finding mail addresses for individuals or groups in directory services.

• Maintaining a group list—for example, adding or removing a name from distribution lists.

• Directing a mail agent to process mail automatically—for example, to reply to each message received with a message announcing you are on vacation for two weeks.

Some of these features depend not only on the mail program but on features of the underlying mail system and mail transport protocols, such as distribution lists.

Social Features

Despite differences in particular implementations, electronic mail technologies share six characteristics that differentiate them socially from other
communication technologies. First, electronic mail is asynchronous. Senders
and receivers do not need to attend to the same communication at the same
time. They can send and receive at their convenience. Asynchrony is not
only a matter of personal convenience; it means communication crosses
time as well as space. Although there are electronic communications
programs for simultaneous communication ("TALK"), they are little used
in organizations at present.

Second, electronic mail is fast. An electronic message can be transmitted
in seconds or minutes down a hall, across a continent, or around the world.
Replies can flow back just as rapidly. Speed is not just a matter of
convenience either. Speed makes possible long-distance conversation,
decision making, and almost any other interaction requiring give and take.

Third, electronic mail is text-based. Messages convey typographic characters, not video images or speech. Only a few of today's mail programs
allow pictures or forms to be transmitted. The text in electronic communication makes it useful for exchanging documents, as well as messages.
But more important, electronic communication looks pretty much alike no
matter what is sent. It lacks social information and reminders of the social
rules and statuses that usually regulate communication.

Fourth, electronic mail has multiple-receiver addressability: someone
can send a message to one, twenty, or hundreds of people wherever they
may be. This attribute means that without respect to physical, temporal, or
social location, people can delegate work, collaborate, form new groups,
and make collective decisions.

Fifth, electronic mail has built-in external memory. The contents of
electronic messages can be stored and retrieved later. This property is
important for social memory. For instance, people can participate in a
group project over months or years and save in memory all of the
interactions of the group. At any time, this group memory can be accessed
by members who want to trace the history of an issue or by newcomers who
want to learn about the group's activities.

Finally, the external memory is computer processable. It can be conveniently searched, edited, partitioned, and shared with others. This attribute
extends the power of social memory by allowing analyses of issue trends,

participation patterns, consensus points, and other social memory characteristics.

Other communication technologies have some of these attributes, as we show in table A.1, but the six attributes taken together comprise a unique and peculiarly social technology. We avoid considering cost as an attribute here because the assumptions one must make to compare costs are quite arbitrary. For instance, a face-to-face conversation is cheap—unless the parties are separated by a continent and must travel to their meeting place. An electronic network is typically expensive to install, but electronic mail is inexpensive to operate insofar as one considers the cost of an additional message or of putting an additional person on the network. Hence cost is

Table A.1
Comparing communication on a computer network with other communication technologies

	Technology Attributes					
	Asynchrony	Fast	Text content only	Multiple address-ability	Externally recorded memory	Computer-processable memory
Meeting	no	yes[a]	no	yes	no[b]	no
Telephone	no	yes[a]	no	no[b]	no[b]	no
Letter	yes	no	no	no[b]	yes	no[c]
Telex	yes	yes	yes	no	yes	no[c]
Facsimile	yes	yes	no	no[b]	yes	no[c]
Voice mail	yes	yes	no	yes	no[b]	no
Electronic mail	yes	yes	yes	yes	yes	yes

a. Although conversation is instantaneous, meetings are fast only if people do not have to travel to the meeting place. Telephone conversations are fast only when both parties are simultaneously available to talk and don't have to play telephone tag.

b. Special actions can be taken to approximate the attribute in question. For example, memory can be provided by recording or transcribing meetings or telephone conversations. Voice messages can be stored. Multiple addressability is achieved with conference calls, certain facsimile machines that can be programmed to dial multiple telephone numbers, and letters that are copied and mailed to several people.

c. Special actions can be taken to improve retrieval properties of paper-based technologies. Vertical filing systems improve the retrievability of paper documents. Imaging systems that "annotate" facsimile images make the resulting documents easier to search. When facsimile or other image-handling technologies are integrated with computers, their retrievability capabilities approach those of electronic communication.

closely tied to scale of use. Furthermore, many electronic networks are installed and maintained principally to support remote access to databases and processing power. In these settings, electronic mail adds function with relatively low marginal cost.

The explosion of facsimile machines in recent years provides an alternative to electronic mail, but one with quite different properties. Facsimile has some advantages over electronic mail: images of all sorts can be transmitted, and any fax machine can talk to any other fax machine because they are connected to the pervasive dial telephone network rather than to isolated computer networks and because they all transmit images in a compatible format. But today's facsimile lacks some important properties that we consider essential for electronic communication. The documents sent or received by facsimile are hard to manipulate: on a personal computer, one can't receive a facsimile document, add three sentences in one paragraph, revise a chart, reformat the results, and then send the revised document onward to a group of reviewers. Facsimile images are expensive to store and hard to search, edit, send to groups, or process by other computer programs (McCarthy 1989). And most fax images never make it into a computer; they are printed on paper and destroyed. Thus fax is convenient for one-time, one-to-one communication, especially when handwritten material or images are required, but it is not as good as electronic mail for collaborative or ongoing efforts. This is changing; improved image quality will allow techniques like optical character recognition to extract computer-processable text from facsimile messages, more personal computers will be outfitted with facsimile interfaces, and we can generally expect electronic mail and facsimile capabilities to fuse into a general form of computer-based communication.

Notes

Introduction

1. See, for these other technologies, such works as de Sola Pool (1977), Chandler (1977), Perrin (1980), Sharpe (1952), White (1962), Stilgoe (1983), Pelto and Muller-Wille (1972), and Barley (1986).
2. See, for instance, Thomas and Carroll (1981), Card, Moran, and Newell (1983), Shneiderman (1987), and Caswell (1988). The technical journals, *Human-Computer Interaction* and *Communications of the ACM* carry many articles on this topic.
3. See, for instance, Uhlig, Farber, and Bair (1979).
4. See Markus (1987), for example, for critical mass arguments or Crawford (1982), Nyce and Groppa (1983), and Caswell (1988) for implementation strategies.

Chapter 1

1. We are not the first to offer social analyses of electronic communication technologies. For a far-ranging early view that in important ways forecasted our work, see Hiltz and Turoff (1978). Studies as far back as the late 1960s began to evaluate the impact of teletyped computer communication on groups (Sinaiko 1963; Chapanis 1972; Short, Williams, and Christie 1976; for a review see Williams 1977). Rice and Associates (1984) have described their more recent research on electronic mail technologies. Another relevant domain is that of general office computing (see Kling 1980; Bikson and Gutek 1983; Turner 1984; Zuboff 1988). We will refer to these and many other sources as they are relevant throughout the text.
2. See Schelling (1978) for an analysis of these processes.
3. Writers who have talked about the difficulty of anticipating things that have never been done before include Bell (1973), Zuboff (1988), and Rule and Attewell (1989).
4. See Beniger (1986) for the history of the Hollerith machine and other early developments in office automation.
5. See Smith and Alexander (1988) for the early development of personal computers and printers.

6. For more extensive reviews of the characteristics of these technologies, see Rice and Associates (1984), Culnan and Markus (1987), Johansen, (1988), and Kraemer and King (1988).

7. Hybels and Barley (1990) provide a labor market explanation of human resource policies in high-technology organizations.

Chapter 2

1. See Caswell (1988:16-17) for more detail.

2. See Meyer and Boone (1987:155) for a value-added analysis of this use of electronic mail.

3. See Kraut, Egido, and Galegher (1990) for the importance of face-to-face meetings in scientific project groups.

4. See Meyer and Boone (1987:210-211) for this story in more detail.

5. Kmetz (1984) describes a nonelectronic form of information buffers in the avionics repair industry.

Chapter 3

1. For example, see Kahn (1952) and Hochstim (1967). For a review of this literature, see Sudman and Bradburn's (1974) discussion of response effects.

2. See Kolnar et al. (1982) and Sundstrom and Sundstrom (1986) for descriptions of how tangible cues in the office reinforce social distinctions.

3. Weizenbaum has been deeply distressed by many developments in the evolving relationship between people and computers. See Weizenbaum (1976).

4. For a review of electronic marketing surveys, see Synodinos and Brennan (1988). A common application of computer interviewing is vocational and career guidance (Sampson 1983). Such programs are used in more than 25 percent of the high schools in the United States and in at least a thousand postsecondary institutions. For instance, see Katz (1984) on SIGI, a program that does career advising. Less common is computer interviewing for therapy, but see, for instance, Wagman (1980) on PLATO DCS, a program for counseling college students; Ghosh, Marks, and Carr (1984), Ghosh and Marks (1987), and Chandler et al. (1988) on computer-based treatment for phobias; Burnett, Taylor, and Agras (1985) on a program for weight control; and Selmi (1983) on computer-assisted therapy for depression.

5. For a review of research on deindividuation, see Forsyth (1983:307-338).

6. See Myers (1987) and Finholt and Sproull (1990) for descriptions of how people can create different electronic personalities.

Chapter 4

1. For a technical discussion of research on groups, see McGrath (1984). A research-based textbook is Forsyth (1983).

2. See, for instance, Berkowitz and Bennis (1961), Dubin and Spray (1964), Berger et al. (1977), Weiner and Goodenough (1977), Ridgeway (1981), Strodtbeck and Lipinski (1985), Kirchler and Davis (1986), Holtgraves (1986), and Jablin (1987).

3. Half the groups first make decisions face to face and then electronically; the other half reverses this order.

4. Others using decision support systems, asynchronous computer conferencing, or other forms of computer-mediated communication, have found similar effects. See, for instance, Zigurs (1987) and Easton (1988). Reviews comparing different forms of computer-mediated communication may be found in Kraemer and King (1988) and Dennis et al. (1988).

Chapter 5

1. See, for instance, Festinger, Schachter, and Back (1950), Newcomb (1961), Monge and Kirste (1980).
2. This literature is reviewed in Fischhoff et al. (1981). Also see Dawes (1988).
3. See Jablin (1987) for a review of research supporting this observation. Managers tend to dominate the conversation, and subordinates expect them to. Further, subordinates are reluctant to convey bad news or negative information to their bosses (Rosen and Tesser 1970; O'Reilly and Roberts 1974; Linde 1988).
4. Research reviews for the past thirty years have failed to find a consistent positive relationship between job satisfaction and performance (Brayfield and Crockett 1955; Vroom 1964; Petty, McGee, and Cavender 1984; Iaffaldano and Muchinsky 1985; Podsakoff and Williams 1986).
5. See, for instance, Mayer and Greeno (1972), Chi and Glaser (1984), Rouse and Morris (1986).

Chapter 6

1. See, for instance, Pettigrew (1972), Allen (1977), Porter, Allen, and Angel (1981), Attewell (1986), and Rule and Brantley (1990).
2. See Innis (1950), Eisenstein (1979), and Katz (1989) for analyses of how earlier communication technologies were introduced and initially controlled by elites.
3. Danziger et al. (1982), Laudon (1986), and Dunlop and Kling (forthcoming) discuss these issues. Rahav (1988) illustrates the potential threats to privacy of databases in his article on Israel's psychiatric case register.

Chapter 7

1. The importance of what one measures is illustrated in Coca-Cola's attempt to change its recipe for Coke. Market share measures indicated that Coke was losing customers. In blind taste experiments, customers preferred the taste of Pepsi. But management had not measured the symbolic importance of Coke to consumers and so was totally surprised by the furor engendered when "old" Coke was removed from the market.

Chapter 8

1. James V. McGee, "Boundary Spanning Systems and Organizational Integration" (seminar at the Graduate School of Industrial Administration, Carnegie Mellon University, May 9, 1990).
2. See Egido (1990) for a review of the failures of video communication.
3. Some research laboratories are beginning to develop experimental video links for informal synchronous interaction at a distance (Root 1988; Abel 1990). It is likely to be years before these become commercially viable.

4. Public networks outside the organizational context may function quite similarly to extend citizen's personal neighborhoods (Glossbrenner 1983).

Chapter 9

1. For more information on interface design, see Shneiderman (1987) and Dumas (1988).

2. For more discussion of organizational dilemmas, see Aram (1976), Hood (1976), Drucker (1977), and McLaren (1982).

3. See Root (1988), Abel (1990), and Borenstein and Thyberg (in press).

References

Abel, M. (1990). Experiences in an exploratory distributed organization. In J. Galegher, R. Kraut, and C. Egido (Eds.), *Intellectual teamwork: Social and technological foundations of cooperative work* (pp. 489–510). Hillsdale, NJ: Erlbaum.

Adams, J. S. (1976). The structure and dynamics of behavior in organizational boundary roles. In M. D. Dunnette (Ed.), *Handbook of industrial and organizational psychology* (pp. 1175–1199). Chicago: Rand-McNally.

Allen, T. J. (1977). *Managing the flow of technology.* Cambridge, MA: The MIT Press.

Aram, J. D. (1976). *Dilemmas of administrative behavior.* Englewood Cliffs, NJ: Prentice-Hall.

Aronson, E. (1966). The psychology of insufficient justification: An analysis of some conflicting data. In S. Feldman (Ed.), *Cognitive consistency* (pp. 115–133). New York: Academic Press.

Aronson, S. H. (1971). The sociology of the telephone. *International Journal of Comparative Sociology, 12*, 153–167.

Attewell, P. (1986). Imperialism within complex organizations. *Sociological Theory, 4*, 115–125.

Barley, S. R. (1986). Technology as an occasion for structuring: Evidence from observations of CT scanners and the social order of radiology departments. *Administrative Science Quarterly, 31*, 78–108.

Barley, S. R., and Williams, L. K. (1985). *Could a funny thing happen on the way to the office of the future?* (ILR Report 23, pp. 11–20). Ithaca, NY: Cornell School of Industrial and Labor Relations.

Becker, F. D. (1986). Loosely-coupled settings: A strategy for computer-aided work decentralization. *Research in Organizational Behavior, 8*, 199–231.

Belasco, W. J. (1979). *Americans on the road: From autocamp to motel, 1910–1945.* Cambridge, MA: The MIT Press.

Bell, D. (1973). *The coming of post-industrialized society.* New York: Basic Books.

Beniger, J. R. (1986). *The control revolution.* Cambridge, MA: Harvard University Press.

Benson, I., Ciborra, C., and Proffitt, S. (1990, October). Social and economic consequences of groupware for flight crew. *Proceedings of the Third Conference on Computer-Supported Cooperative Work* (pp. 119–129). New York: The Association for Computing Machinery.

Berger, J., Fisek, M. H., Norman, R. Z., and Zelditch, M. (1977). *Status characteristics and social interaction.* New York: Elsevier.

Berkowitz , N. H., and Bennis, W. G. (1961). Interaction patterns in formal service-oriented organizations. *Administrative Science Quarterly, 6,* 25–50.

Besston, T., and Tucker, T. (1984). *Hooking in: The underground computer bulletin board workbook and guide.* Westlake Village, CA: ComputerFood Press.

Bikson, T. K., and Gutek, B. A. (1983). *Advanced office systems: An empirical look at utilization and satisfaction* (N-1970–NSF). Santa Monica, CA: The Rand Corporation

Bikson, T. K., Gutek, B. A., and Mankin, D. A. (1987). *Implementing computerized procedures in office settings* (R-3077–NSF/IRIS). Santa Monica, CA: The Rand Corporation.

Binik, Y. M., Westbury, C. F., and Servan-Schreiber, D. (1989). Case histories and shorter communications. *Behavioral Research Therapy, 27*(3), 303–306.

Borenstein, N., and Thyberg, C. (in press). Power, ease of use, and cooperative work in a practical multimedia message system. *The International Journal of Man Machine Studies: Special Issue on Computer-Supported Cooperative Work and Groupware.*

Brayfield, A. H., and Crockett, W. H. (1955). Employee attitudes and employee performance. *Psychological Bulletin, 52,* 396–424.

Burnett, K. F., Taylor, C. B., and Agras, W. S. (1985). Ambulatory computer-assisted therapy for obesity: A new frontier for behavior therapy. *Journal of Consulting Clinical Psychology, 53,* 698–703.

Burns, L. (1989). Matrix management in hospitals: Testing theories of matrix structure and development. *Administrative Science Quarterly, 34*(3), 349–368.

Card, S. K., Moran, T. P., and Newell, A. (1983). *The psychology of human computer interaction.* Hillsdale, NJ: Erlbaum.

Caswell, S. A. (1988) *E-Mail.* Boston: Artech House.

Chandler, A. D., Jr. (1977). *The visible hand: The managerial revolution in American business.* Cambridge, MA: Belknap Press of Harvard University Press.

Chandler, G. M, Burck, H., Sampson, J. P., and Wray, R. (1988). The effectiveness of a generic computer program for systematic desensitization. *Computers in Human Behavior, 4,* 339–346.

Chapanis, A. (1972). Studies in interactive communication: The effects of four communication modes on the behavior of teams during cooperative problem-solving. *Human Factors, 14,* 487–509.

Chi, M. T. M., and Glaser, R. (1984). Problem solving abilities. In R. Steinberg (Ed.), *Human abilities: An information processing approach* (pp. 227–248). San Francisco: Freeman.

Clark, K. B., Chew, W. B., and Fujimoto, T. (1987). Product development in the world auto industry. *Brookings Papers on Economic Activity, 3,* 729–781.

Cohen, W., and Levinthal, D. A. (1990). Absorptive capacity: A new perspective on learning and innovation. *Administrative Science Quarterly, 35,* 128–152.

Connolly, T., Jessup, L. M., and Valacich, J. S. (1990). Idea generation using a GDSS: Effects of anonymity and evaluative tone. *Management Science, 36*(6), 689–703.

Crawford, A. B. (1982). Corporate electronic mail—A communication-intensive application of information technology. *MIS Quarterly, 6,* 1–14.

Culnan , M. J., and Markus, M. L. (1987). Information technologies. In F. M. Jablin, L. L. L. Putnam, K. H. Roberts and L. W. Porter (Eds.), *Handbook of organizational communication* (pp. 420–444). Newbury Park, CA: Sage Publications.

Curtis, B., Krasner, H., and Iscoe, N. (1988). A field study of the software design process for large systems. *Communications of the ACM, 31*(11), 1268–1287.

Danziger, J. N., Dutton, W. H., Kling, R., and Kraemer, K. L. (1982). *Computers and politics: High technology in American local governments.* New York: Columbia University Press.

Danziger, J. N. (1979). Technology and productivity: A contingency analysis of computers in local government. *Administration and Society, 11,* 144–171.

Davis, J. H., and Restle, F. (1963). The analysis of problems and prediction of group problem solving. *Journal of Abnormal and Social Psychology, 66,* 103–116.

Dawes, R. M. (1988). *Rational choice in an uncertain world.* San Diego: Harcourt Brace Jovanovich, Publishers.

Dennis, A. R., George, J. F., Jessup, L. M., Nunamaker, J. F. Jr., and Vogel, D. R. 1988. Information technology to support electronic meetings. *MIS Quarterly* (December), 591–619.

DeSanctis, G., & Gallupe, R. B. (1987). A foundation for the study of group decision support systems. *Management Science, 33,* 589–609.

de Sola Pool, I. (1977). *The social impact of the telephone.* Cambridge, MA: The MIT Press.

Diehl, M., and Stroebe, W. (1987). Productivity loss in brainstorming groups: Toward the solution of a riddle. *Journal of Personality and Social Psychology, 53,* 497–509.

Drucker, P. F. (1977). *An introductory view of management.* New York: Harper and Row.

Dubin, R., and Spray, S. L. (1964). Executive behavior and interaction. *Industrial Relations, 3,* 99–108.

Dubrovsky, V., Kiesler, S., and Sethna, B. (in press). The equalization phenomenon: Status effects in computer-mediated and face-to-face decision making groups. *Human Computer Interaction.*

Dumas, J. S. (1988). *Designing user interfaces for software.* Englewood Cliffs, NJ: Prentice Hall.

Dunlop, C., and Kling, R., (Eds.). (forthcoming). *Computerization and controversy: Value conflicts and social choices.* New York: Academic Press.

Earls, J. (1990). *Social integration by people with physical disabilities: The development of an information technology model based on personal growth and achievement.* Unpublished doctoral dissertation, The University of Wollongong, Wollongong, Australia.

Easton, G. K. (1988). *Group decision support systems vs. face-to-face communication for collaborative group work: An experimental investigation.* Unpublished doctoral dissertation, University of Arizona, Tucson.

Egido, C. (1990). Teleconferencing as a technology to support cooperative work: Its possibilities and limitations. In J. Galegher, R. E. Kraut, and C. Egido (Eds.), *Intellectual teamwork: Social and technological foundations of cooperative work* (pp. 351–371). Hillsdale, NJ: Erlbaum.

Einhorn, H. J., Hogarth, R. M., and Klempner, E. (1977). Quality of group judgment. *Psychological Bulletin, 84*(1), 158–172.

Eisenstein, E. (1979). *The printing press as an agent of change* (Vol. 1). Cambridge: Cambridge University Press.

Electronic Services Unlimited (1987). *Telework: A multi-client study.* New York: Author.

Emmett, R. (1982). VNET or GRIPENET. *Datamation,* 48–58.

Englebart, D. (1989, November). *Bootstrapping organizations into the 21st century.* Paper presented at a seminar at the Software Engineering Institute, Pittsburgh.

Eveland, J. D., and Bikson, T. K. (1988). Work group structures and computer support: A field experiment. *Transactions on Office Information Systems, 6*(4), 354–379.

Fanning, T., and Raphael, B. (1986). Computer teleconferencing: Experience at Hewlett-Packard. *Proceedings of Conference on Computer-Supported Cooperative Work* (pp. 291–306). New York: The Association for Computing Machinery.

Feldman, M. S. (1987). Electronic mail and weak ties in organizations. *Office: Technology and People, 3,* 83–101.

Festinger, L., Schachter, S., and Back, K. (1950). *Social pressures in informal groups.* New York: Harper.

Finholt, T., and Sproull, L. (1990). Electronic groups at work. *Organization Science, 1*(1), 41–64.

Finholt, T., Sproull, L., and Kiesler S. (1990). Communication and performance in ad hoc task groups. In J. Galegher, R. Kraut, and C. Egido (Eds.), *Intellectual teamwork: Social and technological foundations of cooperative work* (pp. 291–325). Hillsdale, NJ: Erlbaum.

Fischer, C. (1985). *Touch someone: The telephone industry discovers sociability, 1876–1940.* Unpublished manuscript, University of California, Berkeley.

Fischhoff, B., and Johnson, S. (1990). The possibility of distributed decision making: Appendix to B. Fischhoff (Ed.), *Distributed decision making: Workshop report*. Washington, DC: National Academy Press.

Fischhoff, B., Lichtenstein, S., Slovic, P., Derby, S. L., and Keeney, R. L. (1981). *Acceptable risk*. New York: University Press.

Fiske, E. B. (1990, January 7). Reform by high-tech. *New York Times*, p. 48.

Forsyth, D. R. (1983). *An introduction to group dynamics*. Monterey, CA: Brooks/Cole Publishing Co.

Fox, J. M. (1982). *Software and its development*. Englewood Cliffs, NJ: Prentice-Hall.

Garbarino, C. (1990). *E-mail delivers Tandem's competitive edge*. Unpublished manuscript, Tandem Computers, Inc., Cupertino, CA.

Geneen, H., and Moscow, A. (1984). *Managing*. Garden City, NY: Doubleday.

Ghosh, A., and Marks, I. M. (1987). Self-treatment of agoraphobia by exposure. *Behavioral Therapy*, *18*, 3–16.

Ghosh, A., Marks, I. M., and Carr, A. C. (1984). Self-exposure treatment for phobias: A controlled study. *Journal of Royal Society of Medicine*, *77*, 483–487.

Glossbrenner, A. (1983). *The complete handbook of personal computer communications: Everything you need to know to go on-line with the world*. New York: St. Martin's Press.

Goldman, M. I. (1987). *Gorbachev's challenge: Economic reform in the age of high technology*. New York: W. W. Norton.

Greif, I. (Ed.). (1988). *Computer-supported cooperative work: A book of readings*. San Mateo, CA: Morgan Kaufmann Publishers.

Halper, M. (1988, November). Portables get raves on the road. *Datamation*, pp. 55–58.

Hannaway, J. (1989). *Signals and signalling: The workings of an administrative system*. New York: Oxford University Press.

Harkness, R. C. (1977). *Technology assessment of telecommunications-transportation interactions*. Menlo Park, CA: Stanford Research Institute.

Hesse, B., Sproull, L., Kiesler, S., and Walsh, J. (1990). *Computer network support for science: The case of oceanography*. Unpublished manuscript, Carnegie Mellon University, Pittsburgh.

Hiltz, S. R., and Turoff, M. (1978). *The network nation: Human communication via computer*. Reading, MA: Addison-Wesley.

Hirschhorn, L. (1985). Information technology and the new services game. In M. Castells (Ed.), *High technology, space, and society*, *28* (pp. 173–188). Urban Affairs Annual Reviews. Beverly Hills, CA: Sage.

Hochstim, J. R. (1967). A critical comparison of three strategies of collecting data from households. *Journal of the American Statistical Association*, *62*, 976–989.

Holtgraves, T. (1986). Language structure in social interaction: Perceptions of direct and indirect speech acts and interactants who use them. *Journal of Personality and Social Psychology, 51*, 305–314.

Hood, C. C. (1976). *The limits to administration.* London: John Wiley and Sons.

Huff, C., and King, R. (1988, August). An experiment in electronic collaboration. In J. D. Goodchilds (Chair), *Interacting by computer: Effects on small group style and structure.* Symposium conducted at the meeting of the American Psychological Association, Atlanta.

Huff, C., Sproull, L., and Kiesler, S. (1989). Computer communication and organizational commitment: Tracing the relationship in a city government. *Journal of Applied Social Psychology, 19*, 1371–1391.

Hybels, R. C., and Barley, S. R. (1990). Co-optation and the legitimation of professional identities: Human resource policies in high technology firms. In L. R. Gomez-Mejia and M. W. Lawless (Eds.), *Organizational issues and high technology management* (pp. 199–213). Greenwich, CT: JAI Press.

Iaffaldano, M. T., and Muchinsky, P. M. (1985). Job satisfaction and job performance: A meta-analysis. *Psychological Bulletin, 97*, 251–273.

Innis, H. (1950). *Empire and communication.* Oxford: Clarendon Press.

Jablin, F. M. (1987). Formal organization structure. In F. M. Jablin, L. L. Putnam, K. H. Roberts and L. W. Porter (Eds.), *Handbook of organizational communication* (pp. 389–419). Newbury Park, CA: Sage.

Janis, I. (1972). *Victims of groupthink.* Boston: Houghton Mifflin.

Johansen, R. (1988). *Groupware: Computer support for business teams.* New York: Free Press.

Kahn, R. L. (1952). *A comparison of two methods of collecting data for social research: The fixed-alternative questionnaire and the open-ended interview.* Unpublished doctoral dissertation, University of Michigan.

Kahneman, D., and Tversky, A. (1979). Prospect theory: An analysis of decisions under risk. *Econometrica, 47*, 262–291.

Katz, E. (1989). *The new media and social segmentation.* Unpublished manuscript, Hebrew University of Jerusalem, Israel.

Katz, M. R. (1984). Computer-assisted guidance: A walkthrough with running comments. *Journal of Counseling and Development, 63*, 153–157.

Kaufman, R. L., Parcel, T. L., Wallace, M., and Form, W. (1988). Looking forward: Responses to organizational and technological change in an ultra-high technology firm. In I. H. Simpson and R. L. Simpson (Eds.), *Research in the sociology of work, 4* (pp. 31–67). Greenwich, CT: JAI Press.

Keegan, W. J. (1974.) Multinational scanning: A study of the information sources utilized by headquarters executives in multinational companies. *Administrative Science Quarterly, 19*, 411–421.

Kiesler, C., and Kiesler, S. (1969). *Conformity.* Reading, MA: Addison-Wesley.

Kiesler, S., Siegel, J., and McGuire, T. W. (1984). Social psychological aspects of computer-mediated communication. *American Psychologist, 39*(10), 1123–1134.

Kiesler, S., and Sproull, L. (1982). Managerial response to changing environments: Perspectives on problem sensing from social cognition. *Administrative Science Quarterly, 27,* 548–570.

Kiesler, S., and Sproull, L. S. (1986). Response effects in the electronic survey. *Public Opinion Quarterly, 50,* 402–413.

Kiesler, S. and Sproull, L. (1987). *Computing and change on campus.* Cambridge: Cambridge University Press.

Kiesler, S., Zubrow, D., Moses, A. M., and Geller, V. (1985). Affect in computer-mediated communication: An experiment in synchronous terminal-to-terminal discussion. *Human Computer Interaction, 1,* 77–104.

King, J. L. (1983). Centralized versus decentralized computing: Organizational considerations and management options. *Computing Surveys, 15*(4), 319–349.

Kinsley, M. (1989, December). Corporate Luddism. *New Republic,* p. 4.

Kirchler, E., & Davis, J. H. (1986). The influence of member status differences and task type on group consensus and member position change. *Journal of Personality and Social Psychology, 51*(1), 83–91.

Kling, R. (1987). Defining the boundaries of computing in complex organizations. In R. Boland and R. Hirschheim (Eds.), *Critical issues in information systems* (pp. 307–362). London: John Wiley.

Kling, R. (1980.) Social analyses of computing: Theoretical perspectives in recent empirical research. *Computing Surveys, 12,* 61–110.

Kmetz, J. (1984). An information processing study of a complex workflow in aircraft electronics repair. *Administrative Science Quarterly, 19,* 255–280.

Kolnar, E., Sundstrom, E., Brady, C., Mandel, D., and Rice R. W. (1982). Status demarcation in the office. *Environment and Behavior, 14,* 561–580.

Kraemer, K. L., and King, J. L. (1988). Computer-based systems for cooperative work and group decision-making. *ACM Computing Surveys, 20*(3), 115–146.

Kraut, R. E. (Ed.) (1987). *Technology and the transformation of white-collar work.* Hillsdale, NJ: Erlbaum.

Kraut, R. E., Egido, J., and Galegher, J. (1990). Patterns of contact and communication in scientific research collaborations. In J. Galegher, R. E. Kraut, and C. Egido (Eds.), *Intellectual teamwork: Social and technological foundations of cooperative work* (pp. 149–171). Hillsdale, NJ: Erlbaum.

Kraut, R. E., Fish, R., Root, R., and Chalfonte, B. (In press). Informal communication in organizations: Form, function, and technology. In S. Oskamp and S. Scacapan (Eds.), *Human reactions to technology,* Claremont Symposium on Applied Social Psychology. Beverly Hills, CA: Sage Publications.

Kraut, R. E., and Streeter, L. A (1990). *Satisfying the need to know: Interpersonal information access.* Unpublished manuscript, Bell Communications Research, Morristown, NJ.

Latane, B., and Darley, J. M. (1968). Group inhibition of bystander intervention in emergencies. *Journal of Personality and Social Psychology, 10*(3), 215–221.

Laudon, K. C. (1986). *Dossier society: Value choices in the design of national information systems.* New York: Columbia University Press.

Laughlin, P. R. (1980). Social combination processes of cooperative problem solving groups on verbal intellective tasks. In M. Fishbein (Ed.), *Progress in social psychology* (pp. 127–155). Hillsdale, NJ: Erlbaum.

Laughlin, P. R., and Ellis, A. L. (1986). Demonstrability and social combination processes on mathematical intellective tasks. *Journal of Experimental Social Psychology, 22*(3), 177–189.

Lederberg, J. (1978). Digital communications and the conduct of science: The new literacy. *IEEE Proceedings, 66*(11), 1314–1319.

Levin, J. A., and Cohen, M. (1985). The world as an international science laboratory: Electronic networks for science instruction and problem solving. *Journal of Computers in Mathematics and Science Teaching, 4,* 33–35.

Lichtenstein, S., Slovic, P., Fischhoff, B., Layman, M., and Combs, B. (1978). Judged frequency of lethal events. *Journal of Experimental Psychology: Human Learning and Memory, 4,* 551–578.

Licklider, J. C. R., and Vezza, A. (1978). Applications of information networks. *IEEE Proceedings, 66,* 1330–1346.

Linde, C. (1988). The quantitative study of communicative success: Politeness and accidents in aviation discourse. *Language and Society, 17,* 375–399.

Litterer, J. (1961). Systematic management: The search for order and integration. *Business History Review, 35,* 461–476.

Lorant, S. (1988). *Pittsburgh, story of an American city.* Lenox, MA: Authors' Edition.

Losada, M., Sanchez, P., and Noble, E. E. (1990). Collaborative technology and group process feedback: Their impact on interactive sequences in meetings. *Proceedings of the Conference on Computer-Supported Cooperative Work* (pp. 53–64). New York: The Association for Computing Machinery.

Lynn, L. (1986). *Office automation in Japan and the United States.* Unpublished manuscript, Case Western Reserve, Cleveland.

McCarthy, J. (1989). Networks considered harmful for electronic mail. *Communications of the ACM, 32*(12), 1389–1390.

McFarlan, F. W., and McKenney, J. L. (1983). *Corporate information systems management.* Homewood, IL: Richard D. Irwin.

McGee, J. V. (1990, May). *Boundary spanning systems and organizational integration.* Seminar at the Graduate School of Industrial Administration, Carnegie Mellon University, Pittsburgh.

McGrath, J. E., and Hollingshead, A. B. (1990). *Effects of technological enhancements on the flow of work in groups: Preliminary report of a systematic review of the research literature* (Report 90–1). Urbana, IL: University of Illinois.

McGrath, J. E. (1984). *Groups: Interaction and performance.* Englewood Cliffs, NJ: Prentice-Hall.

McGuire, T., Kiesler, S., and Siegel, J. (1987). Group and computer-mediated discussion effects in risk decision making. *Journal of Personality and Social Psychology, 52*(5), 917–930.

Mackay, W. (1989). Diversity in the use of electronic mail: A preliminary inquiry. *ACM Transactions on Office Information Systems, 6*(4) 380–397.

Mackay, W., Malone, T., Crowston, K., Rosenblitt, D., Rao, R., and Card, S. (1989). How do experienced information lens users use rules? *Proceedings of the ACM Conference on Human Factors in Computing Systems* (pp. 211–216). Reading: Addison-Wesley.

McLaren , R. I. (1982). *Organizational dilemmas.* New York: Wiley.

Maier, N. R. F., and Solem, A. R. (1952). The contribution of a discussion leader to the quality of group thinking: The effective use of minority opinions. *Human Relations, 5,* 277–288.

Malone, T. (1987). Modeling coordination in organizations and markets. *Management Science, 33,* 1317–1332.

Malone, T. W., Grant, K. R., Turbak, R. A., Brobst, S. A., and Cohen, M. D. (1987). Intelligent information-sharing systems. *Communications of the ACM, 30,* 484–497.

Manasse, M. S. (1990). Complete factorization of the ninth Fermat number. Electronic message, June 15.

Manning, P. K. (1979). Semiotics and loosely coupled organizations. Revised version of a paper presented to the Southern Sociological Society, Atlanta.

March, J. G. (1987). Old colleges, new technology. In S. Kiesler and L. Sproull (Eds.), *Computing and change on campus* (pp. 16–27). Cambridge: Cambridge University Press.

March, J. G., and Sproull, L. S. (1990). Technology, management, and competitive advantage. In P. G. Goodman and L. S. Sproull (Eds.), *Technology and organizations* (pp. 144–173). San Francisco: Jossey-Bass.

March, J. G., Sproull, L. S., and Tamuz, M. (in press). Learning from samples of one or less. *Organization Science, 2.*

Markus, M. L. (1987). Toward a "critical mass" theory of interactive media: Universal access, interdependence and diffusion. *Communication Research, 14,* 491–511.

Markus, M. L., and Pfeffer, J. (1983). Power and the design and implementation of accounting and control systems. *Accounting Organizations and Society, 8*(2/3), 205–213.

Martin, J. (1982). Stories and scripts in organizational settings. In A. H. Hastorf and A. M. Isen (Eds.), *Cognitive social psychology* (pp. 225–305). New York: Elsevier-North Holland.

Maruyama, M. (1963). The second cybernetics: Deviation-amplifying mutual causal processes. *American Scientist, 51*(2), 164–179.

Marwell, G., and Ames, R. (1979). Experiments on the provision of public goods. I. Resources, interest, group size and the free-rider problem. *American Journal of Sociology, 84,* 1335–1360.

Mason, R. O. (1970). *Beyond benefits and costs: A study on methods for evaluating the NASA-ERTS program.* Unpublished manuscript, Southern Methodist University, Dallas.

Mayer, R. E., and Greeno, J. G. (1972). Structural differences between learning outcomes produced by different instructional methods. *Journal of Educational Psychology, 63,* 165–173.

Mead, T. (1990, April). The IS innovator at DuPont. *Datamation,* pp. 61–68.

Meherabian, A. (1971). *Silent messages.* Belmont, CA:Wadsworth.

Messick, D. M., and Brewer, M. B. (1983). Solving social dilemmas: A review. In L. Wheeler and P. Shaver (Eds.), *Review of personality and social psychology* (pp. 11–44). Beverly Hills, CA: Sage.

Metcalf, J., III (1986). Decision making and the Grenada rescue operation. In J. G. March and R.Weissinger-Baylon (Eds.), *Ambiguity and command* (pp. 277–297). Marshfield, MA: Pitman.

Meyer, N. D. and Boone, M. E. (1987). *The information edge.* New York: McGraw-Hill.

Meyer, J. W., and Rowan, B (1977). Institutionalized organizations: Formal structure as myth and ceremony. *American Journal of Sociology, 83,* 340–363.

Mintzberg, H. (1973). *The nature of managerial work.* New York: Harper & Row.

Monaco, C. (1988). The difficult birth of the typewriter. *American Heritage of Invention and Technology, 4,* 11–21.

Monge, P. R., and Kirste, K.K. (1980). Measuring proximity in human organizations. *Social Psychology Quarterly, 43,* 110–115.

Moreland, R. L., and Levine, J.M. (1982). Socialization in small groups: Temporal changes in individual-group relations. *Advances in Experimental Social Psychology, 15,* 137–192.

Morison, E. E. (1966). *Men, machines, and modern times.* Cambridge, MA: The MIT Press.

Myers, D. (1987). Anonymity is part of the magic: Individual manipulation of computer-mediated communication contexts. *Qualitative Sociology, 10*(3), 251–266.

National Research Council, Panel on Information Technology and the Conduct of Research, Committee on Science, Engineering, and Public Policy (1989). *Information technology and the conduct of research: The user's view.* Washington, D.C.: National Academy Press.

National Research Council, Committee on the Effective Implementation of Advanced Manufacturing Technology, Manufacturing Studies Board, Commission on Engineering and Technical Systems (1986). *Human resource practices for implementing advanced manufacturing technology.* Washington, D.C.: National Academy Press.

Newcomb, T. R. (1961). *The acquaintance process.* New York: Holt, Rinehart, and Winston.

Newman, D. (1990). Opportunities for research on the organizational impact of school computers. *Educational Researcher, 19*(3), 8–13.

Nyce, H. E., and Groppa, R. (1983, May). Electronic mail at MIT. *Management Technology,* 65–72.

O'Reilly, C. (1989). Corporations, culture, and commitment: Motivation and social control in organizations. In M. Tushman, C. O'Reilly, and D. Nadler (Eds.), *Management of organizations* (pp. 285–303). New York: Harper and Row.

O'Reilly, C. (1980). Individuals and information overload in organizations: Is more necessarily better? *Academy of Management Journal, 23,* 684–696.

O'Reilly, C., and Roberts, K. (1974). Information filtration in organizations: Three experiments. *Organizational Behavior and Human Performance, 11,* 253–265.

Orton, J. D., and Weick, K. E. (1990). Loosely coupled systems: A reconceptualization. *Academy of Management Review, 15*(2), 203–223.

Ouchi, W. G. (1980). Markets, bureaucracies, and clans. *Administrative Science Quarterly, 25,* 129–140.

Palys, T. S., Boyanowsky, E. O., and Dutton, D. G. (1984). Mobile data access terminals and their implications for policing. *Journal of Social Issues, 40*(3), 113–127.

Pelto, P. J., and Muller-Wille, L. (1972). Snowmobiles: Technological revolution in the Arctic. In H. R. Bernard and P.J. Pelto, (Eds.), *Technology and social change* (pp. 65–199). New York: Macmillan.

Pelz, D. C., and Andrews, F. M. (1976). *Scientists in organizations: Productive climates for research and development.* New York: Wiley.

Perin, C. (in press). The moral fabric of the office: Panopticon discourse and schedule flexibilities. In S. Bacharach, S. R. Barley, and P. S. Tolbert (Eds.), *Research in the sociology of organizations.* Greenwich, CT: JAI Press.

Perrin, N. (1980). *Giving up the gun: Japan's reversion to the sword 1543–1879.* Boulder, CO: Shambhala.

Pettigrew, A. M. (1972). Information control as power resources. *Sociology, 6,* 187–204.

Petty, M. M., McGee, G. W., and Cavender, J. W. (1984). A meta-analysis of the relationships between individual job satisfaction and individual performance. *Academy of Management Review, 9,* 712–721.

Pfeffer, J. (1978). *Organizational design.* Arlington Heights, IL: AHM.

Pfeffer, J. (1981). *Power in Organizations.* Marshfield, MA: Pitman Publishing.

Pfeffer, J., and Leblebici, H. (1977). Information technology and organizational structure. *Pacific Sociological Review, 20*(2), 241–261.

Philip, G., and Young, E. S. (1987). Man-machine interaction by voice: Developments in speech technology Part I: The state-of-the-art. *Journal of Information Science, 13,* 3–14.

Podsakoff, P. M., and Williams, L. J. (1986). The relationship between job performance and job satisfaction. In E. A. Locke (Ed.), *Generalizing from laboratory to field settings* (pp. 207–253). Lexington, MA: Lexington Books.

Poole, M. S., Holmes, M., and DeSanctis, G. (1988). Conflict management and group decision support systems. *Proceedings of the Second Conference on Computer-Supported Cooperative Work* (pp. 227–243). New York: The Association for Computing Machinery.

Porter, L., Allen, R. W., and Angel, H. L. (1981). The politics of upward influence in organizations. In L. L. Cummings and B. M. Staw (Eds.), *Research in organizational behavior, 3* (pp. 109–150). Greenwich, CT: JAI Press.

Rahav, M. (1985). Computers and society, the case of Israel's psychiatric case register. In D. Harper (Ed.), *Proceedings of Two Conferences, June 1984 and June 1985* (pp. 97–100). Rochester, NY: University of Rochester.

Reddy, R. (1990). A technological perspective on new forms of organizations. In P. S. Goodman and L. S. Sproull (Eds.), *Technology and organizations* (pp. 232–253). San Francisco: Jossey-Bass.

Reich, R. B. (1987, August). Bread and circuits. *New Republic, 197*(5), pp. 32–33.

Rice, R., and Associates (1984). *The new media: Communication, research and technology*. Newbury Park, CA.: Sage.

Ridgeway, C. L. (1981). Nonconformity, competence, and influence in groups: A test of two theories. *American Sociological Review, 46*, 333–347.

Ridgway, V. F. (1956). Dysfunctional consequences of performance measurements. *Administrative Science Quarterly, 1*, 240–247.

Roberts, L. G., and Wessler, B. D. (1970). Computer network development to achieve resource sharing. *AFIPS SJCC Proceedings, 36*.

Robey, D., Farrow, D., and Franz, C. R. (1989). Group process and conflict in system development. *Management Science, 35*(10), 1172–1191.

Root, R. (1988). Design of a multi-media vehicle for social browsing. *Proceedings of the Second Conference on Computer-Supported Cooperative Work* (pp. 25–30). New York: The Association for Computing Machinery.

Rosen, S., and Tesser, A. (1970). On reluctance to communicate undesirable information: The MUM effect. *Sociometry, 33*, 253–264.

Rouse, W. B., and Morris, N. M. (1986). On looking into the black box: Prospects and limits in the search for mental models. *Psychological Bulletin, 100*, 349–363.

Rule, J., and Attewell, P. (1989). What do computers do? *Social Problems, 36*(3), 225–241.

Rule, J., and Brantley, P. (1990). *Surveillance in the workplace: A new meaning to "personal" computing*. Unpublished manuscript, State University of New York, Stony Brook.

Sampson, J. P., Jr. (1983). An integrated approach to computer applications in counseling psychology. *The Counseling Psychologist, 11*, 65–74.

Schelling, T. C. (1978). *Micromotives and macrobehavior*. New York: W. W. Norton .

SCIENCEnet Subscribers/Catalog of Services (1988, Fall). Omnet, Inc., 137 Tonawanda Street, Boston, MA 02124.

Selmi, P. M. (1983). *Computer-assisted cognitive-behavior therapy in the treatment of depression*. Unpublished doctoral dissertation, Illinois Institute of Technology.

Servan-Schreiber, D., and Binik, Y. M. (1989). Extending the intelligent tutoring system paradigm: Sex therapy as intelligent tutoring. *Computers in Human Behavior, 5,* 241–259.

Shapiro, N. Z., and Anderson, R. H. (1985). *Toward an ethics and etiquette for electronic mail*. Santa Monica, CA: The Rand Corporation.

Sharpe, L. (1952). Steel axes for stone age Australians. In E. H. Spicer (Ed.), *Human problems in technological change* (pp. 69–90). New York: Russell Sage Foundation.

Sheil, B. A. (1983). Coping with complexity. *Office: Technology and People, 1,* 295–320.

Shneiderman, B. (1987). *Designing the user interface: Strategies for effective human-computer interaction*. Reading, MA: Addison Wesley.

Short, J., Williams, E., and Christie, B. (1976). *The social psychology of telecommunications*. London: Wiley.

Siegel, J., Dubrovsky, V., Kiesler, S., and McGuire, T. (1986). Group processes in computer-mediated communication. *Organizational Behavior and Human Decision Processes, 37,* 157–187.

Simon, H. A. (1973). Applying information technology to organization design. *Public Administration Review, 33,* 268–278.

Sinaiko, H. W. (1963). *Teleconferencing: Preliminary experiments* (Research paper P-108). Arlington, VA: Institute for Defense Analysis.

Sitkin, S. B. (forthcoming). Secrecy norms in organizational settings. In L. D. Browning (Ed.), *Conceptual frontiers in organizational communication*. Albany: State University of New York Press.

Smith, D. K., and R. C. Alexander (1988). *Fumbling the future: How Xerox invented, then ignored, the first personal computer*. New York: William Morrow and Company.

Sproull, L. S. (1983). The nature of managerial attention. In P. Larkey and L. Sproull (Eds.), *Advances in information processing in organizations, 1,* 9–27. Greenwich, CT: JAI Press

Sproull, L., and Kiesler, S. (1986). Reducing social context cues: Electronic mail in organizational communication. *Management Science, 32*(11), 1492–1512.

Stasz, C., and Bikson, T. K. (1989). *Computer-supported cooperative work: Examples and issues in one federal agency*. Santa Monica, CA: Rand Corporation .

Steele, G. (1984). *Common LISP, the language*. Bedford, MA: Digital Press.

Steele, G. L. (1983). *The hacker's dictionary.* New York: Harper & Row.

Stilgoe, J. R. (1983). *Metropolitan corridor: Railroads and the American scene.* New Haven: Yale University Press.

Stohl, C., and Redding, W. C. (1987). Messages and message exchange processes. In F. M. Jablin (Ed.), *Handbook of organizational communication* (pp. 451–502). Newbury Park, CA: Sage.

Stoll, C. (1989). *The cuckoo's egg.* Garden City, N.Y.: Doubleday.

Strassman, P. A. (1985). *Information payoff: The transformation of work in the electronic age.* New York: Free Press.

Strodtbeck, F. L., and Lipinski, R. M. (1985). Becoming first among equals: Moral considerations in jury foreman selection. *Journal of Personality and Social Psychology, 49*(4), 927–936.

Suchman, L. A. (1988). *Plans and situated actions.* Norwood, NJ: Ablex Publishing.

Sudman, S., and Bradburn, N. N. (1974). *Response effects in surveys.* Chicago: Aldine.

Sundstrom, E., and Sundstrom, M. G. (1986). *Workplaces: The psychology of the physical environment in offices and factories.* Cambridge: Cambridge University Press.

Synodinos, N. E., and Brennan, J. M. (1988). Computer interactive interviewing in survey research. *Psychology and marketing* (pp. 117–137). New York: John Wiley and Sons, Inc.

Tamuz, M. (1987). The impact of computer surveillance on air safety reporting. *Columbia Journal of World Business* (Spring), 69–77.

Thoits, P. (1983). Multiple identities and psychological well-being. *American Sociological Review, 48,* 174–187.

Thomas, J., and Carroll, J. (1981). Human factors in communication. *IBM Systems Journal, 20,* 237–263.

Thompson, J. D. (1967). *Organizations in action.* New York: McGraw-Hill.

Thompson, S. (1981). Will it hurt less if I can control it? A complex answer to a simple question. *Psychological Bulletin, 90,* 89–101.

Thorn, B. K., and Connolly, T. (1987). Discretionary databases: A theory and some experimental findings. *Communication Research, 14*(5), 512–528.

Thorngate, W. (1988). On paying attention. In W. Baker, L. Mos, II. Van Rappard, and H. Stam (Eds.), *Recent trends in theoretical psychology* (pp. 247–264). New York: Springer-Verlag.

Travis, P. (1990, January). Why the AT&T network crashed. *Telephony,* 11.

Trevino, L. K., Lengel, R., and Daft, R. L. (1987). Media symbolism, media richness, and media choice in organizations: A symbolic interactionist perspective. *Communication Research, 14*(5), 553–574.

Treybig, J. G. (1985). The take-off company: Self-management and flexible structure. In R. W. Smilor and R. L. Kuhn (Eds.), *Managing take-off in fast growth companies* (pp. 3–18). New York: Praeger.

Turner, J. A. (1984). Computer-mediated work: The interplay between technology and structured jobs. *Communications of the ACM*, 27(12), 1210–1217.

Tushman, M. L. (1977). Special boundary roles in the innovation process. *Administrative Science Quarterly*, 22(4), 587–605.

Tushman, M. L., and Anderson. P. (1986). Technological discontinuities and organizational environments. *Administrative Science Quarterly*, 31, 439–465.

Uhlig, R. D., Farber, D., and Bair, J. H. (1979). *The office-of-the-future: Communications and computers.* Amsterdam: North-Holland Publishers.

Vogel, D. R., and Nunamaker, J. F. (1990). Design and assessment of a group decision support system. In J. Galegher, R. E. Kraut, and C. Egido (Eds.), *Intellectual teamwork: Social and technological foundations of cooperative work* (pp. 511–528). Hillsdale, NJ: Erlbaum.

Von Hippel, E. (1987). Cooperation between rivals: Informal know-how trading. *Research Policy*, 16, 291–302.

Vroom,V. H. (1964). *Work and motivation.* New York: Wiley.

Vroom, V. H., and Yetton, P. W. (1973). *Leadership and decision making.* Pittsburgh: University of Pittsburgh Press.

Wagman, M. (1980). PLATO DCS: An interactive computer system for personal counseling. *Journal of Counseling Psychology*, 27, 16–30.

Wasby, S. (1989). Technology in appellate courts: The ninth circuit's experience with electronic mail. *Judicature*, 73, 90–97.

Waterton, J. J., and Duffy, J. C. (1984). A comparison of computer interviewing techniques and traditional methods in the collection of self-report alcohol consumption data in a field study. *International Statistical Review*, 52, 173–182.

Weick, K. E. (1979). *The social psychology of organizing.* Reading, MA: Addison Wesley.

Weick, K. E. (1976). Educational organizations as loosely-coupled systems. *Administrative Science Quarterly*, 21, 1–19.

Weiner, S. L., and Goodenough, D. R. (1977). A move toward a psychology of conversation. In R. O. Freedle (Ed.), *Discourse production and comprehension* (pp. 213–255). Norwood, NJ: Ablex.

Weisband, S. P. (1989). *Discussion, advocacy and computer-mediated communication effects in group decision making.* Unpublished doctoral dissertation, Carnegie Mellon University.

Weisband, S. P. (in press). Group discussion and first advocacy effects in computer-mediated and face-to-face decision making groups. *Organizational Behavior and Human Decision Processes.*

Weizenbaum, J. (1976). *Computer power and human reason.* San Francisco: Freeman.

Whisler, T. (1970). *The impact of computers on organizations.* New York: Praeger.

White, L., Jr. (1962). *Medieval technology and social change.* London: Oxford University Press.

Williams, E. (1977). Experimental comparisons of face-to-face and mediated communication: A review. *Psychological Bulletin, 84,* 963–976.

Wright, J. P. (1979). *On a clear day you can see General Motors.* New York: Avon.

Yates, J. (1989). *Control through communication: The rise of system in American Management.* Baltimore: Johns Hopkins University Press.

Yates, J. (1982). From press book and pigeonhole to vertical filing: Revolution in storage and access systems for correspondence. *Journal of Business Communication, Summer,* 5–26.

Zigurs, I. (1987). *The effect of computer based support on influence attempts and patterns in small group decision-making.* Unpublished doctoral dissertation, University of Minnesota, Minneapolis.

Zuboff, S. (1988). *In the age of the smart machine.* New York: Basic Books.

Index

Access, 14, 170
  to coworkers, 81–87, 150, 153
  to data, 9, 10, 12, 74, 118, 130
  electronic mail, 177–178
  to expertise, 15, 32
  to management, 87–90, 153–154
  network policy, 162–163
  to people and information, 12, 32–
    33, 80, 107–110, 132–137, 162–
    163
  prohibition of, 137
Accountability, 171
Addressing electronic mail, 41, 178
Administration. *See* Information
  procedures, Management, Organizational structure
Airline reservations systems, 11, 39,
  127, 148
Alerting messages, 128
American Airlines, 148
American Hospital Supply, 146
Analysis, financial, 12. *See also* Costs
Anonymity, 38, 40, 50, 59, 65
Archives, 134, 141. *See also* Data-
  bases
ARPANET, 3, 10, 11, 32, 76
Assignments, task, 26–27, 28
At-home workers, 118, 120–121
AT&T, 127
Attitudes. *See also* Conflict, Psycho-
  logical factors/effects
  employee commitment, 85–86
  moods and feelings, 51–54
  toward networks, 14
Austek, 151–152

Behavioral factors. *See* Psychological
  factors/effects, Social control, Social
  effects
Bell Communications Research, 128–
  129, 160
Beneficial Finance, 31
Black and Decker, 149–150
Brainstorming, 25, 58, 59, 71, 73
Bulletin boards, electronic, 11, 129–
  131, 138–139. *See also* Electronic
  groups
Bureaucracy, 154

Calendar, electronic, 75
Carnegie Mellon University, xii–xiii,
  114
City government, 85–86, 90, 103
Class-based social forums, 139–140
Classification of mail, 139–140, 181.
  See also Filters; Folders, mail
Cohesiveness, group, 57
Commitment, employee, 73–74, 79–
  80, 85–86, 98, 100–101, 119
Common LISP, 32, 76
Communities, electronic, x, 11, 13,
  143–145
Computer-based communication
  terminology, 10
Computer-supported cooperative
  work (CSCW), 70–72. *See also*
  Group decision support systems
Conferences, computer, 11, 43, 59–
  63, 110
  real time, 60, 64, 70–71, 74–75
Confidentiality of data, 111, 163. *See
  also* Access, Information sharing,
  Privacy

Conflict, 54, 105–106, 107, 170. *See also* Flaming
consensus and, 64–65, 66, 68
control of projects, 155–156
procedures and, 130–131
social control and, 113–114
Consensus, decision making, 64–65
Control. *See* Information control, Performance control, Privacy, Social control
Control of projects, 155
Coordination
administrative systems, 144
costs, 25–26, 130, 167
in groups, 25–31, 31–32, 126
large project groups, 127–129, 132–133
Copying, 153–154
Corporate communications offices, 82
Costs
assessment of new technologies, 1, 2, 4, 8, 33–34
coordination, 25–26, 31
electronic mail compared with hard copy, 21–23, 183
electronic mail compared with telephone, 21–23, 183
information processing and transmission, 23, 35
installation of networks, 168–171
message reply, 34
network start-up, 168–171
switching, 148–149
Cues, social context, 38–41, 122
adding, 51–53, 171–173
temporal, 52–53
Customer assistance, 149–150. *See also* Services

Data-based communication, 12–15
Databases, 9, 10, 12, 13, 72, 74, 107, 118, 119, 123, 128, 130, 170, 184. *See also* Archives
Data processing, 9, 12, 13
Decision making. *See also* Group dynamics
centralization of, 104–106
in dispersed groups, 73–74
GDSS, 70–72
in small groups, 61–69
tools for, 70–72

Delegation of responsibility, 116
Democracy, 13, 105–106
Designated experts, 140–141
Design of information procedures. *See* Information procedures
Development projects. *See also* Large project groups
information sharing, 132–133
software, 155
Deviation amplification, 2–3, 8, 11–12
DIALOG, 43–44
Digests, procedure design, 136–137
Digital Equipment Corporation, 23, 24, 160
Disabled employees, 97
Discussion groups, 58, 90–94, 100–101. *See also* Electronic groups
Disputes/dissent. *See* Conflict
Distribution lists (DLs), 16, 81, 82, 83, 90–91, 138–139. *See also* Electronic groups
Does-anybody-know messages, 133–136, 139, 141
Du Pont, 104–105, 106, 147–148

Educational organizations, xi, 4, 32, 45, 163–164. *See also* Instruction
Efficiency effects, 1–3, 21–24, 119. *See also* Two-level perspective
accelerating information flow, 21–22
large group coordination, 127
regularizing information flow, 23–24
Egocentrism, 57
reducing, 91, 155–156
Electronic calendar, 75
Electronic communication terminology, 11
Electronic data interchange (EDI), 10, 146, 147, 148
first-level effects, 22
regularization of relationships, 149–150
Electronic groups, 70–76. *See also* Bulletin boards, electronic; Distribution lists; Group dynamics
administration of, 167–168
compared with face-to-face groups, 59–74
decision making in, 61–69

discussion groups, 58, 90–94, 100–101
distributed groups, 31–33, 73–74
subgroup structures, 155–156
Electronic mail, 11. *See also* Bulletin boards, electronic; Distribution lists; Electronic groups
access, 51, 177–178
addresses, 41, 178
classification, 139–140
compared with other technologies, 13, 40–42, 183
extracurricular, 91, 93–94, 100–101, 139–140, 149
filters, 76, 115, 137–140, 169
group mail, 25, 140, 180
interface features, 39–40, 74–77, 138, 163, 165, 181
mandatory procedures, 140
naming, 41, 178
and organizational structures, 153–154
social features, 42–50, 182–184
transport, 178–180
Electronic surveys/interviews, 44–49
ELIZA, 44
Emotional content. *See* Psychological factors/effects
Employees. *See also* Managers and executives, Peripheral employees, Sales
field personnel, 170–171
home-based, 118, 120–121
on-the-road, 10, 118, 119–120
Employee satisfaction, 81–94, 115, 121
Ephemeral communication, 42
Etiquette, 38–39, 51, 54, 55, 165. *See also* Norms
Experimental groups, 58–70
Expert locator, 128
Experts. *See also* Access
administration of electronic groups, 167–168
designated, 140–141
queries, "does anybody know," 133–134
Expert systems, 12, 45–46
Extracurricular mail, 91, 93–94, 100–101, 139–140, 149

Face-to-face communication
compared with electronic communication, 13, 40–42, 55–69, 72–74, 183
decision-making quality, 67
group dynamics, 58
need for, 30–31
status as factor in, 60
Facsimile, 30, 183, 184
Field personnel, 170–171
Filters, 76, 115. *See also* Classification of mail
information management, 169
procedure design, 137–140
Financial analysis, 12
First-level effects, 6, 15, 21–24, 119. *See also* Efficiency effects
Flaming, 49–50, 54, 65, 114
Folders, mail, 76, 139–140
Folklore, 133–134
Forecasting, 13
Foremost-McKesson, 147
Forums
network policy, 163–165
procedure design, 137–140
social forums, 12, 14
Future trends, xii, 53–54, 171–173

General Motors, 14, 38
General-purpose structures, 156
Government, city, 85
Government agencies, 136–137
GRIPENET, 113
Group decision support systems (GDSS), 59, 70–72
Group dynamics
appropriateness of electronic groups, 72–73
consensus, 64–65
decision quality, 65–69
decision time frames, 69
design and management of groups, 70–76
general-purpose versus special-purpose tools, 74–76
participants, 59–64
Group extremitization, 57
Group mail, 25, 140, 180. *See also* Electronic mail
Group projects, large. *See* Large project groups

Groups. *See* Electronic groups
Groupthink, 57

Hewlett-Packard, 31
Hierarchy
  communicating in, 38, 87–90, 104–
    106, 109–110, 119–120, 153–154
  dynamic structures, 154–155
  information flow, 153
  responses to new technology, 14,
    174–175
  status effects, 61–63
Historical perspective, x, 2–3
  communication technologies, 3, 6–7,
    43
  computers, 8–9
  information control, 104–106
  information procedures, 125–126,
    131
  networks, 10–11
  social effects, 5, 39
  technology and organizational
    structure, 143–145
Human resources, 14–15, 32, 46, 82,
    175. *See also* Employees, People,
    Peripheral employees, Psychological
    factors/effects

IBM, 9, 113, 128
Idea-based communication, 12–15
Influence. *See* Information control,
    Social control
Informal communication, 132–133.
    See also Extracurricular mail
Information control. *See also* Access,
    Privacy
  complications of, 75, 114–117, 120,
    133, 170
  computers and, 106–107, 126, 128
  hierarchical communications, 109–
    110, 119–120
  rate of information transfer, 107–
    110
  restriction of access to information,
    110–111
  secrecy, 111
  and systematic management, 104–
    106
Information flow
  accelerating, 21–23
  design of procedures. (*see* Informa-
    tion procedures)

efficiency gains, 21–24
  encouragement of, 165–166
  regularizing, 23–24
Information overload, 115–116, 134,
    169–170, 171
Information procedures
  designated experts, 140–141
  digests and reviews, 136–137
  distribution procedures, 129
  filters and forums, 137–140
  group mail procedures, 140
  information sharing, 132–141
  limitations of routine procedures,
    129–131
  mandatory procedures, 140
  queries, 132–136
  reporting procedures, 27, 29, 104–
    106, 130–131
  routines via computer, 126–129
Information processing costs, 35
Information sharing. *See also* Access,
    Privacy
  incentives for, 165
  limitations of, 129–131, 170
  procedures for, 132–141
  self-disclosure, 44–49
Innovation, 13, 33, 59, 72, 99–100,
    105–106, 131
Inquiries, 132–136, 139, 141
Instruction, 4, 54, 59, 118, 166–168
Interactive systems, control issues in,
    107–109
Interdependence, 5, 145–150, 170–
    171
Interface, electronic mail, 39–40, 74–
    77, 138, 163, 165, 166–168, 181
Interorganizational communication,
    145–150, 172
Interviews, computer. *See* Electronic
    surveys/interviews
Inventory management, 149–150
ITT, 40

Japan, 6, 79, 132–133, 151
Job satisfaction. *See* Employee
    satisfaction
Just-in-time manufacturing, 146

Large project groups, 164
  coordinating, 32, 76, 127, 128–129,
    130
  information sharing, 132

Mail, electronic. *See* Electronic mail
Management. *See also* Hierarchy,
  Information control, Organizational
  structure, Social control
  attitudes toward networks, 14
  complications of information
    control, 116
  electronic groups, 26–30, 70–76
  parallel, 132–133
  peripheral employee communications
    with, 87–90
  responses to new technology, 14,
    160, 174–175
Management information systems.
  See Archives, Databases, Informa-
    tion procedures
Management policies
  for electronic groups, 76, 165
  for information control, 103, 110,
    114–115, 123
  for information exchange, 15, 51,
    80, 101, 162
  pricing, 137–138
Managers and executives. *See also*
  Hierarchy
  cost savings for, 23
  in meetings, 57–58, 60–61
  product managers, 16, 153–154
  software development, 26–30, 155
Manufacturers Hanover Trust
  (MHT), 99
Manufacturing, 104–105, 129, 132–
  133, 143–144, 146, 149–150, 156
Marketing/market research. *See*
  Electronic surveys/interviews, Sales
Miles Laboratories, 119
Misinformation, 116–117
Modeling programs, 12, 13
Moods, 51–54
Morale, 115. *See also* Commitment,
  employee; Satisfaction, employee
Motivation. *See* Attitudes; Commit-
  ment, employee; Participation;
  Satisfaction, employee

Naming, electronic mail, 41, 178
NASA, 57, 128
National Research Council, 9, 174
Networked databases, 72, 130. *See
  also* Databases

Networks, 12–13
  history of, 10–11
  installation of, 166–168
  terminology, 10
Norms, ix, 37–38, 40–41, 54, 139–
  140, 152, 165

Office work, 6, 107, 108, 116–117,
  120, 144
OMNET, 164, 168
Opportunity cost, 169–170
Order processing, 128, 146, 149–150
Organizational change, ix, 14–15,
  173–175
Organizational culture, 14, 109–110,
  114, 121
Organizational structure. *See also*
  Hierarchy, Subunits
  changes in, 5, 7, 143–145, 173–175
  conventional, 159–160
  dynamic, 15, 154
  electronic groups, 155–156
  nineteenth-century technology, 143–
    144
  organizational interdependence, 145–
    150
  subunit separation, 150–153
  task-specific, 156–157
  technology and, 143–145

Parallel management, 132–133
Participation. *See also* Access,
  Peripheral employees
  commitment, 85–86
  control, 110, 112–114
  differential benefits of, 84, 86–87,
    95–98
  effects, 80, 87, 95–100
  in groups, 30, 59–64, 90–95
  organizational culture, 14
  in organizations, 73, 79–80
  policies, 14, 162–166
  voluntary, 136–137
People, 14, 162. *See also* Employees,
  Participation, Peripheral employees,
  Psychological factors/effects
  network policy, 162
  as network resource, 12–15
  organization elements, 131
Performance. *See also* Productivity
  and control, 106, 108

Performance, *continued*
and efficiency, 21–24
group, 1, 59, 73
office-based versus home-based
workers, 120–121
peripheral employees, 95–101
quality of, 29–30, 65–69, 86, 95–98,
132–133
Performance control, 112, 117, 119,
121
Peripheral employees. *See also* Social
control
electronic discussion groups, 90–94
extracurricular mail, 100–101
information and emotional connections, 84–87
management, communication with,
87–90
performance benefits, 95–98
short-term versus long-term benefits
of communications, 98–100
Personas, 50–51, 52
Policies. *See* Information control;
Management policies; Social control
Power. *See* Hierarchy, Information
control, Social control
Pricing policies, 137–138
Privacy, 39, 45, 49, 163
Problem solving, 13, 19, 68, 72, 73,
99. *See also* Decision making,
Information procedures
Procedures. *See* Information
procedures
Process loss, 25
Procurement, 146
Productivity
gains in (*see* Efficiency effects,
Performance, Two-level perspective)
office-based versus home-based
workers, 120–121
Prohibition, 109–110, 137, 165
Psychological factors/effects. See also
Attitudes; Cues, social context;
Group dynamics; Norms; Participa-
tion
anonymity, 38, 40, 50, 65
commitment, 73–74, 85–86
control, 74–75, 112–114, 116
deindividuation (*see* Flaming)
ephemeral communication, 42
flaming, 49–50, 65, 114

information effects, 83, 116
information overload, 115–116
information sharing, 30, 34, 74,
129–131, 153–154, 160–161, 171
management, 160
moods and feelings, 51–54
participation in groups, 59–64
persuasion, 73
psychological neighborhood, 151
relationships, 79, 149, 150–153
risk taking, 64–65, 67
self-disclosure, 38, 39, 44–49
social differences, 43–44
social information in communication, 40–41, 52–53
social regulation in communication,
49–54, 65–66, 121
status and group behavior, 60–64,
66–67, 73
switching costs, 148–149
telework, 121–122
text, effects of, 40–41
Public electronic communication,
172–173

Queries, 132–136, 139, 141

Rand Corporation, 84, 155
Reference groups, 113
Remote employees, 116–122
Research and development, 132–133,
154
Restrictions, effects of, 165
Retirement planning, 84–85
Reviews, procedure design, 136–137
Risk, decision making, 66–67
Roles, 5
Routine procedures
computerized, 126–129
limitations of, 129–130

Sales, 10, 11, 16–17, 19, 72, 119,
135, 145, 147, 149–150
Satisfaction, employee, 115, 121
Scanning procedures, 129
Scheduling
design of procedures, 26, 126–127
electronic calendar, 75
social effects of, 26
Second-level effects. *See* Social effects
Secrecy, 111. *See also* Privacy

Services, 13, 24, 107, 108, 119, 149, 167–168
  customer assistance, 149–150, 163–164
  employee, 165–166, 168
  financial, x, 2, 31, 72, 107, 108, 111
  government organizations, 8, 32, 57, 125–126
  health, 39, 119, 127, 146, 147
  police, 107–108, 109
  project, 128
  restaurants, xi, 39
  travel, 12, 39, 127, 148, 149
Security, 111
Self-disclosure, 38, 39, 44–49. *See also* Privacy
Sexpert, 46–48
Simulation programs, 12
Skills acquisition, 99, 100–101
Social boundaries, 42–43
Social control
  complications of information control, 114–117
  employees on the road, 119–120
  home-based workers, 120–121
  information overload, 115–116
  misinformation, 116–117
  remote superiors, 117–118
  remote workers, 116–122
Social effects, 6. *See also* Historical perspective, Psychological factors/ effects, Theory, Two-level perspective
  boundary spanning, ix, 31–33, 42–44
  communication technology, 4–5, 7, 11, 15–16, 105–106
  distributed groups, 31–33
  drawbacks of networks, 33–35
  of electronic mail, 182–184
  future trends, 171–172
  information control, 108–110
  nature of, 1–3, 6–7, 35, 161
  new businesses, 147
  organizational interdependence, 145–150, 160
  organizational structures, 143–145, 154–155, 156
  peripheral employee. *See* Peripheral employees

relationships, 153–154
reporting, 27, 29
scheduling, 26
social control of work, 118–122
social differences, 43–44
social regulation in communication, 49–54, 65–66, 121
task assignments, 26–27, 28
Social forums, 139–140
Social information in text, 40–43
Social roles, 5
Software
  electronic mail, 181, 182
  filters (*see* Filters)
Software development groups, 127–129, 130, 155
Status, 60–64, 66–67
Strategic planning, 174
Structure of information, 130
Structure of organizations. *See* Organizational structure
Subunits
  communication and, 151–152
  effects of networks, 159
  organization elements, 131
  separation of, 150–153
  structures, 25, 155
Supply delivery, 146
Supply management, 147–148
Surveys, electronic, 44–49
Switching costs, 148–149

Tandem Computers, Inc., 14, 20, 135, 141, 152
Task assignments, 26–27, 28
Teams, 154. *See also* Large project groups
Technical components, 12–15
Technology feedback, 2
Telecom Canada, 153
Telephone communications, electronic mail versus, 21
Terminology
  computer-based communications, 10–11
  group dynamics, 57
Text, social information of, 40–43
Theory. *See also* Group dynamics, Two-level perspective
  boundary spanning, ix, 31–33, 42–44

Theory *continued*
  cues, social context, 38–41, 122
  differential benefits, 95
  social information in communica-
    tion, 40–49, 52–53, 61
  social regulation in communication,
    49–54, 65–66, 121
Therapy, 44, 46–48
Time
  efficiency gains, 15
  temporal cues, 52–53
  time for decision making, 69
  transaction time, reduction of, 24
Training. *See* Instruction
Transmission costs, 35
Transport, electronic mail, 178–180
Traveling workers, 118, 119–120
Two-level perspective. *See also*
  Efficiency effects, Social effects
  communication technology at two
    levels, 3–5
  data processing, 9
  deviation amplification, 11–12
  early experience with technology,
    10–11
  first-level and second-level effects, 3
  historical experience, 6–8
  new technology, 8
  technical and human components,
    12–15

University of Arizona, 58
Users. *See* People
U.S. Forest Service, 136–137
USSR, 105–106

Visual information, 53
VNET, 113

Workers. *See* Employees